DEMOCRACY
A Worldwide Survey

Edited by
Robert Wesson

PRAEGER

New York
Westport, Connecticut
London

Library of Congress Cataloging-in-Publication Data

Democracy: a worldwide survey.

  Bibliography: p.
  Includes index.
  1. Democracy — History — 20th century.
  2. Authoritarianism — History — 20th century.
I. Wesson, Robert G.
JC421.D46   1987   321.8′09′04   86–30443
ISBN 0–275–92440–8 (alk. paper)

Library of Congress Catalog Card Number: 86-30443
ISBN: 0-275-92440-8

First published in 1987

Praeger Publishers, One Madison Avenue, New York, NY 10010
A division of Greenwood Press, Inc.

Printed in the United States of America

∞

The paper used in this book complies with the Permanent
Paper Standard issued by the National Information Standards
Organization (Z39.48-1984).

10 9 8 7 6 5 4 3 2

Contents

Preface

One of the more encouraging facts in the sometimes dismal political panorama of the day is the rising awareness of human rights and democratic values. This has been growing since the 1970s, when rights abroad became a major concern of U.S. foreign policy. A landmark was the Helsinki Accord of 1975, acknowledging that human rights are not purely an internal matter but that governments have some international responsibility (at least in theory) for the way they treat their citizens. But humanitarian concern for human rights is inseparable from something that had commonly been treated as an internal matter of the nations involved: democracy or the lack of it. Human rights are part, a good part, of democracy, and they can be assured only by legal, responsible, that is, democratic governments.

The idea that we would like to see other peoples free and democratic is as old as the United States, but only recently has it become an important goal of foreign policy to do what may judiciously be done to propagate freedom and democracy. This has been accompanied by increased attention to the conditions and prospects of democracy worldwide, especially in the many nations that are somewhere between stable democracy, in which political rights are taken for granted and absolutist states, where democracy is hardly an aspiration.

It is the purpose of this volume to survey the status of democracy, or movement toward or away from it, during the year just past. Yearbooks of human rights, especially those published by the State Department, Amnesty International, and Freedom House, serve an admirable purpose, and much can be learned from them about the status of democracy worldwide. But the question of democracy is broader, and a more analytical discussion of political developments seems necessary. For this reason, the contributors to the present volume have given less attention to specifics of violations or observation of political and civil rights, and more to the political situation, institutions, and outlook.

Eight scholars have written on the regions into which it seemed most suitable to carve the world; namely, Western Europe, North America, Latin America (with the Caribbean), Sub-Saharan Africa,

North Africa and the Near East, South Asia, East Asia (and the Pacific), and the Soviet Union and Eastern Europe. Of these regions, the first two are solidly democratic; the authors, Dennis Kavanagh and Martin Wattenberg, report more signs of health than ailment, although democracy remains everywhere imperfect. John Martz sees Latin America predominantly and promisingly democratic; the holdout dictatorships or military regimes are clearly contrary to the prevalent trend. Sub-Saharan Africa, viewed by Larry Diamond, is somewhat like the poorest parts of Latin America; democracy is very limited, but it is a fairly widespread ideal, and there are signs here and there of movement toward it. As detailed by Glenn Perry, the Islamic region of North Africa and the Near East likewise contains little democracy, aside from partly Europeanized Turkey and the European-originated enclave of Israel. This is the chief arena of the only dynamic antidemocratic ideology in the present world, Islamic fundamentalism. South Asia, discussed by Douglas Makeig, shows more democratic institutions, especially in India, with a population equal to those of Africa and Latin America together, and there has been some movement toward democracy in two other populous countries, Pakistan and Bangladesh. East Asia, covered by Edward Olsen, is the most diverse of our regions, with a major democracy in Japan, several absolutist-totalitarian regimes in China and its neighbors, and many others somewhere between; but so far as there is change, it is nearly all in the direction of slightly more open, if not democratic, systems. Finally, the Soviet Union and its satellites, described by David Powell, are quite undemocratic if not antidemocratic; but here again there are indications of some movement toward slackening of authoritarian ways.

As this volume is a first attempt to cover this expanse, it includes a good deal of historical background, although attention is centered on events of 1985. It is intended in future editions to concentrate more closely on the events and developments of the single year just past. No account is taken here of events or changes after December 31, 1985.

A common adjunct of description is classification, and the contributors have attempted to place countries in categories of democracy and nondemocracy. This is necessarily somewhat arbitrary, as there are always countries the classification of which is very doubtful; we apologize for any injustice that may be committed. Of the five categories here used, "stable democracy" is perhaps the least equivocal. It includes simply countries with governments based on free and fair elections, enjoying freedom of expression and civil rights, whose people would be incredulous if they heard on the morning news that the government had been taken over by a coup of any kind. There are 28 countries listed in this category.

Next to them are "insecure democracies," in which the powers of state are all theoretically based legally on popular choice but democratic institutions function less well or are subject to infringement—as in less than honest elections—or are less to be taken for granted. Typically, the military stands behind the government, formally under civilian command but in practice a largely self-directed organization. People know that if the soldiers felt it necessary or desirable, they could oust the civilian government, as they have probably done in the past, and they would not be terribly surprised if in the next month or year the democratic state were pushed aside. In this group of 26 countries belong the countries in which military rulers have recently turned administration over to elected civilians, such as Brazil and Peru, plus India, whose democracy could be legally set aside by determination of the ruling party, and Botswana, in which one cannot guess the result if the ruling party were unable to win a general election.

"Partial democracies" follow, those in which there are genuine democratic elements mixed with authoritarian powers. The authoritarian sector may be monarchic, as in Nepal. In countries with a historical background of traditional monarch, it is usually comprised of, or supported by, members of the military, as in Pakistan, or it may be a one-party civilian regime, as in Mexico. Other examples of seriously flawed democracy are Sri Lanka, torn by civil war, or Singapore, with a dictatorial but not all-powerful prime minister. Partial democracy bespeaks reality throughout much of the world, where societies are basically undemocratic but real concessions are made to pressures and aspirations for democracy. There are 18 in this group.

"Limited authoritarian" regimes are those that have been called "merely authoritarian" in contrast to communist-totalitarian regimes. These are dictatorships that are not exceptionally pervasive, leaving many or most activities to private discretion, allowing the press, for example, to publish freely as long as it refrains from serious criticism of the leader, and tolerating some aspects of constitutional government, such as an elected assembly with little power.

An example is the government of the Republic of China on Taiwan, which holds elections of some importance but hardly proposes sharing power with an opposition, or that of Pinochet in Chile, where police power is slightly mitigated by more or less independent courts and there is some freedom of criticism in the press. Paraguay, where General Stroessner has regularly allowed the people to reelect him, is another example. Yugoslavia must be placed also in that category, despite the monopoly of the communist "League," because the federal structure limits political power. These 48 states are more numerous than the partial democracies from which it is often difficult to distinguish them.

"Absolutist or totalitarian" states, of which we list 39, are those in which there are no rights against officialdom, and no constitution that the rulers cannot change to suit their convenience; democracy is not in consideration at all. If there are elections, they are for show and have no effect on political power. Quite unlimited governments are apt to be unrestrainedly brutal, and brutality obviously affirms power; but the primary characteristic is fullness of political power. It is possible to imagine a benevolent despotism, but it would still be a despotism. Saudi Arabia must thus be classified as absolutist, although it ordinarily does not weigh extremely harshly on its people but usually follows traditional ways.

The most prominent of absolutist states are those also called "totalitarian," which in current practice means "communist." These are, of course, the Marxist–Leninist powers headed by the Soviet Union, in which the authority of the ruling party (in practice, of the leadership of the party) is in theory absolute and in practice limited only by incompetence or practical necessity.

It may seem inappropriate to lump conservative Arab kingdoms and old-fashioned dictatorships, such as those of Duvalier in Haiti or Mobutu in Zaire, with ostensibly revolutionary-egalitarian countries, but their political essence is not totally different. Revolutionary regimes, although continuing to proclaim ideals of social renovation, readily turn into self-serving apparatuses increasingly similar to dictatorships with less rationale of utopian purpose; the conservatism of authoritarian regimes is closely related to their age. On the other hand, crude dictators achieving power by coup may see fit (depending on political circumstances) to look to the Soviet Union, take over more or less of its organizational methods, and officially adopt

Marxism–Leninism without much altering the nature of their rule except to make it more thorough.

Generally speaking, Marxist–Leninist regimes are more total, intrusive, or penetrating, and seek to direct all aspects of life, as in the typical communist state. But the distinction is not clear; for example, the Islamic government of Libya is more enveloping and demanding than the Marxist–Leninist regimes of Hungary and Yugoslavia. Brutality likewise fails to distinguish Marxist–Leninist and non–Marxist absolutism. There are nightmarish cases in both groups, such as the Khmer Rouge in Kampuchea and the Idi Amin government of Uganda, both happily extinct. Moreover, a Marxist–Leninist government with no place for rights of citizens may be fairly legalistic, as in the case of Czechoslovakia, like many non–Marxist absolutisms. The essential fact is autocratic power, regardless of the assumption of a utopian mission and modernized forms of mobilization and control.

COUNTRIES OF THE WORLD

Stable Democracies

Western Europe: Austria, Belgium, Denmark, Finland, France, Germany (West), Iceland, Ireland, Italy, Luxembourg, Netherlands, Norway, Portugal, Spain, Sweden, Switzerland, United Kingdom

North America: Canada, United States

Latin America: Barbados, Colombia, Costa Rica, Trinidad-Tobago, Venezuela

North Africa and Near East: Israel

East Asia–Pacific: Australia, Japan, New Zealand

Insecure Democracies

Western Europe: Greece, Malta

Latin America: Argentina, Antigua, Bahamas, Belize, Bolivia, Brazil, Dominican Republic, Ecuador, El Salvador, Grenada, Honduras, Jamaica, Peru, St. Kitts–Nevis, St. Lucia, St. Vincent–Grenadines, Uruguay

Africa: Botswana, Mauritius
North Africa–Near East: Cyprus
South Asia: India
East Asia–Pacific: Fiji, Papua New Guinea

Partial Democracies

Latin America: Guatemala, Honduras, Mexico, Panama
Africa: Gambia, Senegal, Zimbabwe
North Africa–Near East: Lebanon, Turkey
South Asia: Maldives, Nepal, Pakistan, Sri Lanka
East Asia–Pacific: Malaysia, Philippines, Singapore, Thailand

Limited Authoritarianisms

Latin America: Chile, Guyana, Nicaragua, Paraguay, Suriname
Africa: Burkina Fasso, Burundi, Cameroon, Cape Verde, Chad, Comoros, Djibouti, Ghana, Guinea, Ivory Coast, Kenya, Lesotho, Liberia, Madagascar, Mali, Nigeria, Rwanda, Seychelles, Sierra Leone, South Africa, Swaziland, Tanzania, Uganda, Zambia
North Africa–Near East: Algeria, Egypt, Iran, Jordan, Kuwait, Mauritania, Morocco, North Yemen, Sudan, Syria, Tunisia
South Asia: Bangladesh, Bhutan
East Asia: Indonesia, Korea (South), Taiwan
Soviet Union–Eastern Europe: Hungary, Poland, Yugoslavia

Absolutisms

Latin America: Cuba, Haiti
Africa: Angola, Benin, Central African Republic, Congo (Brazzaville), Equatorial Guinea, Ethiopia, Gabon, Guinea-Bissau, Malawi, Mozambique, Niger, Sao Tome–Principe, Somalia, Togo, Zaire
North Africa–Near East: Afghanistan, Iraq, Libya, Oman, Qatar, Saudi Arabia, South Yemen, United Arab Emirates

East Asia–Pacific: Brunei, Burma, China, Kampuchea, Korea (North),
    Laos, Vietnam
Soviet–Eastern Europe: Albania, Bulgaria, Czechoslovakia, Germany
    (East), Mongolia, Romania, Soviet Union

Introduction

Not infrequently, observers, to eschew ethnocentricity, insist that we should not insist on our particular kind of democracy but should give others credit for other varieties, such as one-party democracy, or even Soviet democracy. But democracy is a fairly coherent concept, simple in essentials and in spirit, however complicated in detail. It is universally applicable; and there is no more reason to credit dictators with being democratic, however much they use the word, than to assume that libertines are chaste because they claim chastity. The comparison is the more appropriate because democracy is commonly considered a virtue, and most political leaders nowadays want to cloak themselves in it.

There are many reasons why democratic institutions have prospered more in certain places than others. Sometimes there is an obvious immediate answer. For example, the eastern part of Germany became an absolutist-totalitarian state after World War II and the western part became democratic by virtue of the demarcation between zones of anti–Nazi armies. Causes for the democratization of Spain after Franco are less simple and subject to different weighings, but they seem fairly clear, including the great expansion and diversification of the Spanish economy after World War II, the influence of millions of Spaniards familiar with European democracy by virtue of working abroad, some tradition of democratic or at least nonauthoritarian institutions going back to the free states of pre-imperial Spain, the feeling of elites that democracy was necessary for Spain's development, and by no means least the personality of King Juan Carlos. But to assign comparative weights to these factors or to make clear why so many Spaniards were willing to cede part or all of their political power is beyond our analytical capacities; nor can we be sure that less obvious factors may not have been equally or more important.

There is a close association between democracy and material prosperity. This is understandable inasmuch as the prosperous modern society in its complexity defies central direction, has abundant means of communication, is socially mobile, and has many groups and organizations through which citizens may have some political influence. Yet the enormous economic development of such countries as Mexico and the Soviet Union in the past 70 years has not brought them visibly closer to a democratic political system. It is also obvious that a homogeneous society can more easily rule itself democratically than a divided one. Yet India, one of the world's very poor and very fractured countries is one of the very few democracies outside the West European–American sphere. No one can say just why India has been so exceptional, although one can point to some obvious factors: the British ruled the country long enough to implant a legalistic mentality in at least some of the educated; an efficient civil service and a class of politicians, lawyers, and so forth interested in democracy had developed; and the preparation for independence was long and gradual, turning power over to a party that had been working for the popular cause for a generation and has continued to govern (with a brief interruption) until now. The military has been kept out of politics, unlike the situation in neighboring countries, in part by its organizational structure. Moreover, an undemocratic institution, the caste system, has lent structure and stability to Indian society and has inculcated resignation, thereby contributing to making democracy workable.

An opposite example is Argentina, which has enjoyed all the obvious conditions for democracy yet has seen little of it since 1930. In the 1920s Argentina, with a population of overwhelmingly European background, with no troublesome ethnic or other divisions, geographically unified, well endowed with resources, especially land, and a high level of literacy, was one of the most prosperous countries of the world and seemed to have entered its democratic maturity. Yet in 1930 a military coup shattered complacency, and the country entered a long period of political breakdown and economic failure, reducing it to mediocre Third World status with a per capita income a small fraction of that of nations it once surpassed. Argentines have sought in vain for answers ever since. Some factors, however, seem to stand out. In 1912, the Argentine elite, predominantly landholders, enfranchised the masses and made way for a democratic electoral system. They did so under the pressure of considerable national ferment but in the conviction that they could continue to govern despite concessions to democracy, a conviction nourished by the great successes of the previous several decades. However, honest elections brought to power the opposition party and threatened the position of the conservatives. The incompetence of the president and the onset of the depression in 1930 led the military to remove the president. The concessions to free elections made in 1912 were in effect withdrawn, and Argentina was ruled by force and fraud by elites not prepared to sacrifice their position. The military felt called upon to take charge, and the need to conciliate laboring masses led to demagogic dictatorship under Peronism, deep political divisions, and a condition where democracy seemed to mean victory for elements unacceptable to the conservatives or military or both. Authoritarian regimes could not govern effectively because contrary forces were too strong; democratic regimes lacked coherence and were unable to tame the military. The economy stagnated. This is certainly an oversimplified scheme and perhaps an unrealistic one, but it illustrates the complexity of causation and the difficulty of generalization.

Nonetheless, however defective our understanding of causation, the general meaning of democracy is clear. However varied its institutions, the essence is recognizably the same everywhere, from Japan to India to Scandinavia to the United States. It is the responsibility of the people who have political power to those who do not.

This entails many things, principally: mechanisms whereby the people can place governors in office or remove them, meaning in practice honest elections; impartial laws governing all alike, with basic rules (a constitution) specifying the powers and relations of political bodies; freedom to criticize those in power and to organize for political action or defense of interests; indefeasible rights of private parties against political powers; and a system of courts more or less independent of administrative authorities capable of protecting rights and impartially applying the law. These things form a mutually supporting framework of government. It is difficult to assure the existence of any one of them without the others, and the failure of any one would endanger the entirety of the structure.

Democracy is a set of institutions to regularize government by consent instead of imposition. Democratic states always have an elected head of government, almost always chosen by popular vote. They also have a more or less numerous body empowered to sanction laws and budgets, commonly with two chambers for balance. The administrative staff of the state is largely protected from political dismissal and is usually selected, except at the top level, by nonpolitical criteria. And there is, as noted, a judicial system largely sheltered from political pressures.

The chief ingredients of the democratic complex are those celebrated by the French Revolution, "Liberty, Equality, Fraternity," a better word for the last being "community." Freedom implies a noncoercive government that allows its citizens generally to do as they please as long as they do not infringe on the welfare or rights of others. It particularly means latitude for political expression or open competition for political influence. Freedom for individuals and organizations is desirable and indispensable in order to check the government; but in the modern spirit, freedom is a value in itself, part of the human fulfillment, and an essential ingredient of the healthy society.

Equality refers primarily to political rights for all mature and responsible persons, practically the basic condition of modern democracy. However, the broader equality, or minimal inequality, of economic and social condition is a major democratic value and a condition of the depth and reality of democracy. Political equality is always hedged by inequality of resources and status; the democratic order requires that there be a large group of persons of more or less middling condition who see themselves as reasonably equal. Inequality makes different values and divides classes and other groups, impeding the functioning of the democratic apparatus; but the complicated democratic structure of government requires considerable consensus, or agreement to accept the rules of the political game, even if it may be contrary to one's immediate interests. The consensus, in turn, must rest on a sense of community. The more people share basic values and the closer they are in their sense of justice and desire to make the shared system function properly, the more secure the democratic order.

Democracy gives formal equality to people in unequal societies and sanctions rights for persons who would otherwise lack them. In this fashion it benefits most strongly the underprivileged. Indeed, the vote may be almost the sole possession (possibly for sale on voting day) of the poor in a country like India, and it is their chief protection, feeble as it may be, against abuses of authority, from haughty village police to landlords who might dispossess them. It is also their chief way of exerting some kind of pressure on the powers of state to provide them with roads, schools, protection, and so forth. The altruism of leaders is problematic unless they have to answer to the people.

From this it may be inferred that democracy is principally desired and fought for by the nonpossessing classes, while the possessing or privileged classes tend to support undemocratic regimes. Reality, however, is more complex. Movement toward democracy has seldom been propelled primarily by the masses, who in any case are impotent unless mobilized, probably led by educated persons of middle-class origin. The masses, urban and rural, probably support democratization, but it is not likely to have top priority for those whose great problem is earning their subsistence; they cannot be the builders of the democratic state.

Those who press for democracy in undemocratic societies are first of all those who are aware that it is the way of the most prosperous and culturally advanced societies, and it is natural to suppose that democratization is helpful for progress and industrialization. Elites wish their country to be regarded as politically advanced, that is, democratic. They can move, however, only so far as they are supported by those who feel cheated by the authoritarian order or disillusioned by it. This includes intellectuals of various kinds, such as students, teachers, writers, artists, and journalists, who want freedom for themselves and a state corresponding to their ideas of justice. It also includes professionals, such as lawyers and judges, who can work best in a democracy. Labor leaders also want freedom to act with and on behalf of workers. Entrepreneurs, especially small ones, want the relative security and freedom from arbitrary regulation that they are more likely to find in a democratic state than any other. People concerned with minority rights also want and need democracy as the only real guarantee of rights.

Pluralism, like equality and community, is a vital part of democracy. It is almost a synonym for democracy, because a society organized pluralistically is inevitably constitutional and more or less democratic. Historically democracy has grown up from the expansion of rights of various components of feudal society. For democracy to be a reality, it is essential that there be competitive centers of power offsetting one another, in the framework of the state and outside it; if there were not, the one big organization of administration would be excessively dominant. A traditional order may be pluralistic, with positions based on traditional or feudalistic rights or fixed divisions such as castes, but it is apparently not possible for a modern society to be really pluralistic without a constitutional and legitimate basis, that is, without democracy.

There are many forms of pluralism: autonomous powers and agencies of the state; local or federal self-government; organized ethnic, religious, or other groups; private associations; and economic groups and enterprises. Basic to most pluralism is private property, which always wields some influence, at times a great deal. Sometimes democracy seems to amount to a scheme for harmonizing or mediating among sectors or private interests.

Viewed a little differently, democracy may also be defined succinctly as fair government, that is, government without discriminations or political advantages for any person or groups, applying the same rules to all. This not only means that opponents of the state should be able to speak out like its supporters, but also that the state, which should represent all, does not give unwarranted advantages to any particular group. It is unfair, for example, to use government-controlled broadcasting facilities to favor one party, or to allocate newsprint to conformist papers. Broadly speaking, to ask whether any procedure is fair is the same as asking whether it is democratic.

No state is fair in the sense that all have equal chances, but the democracy cannot have institutions assigning power to a self-selected minority (as in party-ruled states), nor does a group hold the state by virtue of having guns (as in a military dictatorship), nor does an individual dominate essentially by fraud or bullying (as in many dictatorships), or by reason of birth (as in hereditary monarchies). Instead, all are considered to be equal citizens with equal basic rights. Nothing less is fair in the modern outlook.

A consequence is that the democratic state does something to help the needier sectors for the sake of economic fairness. The democracy always has some purpose of redistribution from the richer to the poorer through benefits or social programs of some kind, from noncontributory pensions to free education. In some cases, especially as in Scandinavia, the state rechannels a large fraction of the national income. Some authoritarian states, on the other hand, seem to have functioned chiefly to take from the poor and give to the rich.

Nondemocratic government is almost by definition more or less arbitrary, that is, based on no generally accepted philosophical values. Thus, the only reason Jean–Claude Duvalier was president-for-life of Haiti is that he is the son of the previous dictator; and there is no reason in Marxism or any broader theory why the Communist party and not another should have control of the Soviet Union. And arbitrary, unfair, more or less exploitative government is probably the largest single reason that most of the world is very poor, much poorer than it needs to be in terms of the resources and technology readily available.

To some extent, democracy can be called good government. So far as freedom is esteemed for itself, the democratic state may claim superiority. Happiness is not measurable and freedom certainly has its burdens as well as its rewards. But it seems clear that people are usually more creative when less coerced, and hence fulfill more of their human potentialities.

Democracy is rather closely associated with material abundance. All the advanced industrial countries are securely democratic, except some held under Marxist-Leninist party rule by military force, such as East Germany and Czechoslovakia, and these are much less prosperous than countries of similar background in Western Europe. Broadly speaking, people are more productive when there is a free flow of information, the state is unoppressive and predictable, and commercial values outweigh political; these conditions are seldom to be maintained except in a democratic order. The advantages of central control of flow of resources in an authoritarian state are undone by the inability of the central planners to make rational choices in countless complicated situations. The potential advantages of the strong state are also offset by the prevalence of corruption, which wastes resources and frustrates orderly government. The only reliable means of coping with corruption is freedom to criticize and to hold officeholders responsible, that is, democracy.

This is far from claiming that democracy is a perfect system of government—aside from the fact that no state is ideally democratic. By etymology, it means rule by the people, but all democracies are seriously flawed in that the popular will or the needs of the community, as best the leadership can perceive them, are not the only, perhaps not even the chief guide to the policies of the state. There are many reasons for this, such as the difficulty of determining the will of the people by elections at considerable intervals when numerous policy questions are at stake, disinterest in many issues, incompetence of the masses in technical questions, and the ability of well-organized and well-financed groups to outpressure broader preferences, as well as uncertainty just how the desires of the people are best to be implemented or their needs filled. But even a quite defective democracy should serve to check the state, to keep officeholders more or less attentive to those under them, to restrain abuses of power, and to renew political elites.

Democratic government thus has two sides, the limitation of arbitrary power of government (or protection of the rights of people and organizations) and the compliance of government with the will of the people. These are inseparably linked. A state may claim (as Marxist-Leninist states do) to be serving the people without being democratic in the institutional sense, but it is very hard to imagine that the holders of political power will consistently sacrifice their interests to those of the unofficial masses unless there are institutions giving effect to the will of the citizenry, with respect for rights and political freedom.

It is probably easier, however, to make progress toward the observance of human and civil rights and a rule of law than toward the implementation of the popular will through democratic processes. Indeed, it is probably realistic to think of democracy, at least in countries where it is incipient and tentative, more in terms of people limiting power than of people exercising power. It is certainly informative to focus on the former aspect, especially if one considers the state of democracy—or steps toward it—in the nondemocratic majority of states in the world. Historically, modern democracy arose from the need of kings to secure the support of their subjects, both nobles and commoners, especially for the levying of taxes. The monarch had consequently to establish councils more or less representative of the estates of the realm, and to make concessions to these bodies of powers in return for revenues, that is, to share his authority with them—a process that continued in Europe until the monarch was left with only a ceremonial position.

Where democracy is a widespread aspiration, as in Argentina or Brazil, a military regime may simply walk away and turn the government over to elected civilians; but in many places, where democracy is not familiar, the process has to be more like the clipping of powers of the European monarchs in the slow growth of modern democracy. In this view, any relaxation or concession made to people outside the official structures constitutes an edging in the direction of democracy. For example, permitting slightly realistic elections may nurture expectations of genuine elections to bodies with real authority. Inviting people to make money for themselves, as in the China of Deng Xiaoping, invites them to make themselves independent of the state, thinking and acting on their own, perhaps exerting some influence through economic power. It also nourishes nonpolitical values and undermines ideology. Conceivably accumulation of such concessions might ultimately lead a totalitarian ruling party to admit democratic competition for power.

History has yet to provide an example of a modern absolutism softening enough to give way to an open political system. But movement toward a more relaxed authoritarianism or partial democracy is probably always positive in terms of humane values. A modicum of freedom is much more promising than none at all. Probably nearly all outside observers would agree that life is materially and mentally more rewarding in Hungary than in Romania. Likewise the relative freedom of Mexico's partial democracy has been decidedly beneficial, despite its limitations, and the political system has performed well, at least until the oil boom poured excess riches into it.

If democracy is always desirable when scarce or absent, this does not imply that the maximum of democracy is necessarily the best for most peoples. Authoritarianism has values, and it is questionable, especially in much divided or grossly unequal societies, just how much democracy is desirable or sustainable. But it seems clear that most of the world would be better governed, and consequently would enjoy greater material well-being as well as more freedom, if governments were less authoritarian and more democratic. It is consequently reasonable to regard the progress of democracy as valuable, promising more rational societies, more autonomy and creativity, and better quality of life. Indeed, hardly anything is more important, and it is no great exaggeration to say that the health of democracy is equivalent to the health of humanity. What the writers of the following chapters seek to do is to evaluate the political health of the world.

1   Western Europe

Dennis A. Kavanagh

Western Europe has been the birthplace for many values that have contributed to liberal democracy. These include direct democracy (in the Greek city-states), Roman law, the Reformation, the rise of industrialism, and liberalism. At the same time the region has nourished antidemocratic ideologies. After 1815, for example, there emerged in France a school of right-wing philosophers who wanted to restore the values associated with the Catholic church, the Crown, and the hierarchy, which had been overturned by the 1789 Revolution. At the turn of the century, elitists like Mosca, Pareto, and Michels dismissed the possibilities of democracy and proclaimed the inevitability of rule by an elite, regardless of any political arrangements.

The experience of the region after the 1919 Versailles peace treaty was discouraging for believers in the progress of democracy. Although immediately after the defeat of the more militaristic-authoritarian Central Powers, many new states were erected with democratic constitutions, most of these soon gave way to dictatorships, especially in Eastern and Southern Europe. Democratic regimes were replaced by authoritarian or totalitarian regimes in Portugal, Greece, Germany, Italy, Austria, and Spain. Only in Britain and Scandinavia was democracy secure. Challenges were posed by the rise of Fascism and of Communism; both ideologies were anti-individualist and hostile to the idea of limited government or a pluralistic society.

These developments drew attention to the shortcomings of democratic political institutions, multiparty politics, and extreme proportional representation, and to the important part played by legacies of history, national character (particularly in the case of Germany), and the "loads" imposed on the system by economic crises, cleavages, and low legitimacy. As recently as 1956 a major student[1] of comparative government contrasted Anglo–American societies, as model democracies, with the unstable democracies of continental Europe (France, Italy, and prewar Germany).

For purposes of this chapter we treat Western Europe as consisting of 19 states. They are the five Nordic states of Finland, Norway, Sweden, Denmark, and Iceland; 11 continental European (France, Italy, Germany, Switzerland, Luxembourg, the Netherlands, Belgium, Greece, Spain, Portugal, and Austria); three island states, Britain, the Republic of Ireland, and Malta. Usage of the term Western Europe, and the assumption that there are sufficient important similarities across the states to justify the term, is a recent development. The postwar geographical and political division in Europe between the Soviet Union and her socialist neighbors in the East and the other states has meant that, almost by default, the latter are now regarded as Western European.

The outstanding feature of the Western European states is that they are all liberal-democratic, despite great differences in their national histories, party systems, and political institutions. We may distinguish between those such as Britain, Switzerland, and Sweden, which have durable histories as liberal democracies; West Germany, Italy, and Austria, which have checkered records, the Netherlands, Norway, Denmark, France, and Belgium, which were occupied in the Second World War; and Spain, Portugal, and Greece, all of which were under military rule a decade ago and have attained democratic status only recently. The last states may be termed democratic latecomers; they have been plagued by political divisions, instability, and rule by men on horseback. In the 1980s, for the first time in the history of the region, one can refer to democracy as the political norm.

A recent survey of democracy found that only 23 states have continuously permitted competitive elections since 1948.[2] Of the 21, 6 states are Anglo-American (Britain, the United States, Australia, New Zealand, Canada, and Ireland). Fifteen are Western European (the notable exclusions from this list are Spain, Portugal, and Greece). Israel and Japan complete the list. There is some justification for

regarding liberal democracy as a phenomenon that is largely geographical (Western European), or cultural (Anglo-American), and
located in the twentieth century.

In a famous article Lipset[3] stated that "The more well-to-do a
nation, the greater the chances that it will sustain democracy." His
research and later studies showed an association between stable
democracy and high levels of national wealth, industrialism, education, urbanization, and communications. Several facts tend to confirm this thesis.

The Western European states are highly industrialized and comparatively affluent. Greece, Spain, Portugal, and Ireland are the least
industrialized (they are the only states in the region with at least
one fifth of the work force in agriculture) and are also the poorest
states in Western Europe. Three of them have been the least successful as democracies in the region in the twentieth century. In Portugal
and Spain dictatorships were formed in the interwar years, a time
when liberal democracy was retreating in Europe. The Portuguese
dictatorship lasted nearly 50 years, until a left-wing army coup in
1974 paved the way for democracy. In Spain the monarchy was
restored after the death of General Francisco Franco in 1975, and
competitive elections followed in 1977. In Greece the army has
regularly intervened in politics in the twentieth century and there
was a military dictatorship between 1967 and 1974, the only successful challenge to liberal democracy in postwar Western Europe. However, these states have made rapid progress in economic modernization and their per capita income has increased greatly in the past
decade.

The variety of political models of democracy in Western Europe
presents a challenge to the student of politics. The Scandinavian
societies, for example, are among the most affluent in the world.
They are also highly collectivist in their political cultures; and, as a
result of nearly half a century of Social Democratic dominance in
government, they rank near the top in terms of public spending,
welfare provision, and taxation. The Netherlands, Belgium, Austria,
and Switzerland have attracted attention because they have combined political stability in the postwar period with social fragmentation, as groups have formed mutually exclusive *zuilen, familles
spirituelles,* or *lager.* They are characterized by grand coalitions (on
the Swiss seven-member Federal Council informal rules govern the
allocation of seats between parties and language groups according

to their popular support), minority representation, proportionalism, federalism, and decentralization. Lijphart[4] calls these polities consensus systems, because they try to take account of, or represent, minorities.

Britain, of course, has long been regarded as a model stable democracy. In contrast to the Western European norm of coalition governments and proportional electoral systems the majoritarian British system of government has emerged from the dominance of two parties and the first-past-the-post electoral system.

In France the Fifth Republic has been perhaps the most legitimate regime the country had had since 1789. It has restored stability to France by combining a strong directly elected president with a simpler party system, in which a leftist political "stream" (Socialists and Communists) opposes a rightist "stream" (Gaullists and Giscardians). Moreover, the institutions of the regime now appear to be accepted by all sections of French society. Similarly, the modern West German state has gained legitimacy from impressive economic recovery. The simplification of the party system and the new constitution have also played a part in preventing a recurrence of the instability of Weimar. German economic efficiency has long been admired; it is new that many political commentators regard its political system as a model liberal democracy.

ELECTIONS AND FORMATION OF GOVERNMENTS

All Western European states have universal suffrage, though Switzerland granted the vote to women only in 1971. There is a good deal of similarity in the conditions of voting; age (normally 18) is the chief ground for limiting the vote. Richard Rose observes that the election rules are fair to all candidates and all parties, and "The requirements for securing a place on a ballot are few, and disqualifications of anti-system parties or adult citizens virtually non-existent."[5]

Opportunities for casting a vote vary widely in Western European states.[6] Some two-thirds of the states provide for the holding of referendums and 12 have held at least one referendum since 1945, mostly in connection with the country's application for membership of the European Economic Community. In four states—Belgium, Italy, Spain, and Switzerland—there is provision for direct election of the upper legislative house. In other states the upper house is indirectly chosen, or composed of appointed and hereditary members (as in Britain), or does not exist. All states, except for Portugal, Britain, France, Spain, and Norway, allow voters to choose at elections between candidates of the same party. Electoral turnout varies widely between states, with a handful of states regularly having turnouts in excess of 90 percent (Table 1.1).

The variety of institutional arrangements for choosing governments demonstrates that democracy is compatible with many types of systems. There is the predominantly two-party system in Britain, the emerging two blocs in Germany and France, and the extreme multipartism of Denmark, Belgium, and the Netherlands. The British one-party majority government is not found anywhere else on the Continent as a regular feature. Even in France and West Germany, where Socialists and Christian Democrats have had a majority of seats, they have opted for sharing power in coalitions. (In France, the Communists were members of the government until 1984, when they broke with the Socialists.) Denmark has had frequent spells of minority governments since 1945. One may distinguish between countries in which elections normally directly determine the composition of government and those in which bargaining between parties follows an election to determine the composition of a government. To a large extent the decisiveness of elections for the formation of governments depends on whether one party or group of parties emerges with a majority of seats. Table 1.2 shows a fairly even division between the two types of states in the region.

Table 1.1. Average Turnout Rates in General Elections Since 1945

%	Countries
90%+	Luxembourg*, Italy*, Belgium*, Austria
80–89%	Denmark, Sweden, Norway
75–79.9%	France, Britain, Greece, Finland, Spain
70–74.9%	Ireland
Below 70%	Switzerland

* = compulsory voting

Source: Ivor Crewe, "Electoral Participation," in *Dunleavy at the Polls,* ed. D. Butler et al. (Washington, DC: American Enterprise Institute), pp. 234–37.

Table 1.2. Election Outcomes and the Formation of Governments

(A) States in which elections normally determine the composition of government	(B) States in which inter-party bargaining determines the composition of government
Austria	Belgium
Britain	Denmark
France (Fifth Republic)	Finland
Ireland	Italy
Norway	Netherlands
Spain	Portugal
Sweden	France (Fourth Republic)
Switzerland	Greece
	Luxembourg

Source: Anthony King, "What Do Elections Decide," in *Democracy at the Polls,* ed. D. Butler et al. (Washington, DC: American Enterprise Institute, 1981), p. 281.

RECENT EVENTS

By tradition, the southern part of the region has been democracy's weak area. Interestingly, at the beginning of 1985, four of the five mainly Socialist governments in Western Europe were found in the south and three of the states held general elections in 1985. In both Portugal and Greece these confirmed the country's transition from dictatorship. In Portugal the centrist Social Democrats replaced the Socialists as the largest party and dominated the new government. The 1985 election produced the eighth government that Portugal has had in nine years. Multipartism and the absence of a clear majority party have led to fragile coalition or minority governments. This governmental instability has not helped the country find effective policies for coping with mounting economic difficulties.

Greece is the only Western European state considered that has actually abandoned democracy in the postwar period (1967–74). Interventions by the military and the monarchy have been regular features of Greek politics in the twentieth century, however anach-

ronistic they appear. These two obstacles to constitutional government have since been removed. The monarchy was abolished in a
referendum in 1973; and a party of the center-right, the New Democrats, won the first elections. The army was humiliated by its defeat
in Cyprus in 1974, and it was widely criticized for its abuse of human
rights. In 1984 the Greek version of the U.S. Central Intelligence
Agency, the KYP, was brought under government control, and the
files on the political views of many Greeks were destroyed. In
November 1984 a law outlawing torture was adopted unanimously
by Parliament.

In 1981 the Socialist Pasok party had displaced the New Democrats, and the government party increased its lead in elections in
1985. The state-controlled radio and television provide a black and
white view of political life, with regular attacks on "the Right,"
"Capitalism," "Imperialism," the United States, and the European
Community. According to one expert the government-controlled
media conduct "a propaganda campaign the like of which would
have made even the dictatorship blush."[7] Many neutral observers
of the 1985 election campaign were dismayed by the blatant way in
which the government-controlled television and radio gave massive
exposure to government spokesmen and little attention to the New
Democracy party.

In Spain the post-Franco constitution, based on a constitutional
monarchy and parliamentary democracy, was approved in a referendum in 1978, and the system appeared to be well established by
1985. It is not surprising that, after a gap of nearly 50 years in nor-
mal political participation, there has been great electoral volatility,
and the political parties have taken some time to establish themselves.
The breakup of the center-led coalition government in 1982 was
followed by a strong Socialist government led by Felipe Gonzalez.
An extreme example of a "flash" party has been seen in the fortunes
of the Unión Centro Democrático (UCD). This was the main party
of government until 1982 when it fell from a 35 percent share of the
vote gained in 1979 to a mere 7 percent. Terrorism continues to be a
problem, with the frequent bombings of ETA, the Basque separatist
organization. Retaliatory outrages have also been committed by the
Anti-Terrorist Liberation Group. Civil libertarians were concerned
about the Constitutional Tribunal's ruling that abortion in Spain
(allowed in a 1983 act) is incompatible with the constitution. The
Emergence in 1982 of the Socialists with 46 percent of the vote

(and a majority of seats) and a moderate rightist-center party, Alianza Popular (AP), with 25 percent, has provided some degree of effective choice for the electorate.

In France, attention in 1985 concentrated on two developments. The first was the sinking in Auckland, New Zealand, in July, of the environmentalist Greenpeace vessel Rainbow Warrior by the French secret service. At the outset the government denied all knowledge of the incident, but it was well known that the French government resented Greenpeace monitoring its nuclear testing in the Pacific. It gradually emerged that the secret service had authorized the operation and, after the resignation of the head of overseas intelligence, M. Maurice Lacoste, and the minister of defense, M. Charles Hernu, commentators speculated that responsibility might lie within the presidential palace. Others wondered, however, if this was a plot by the secret service to discredit the government. It was the investigative journalism of *Le Monde* rather than Parliament that exposed the outrage and the cover-up.

The possible tension inherent in the Fifth Republic's dual executive moved nearer to crisis point in 1985. Since 1958 the president has always operated with a prime minister and cabinet broadly acceptable to him. In 1984 and 1985 election results and opinion polls all pointed to a clear defeat for the Socialists in the next general election, due in March 1986. But President François Mitterand would still have two years of his term to run. How would he cope with a government of the opposition? Would he dissolve Parliament again?

In some desperation the Socialists introduced proportional representation with the intention of fragmenting the parliamentary strength of the parties of the right. This carried on a French tradition whereby governments exploit the electoral system for their own ends. In the Fourth Republic center parties had used the system to weaken the extreme left and right. In the Fifth Republic the second ballot had been adopted in 1958, in part to isolate the Communists. One welcome development under Mitterand has been a less blatant Elysée control of the state-run French television, ORTF.

After the government backed down in 1984 over the plans for greater state control over church schools, the opposition demanded a referendum on the issue. This promised to re-ignite the old church-state divisions that had plagued the Third and Fourth Republics. President Mitterand countered by proposing a constitutional amendment that would allow referenda to be held on bills that affect basic freedoms. The opposition blocked the measure in the Senate, but not before losing face. The right-wing National Front, led by M. Jean-Marie Le Pen, continued to prosper. At a time of rising unemployment its crude anti-immigrant policy attracted support and forced a tougher response by other right-wing parties.

In the German Federal Republic (FRG), the Social Democrats appeared to have recovered some ground and there were signs of a rapprochement with the Greens for the next general election. Employees in the public service are still required to take a loyalty oath to uphold the constitution. Only rarely are prominent dissenters refused employment, but the publicity is invariably embarrassing for the government. The memory of Weimar was so sharp that the Basic Law, the postwar constitution, declared ineligible any parties that sought to destroy the democratic system or endanger the existence of the Federal Republic. Under this clause the authorities in the 1950s banned the Communist and neo-Nazi parties. The ban remains in effect, more in letter than spirit, as other Communist and neo-Nazi parties have been formed.

In Italy, Mr. Bettino Craxi, a Socialist, led a party with only 11 percent of the votes but he proved a capable prime minister of the coalition government. His defense minister, Mr. Giovanni Spadolini, openly dissented from the government's release of a Palestine Liberation Organization (PLO) terrorist who had helped to seize the Italian liner *Achille Lauro,* and prompted the collapse of the government. But Mr. Craxi was able to form a new, broadly similar, government. In 1984 the government had agreed to a revision of the 1929 Concordat with the Vatican. The new terms took account of the more secular Italian society; religious instruction in schools was made optional, and Catholicism ceased to be the state religion.

Belgium has had a postwar history of short-lived coalition governments, with divisions between Socialists, Christians, and Liberals. In recent years the linguistic-cultural conflicts between the French-speaking Walloons and Dutch-speaking Flemings have threatened to break up the country. To date, the grant of considerable autonomy to the separate regions and division of the main parties into French and Dutch versions, have kept the state intact. The constitution was amended in 1970 to require cabinets to have equal numbers of French- and Dutch-speaking members. Postwar governments have lasted an average of a year, but the outgoing administration led by Mr. Wilfried Martens survived nearly four years until its fall in the summer. In the general election, the outgoing center-right parties were returned with a majority; the dominant Social Christians made gains that more than compensated for the Liberal losses. There were losses for the French-speaking group, Dutch-speaking Volkes-unie in Flanders, anti-immigrant parties, and the Communists, who lost their two seats in Parliament.

The Belgian election result rebutted those who feared that economic decline leads to support for extreme or antisystem parties. In spite of suffering one of the highest rates of unemployment (13.3 percent) in Western Europe, Belgians in effect voted for another dose of austerity economic policies by remaining faithful to the center parties. But sectionalism continued to be a threat, as different parties dominated different regions: Social Christians in Flanders, Liberals in Brussels, and Socialists in Wallonia.

General elections were held in Norway and Sweden. In both cases the incumbent government retained power, albeit narrowly. In Norway, the Conservative-led coalition, which in 1981 interrupted Labour's 50 years in office, was returned, with a majority of one seat over Labour and leftist-Socialists. The Conservatives (50 seats) and Labour (71 seats) had three-quarters of the seats. A crucial two seats were held by the anti-tax Justice party. The classic British device of a parliamentary dissolution as a way out of a deadlock is not available in Norway.

In Sweden, the "bourgeois" parties (Center, Liberal, and Conservative) had managed to oust the Social Democrats in 1976, after the latter had been in office for 44 years. But their coalition formed a fragile alternative to the Social Democrats. The Palme-led Social Democrats regained office in 1982 and held on in the general election in September 1985.

In Denmark, the center-right has made electoral progress. In 1981 the Conservatives controlled the prime ministership for the first time since 1905. As in Norway and Sweden, there has emerged a more competitive balance between the blocs of the left and right, and a challenge to the traditional dominance of Socialist parties. In Denmark this has been accompanied by a fragmentation of the party system in the wake of the referendum on Danish membership in the EEC in 1972. There were five parties in Parliament in 1971, 11 in 1977, and ten in 1985.

In Britain, perhaps the major complaint has been about the effect of the first-past-the-post electoral system. In an era of three-party politics, this has reached a new level of unfairness. In the 1983 general election, the new Alliance party (of the Liberals and Social Democrats) got a mere 3.5 percent of seats in the House of Commons for 25.4 percent of the popular votes. The Conservative government achieved its landslide of 61 percent of seats with 42 percent of the vote. By contrast, virtually all other Western European electoral systems pay some respect to the idea of equality of votes. The disproportional British result is perhaps only tolerated in a relatively united and consensual society.

Civil libertarians had a number of criticisms of the government. In 1984 the government debarred security workers at the Government Communications Centre from membership in a trade union. Recently an appeal against this policy was carried to the European Commission of Human Rights. A year-long strike by most of the country's coal miners ended in April 1985 only after many bloody confrontations between police and strikers, in which the police and courts had allegedly been used to undermine the strike. An act to abolish the Greater London Council and a number of other elected local governments became law. Such a measure would have been unthinkable in a federal system.

Northern Ireland continued in a state of "exception." The Prevention of Terrorism Act (Temporary Provision), introduced in 1976 and renewed for the lifetime of each Parliament, gives sweeping power to the police and authorities, including the arrest and detention of suspects. There are also trials without jury for suspected terrorists. In November 1985 a historic agreement was made between the governments of the United Kingdom and Ireland to establish a conference that would discuss relations between Dublin and Northern Ireland. Protestant Unionists were furious at what they regarded as a sellout, and all 15 Unionist members of Parliament (MP) resigned their seats in the House of Commons. They hoped to force the holding of by-elections on the same day, so making the elections into a referendum. They objected to the possible intervention of the Dublin government in the affairs of the province and were not assuaged by assurances that the Irish government agreed that a united Ireland could only be achieved with the assent of the majority in the North.

The dark spot on the democratic front is Malta, whose population (360,000) and size are too small to command much attention by students of politics. The grant of independence from the British in 1964 did not ease the bitter rivalry between the Nationalist and

Labour parties. The Nationalists had a narrow majority in government from 1964 to 1971, but since then Labour has been in office. In recent years society has become more polarized, and the level of violence at political gatherings has increased. Both parties accuse each other of using thugs to break up meetings. In the 1981 election the Nationalists gained 51 percent of the vote but got fewer seats as a result of gerrymandered districts. Between December 1981 and March 1983 the Nationalists boycotted Parliament, and since then there have been frequent walkouts by opposition MPs.

These events have increased the resistance of the opposition party and the Catholic church to government policies. In 1984 the European Parliament condemned the activity of Labour-led gangs that had sacked the Nationalist party headquarters. There were serious cases of political bias in the state-controlled broadcasting media. The General Workers' Union ordered its reporters to boycott the activities of the Nationalists. When the Nationalists advised their supporters to boycott goods advertised on the broadcasting media, the government informed businessmen that they would be refused import permits if they did not advertise.

In December 1984 Dom Mintoff stepped down as prime minister and was replaced by Mifsud-Bonnici, who had earlier declared that Malta "needs a one-party state." As minister of education, Bonnici had led the offensive against the Catholic church schools that, in contrast to the state schools, charged fees. The government introduced legislation to close any schools that charged fees and regulations that amounted to state control.

In the 1983 elections the Austrian Socialist party lost the overall majority that it had enjoyed since 1971. It then formed a coalition with the Freedom party. The activities of far-right parties caused some concern; and in 1984 the government banned a meeting that was to launch a neo-Nazi party, the National Front. The significance of the move was reduced by the fact that a number of other far-right parties existed.

In Finland, interest centered on the split in the Communist party (Democratic League). The major group was the Euro-Communists, who favored some accommodation with democratic procedures and opposed the more Stalinist minority supported by Moscow. Government is in the hands of a complex center-left coalition of Social Democratic, Center, Rural, and Swedish People's parties. Unstable center-left coalitions are the rule in Finland, but some stability is provided by a strong, elected president.

THREATS TO DEMOCRACY

Many forces that have been a threat to liberal democratic regimes in the region have weakened recently. In Italy and France, the Communist parties are no longer the formidable challenge they appeared at the height of the Cold War. These parties, plus the Spanish party, shared the label of Euro-Communism in the late 1970s, and formally accepted many liberal-democratic procedures. The easing of the Cold War between East and West from the mid-1950s made them appear less outsiders in France and Italy. The parties agreed that the transition to socialism could be achieved peacefully, diluted their old claims that it required "the dictatorship of the proletariat," and loosened ties with Moscow. In France, the Communist party has been in decline for many years. It gained little from membership in the Socialist-dominated government formed in 1981, departed in 1984, and slumped to 11 percent of the vote in the 1984 elections for the European Parliament. In Italy the Communists have accepted the country's membership in the North Atlantic Treaty Organization (NATO), the EEC, and the mixed economy. Although its electoral support in 1983 (29.9 percent) has fallen back from its 1976 level (34.4 percent), the permanent exclusion from power of the second largest party has produced immobility in the Italian party system and short-lived coalitions.

There have been various leftist splinter parties claiming to be faithful heirs to Marx and Trotsky. Invariably, they allege that Communist parties have compromised their principles; and, like the PSU in France and the Socialist Workers party (SWP) in Britain, they are dedicated to fighting the class war and overthrowing capitalism. They attract a trivial number of votes in elections.

Parties of the extreme right have also failed to progress, except in France. Nazi and Fascist parties in Italy and West Germany attract minuscule support, although the rightist MSI in Italy is important. Parties of the far right campaign on hostility to immigrants, anticommunism, and rabid nationalism.

In the late nineteenth century some spokesmen for the Catholic church were unsympathetic to democracy. Until recently in France, Italy, Spain, and Portugal the claims of the church, particularly on control of schools, caused further division between left and right. But the modern church has proved more willing to accept values of liberalism and democracy. Indeed, its support for moderate center-right Christian Democratic parties in Italy and West Germany has been important in promoting political stability in these countries. Only in Malta can the church complain of being persecuted. Religion-based parties in the Netherlands have steadily lost electoral support, and the political power of the church in Italy and Spain has diminished. Religion has been a political issue only in Northern Ireland, where rivalries between Catholics and Protestants, and rival national loyalties to Ireland and Britain have brought about emergency rule and the lapse of liberal democratic procedures.

The main postwar threat to democracy in Western Europe has come from the army, particularly in southern Europe, and in France in 1958. Yet Greece, Spain, and Portugal have made relatively bloodless transitions from dictatorships in 1974 and 1975. In Portugal the withdrawal of the armed forces from politics was confirmed by the abolition in 1982 of the Council of Revolution, a military-dominated body set up to guarantee the spirit of the Revolution of April 1974. In Spain, notwithstanding the attempted coup in February 1981, the army has lost influence. In all Western European states, military intervention is a remote possibility because the level of integration of the armed forces with society is high, the political culture denies legitimacy to a takeover,[8] and the "linkage" (e.g., NATO, EEC, etc.) between liberal democratic states is increasing. In the early years of the EEC, Spain, Greece, and Portugal were not politically acceptable because they were not democracies. Greece was admitted in 1981; Spain and Portugal joined on January 1, 1986. Absorption in a wider community of democratic states is likely to prove a force for strengthening democracy.

The problem of urban terrorism by extremist political groups has been more troublesome. It has been most marked in former dictatorships. In Spain, the Basque separatist group ETA, in Italy the "Red Brigade," and in Germany extreme left-wing groups have used terrorism as a means of attempting political destabilization. In Northern Ireland terror and murder have regularly been employed by the Irish Republican Army (IRA) and various Protestant Ulster "defense" groups. Indeed, the more significant threat stems from the coincidence of terrorism with nationalism, as in Northern Ireland. The largest antisystem vote in the region is given to nationalist parties in Belgium (Table 1.3).

The motives of extremist groups include separatism, nationalism, and extreme left and right ideologies. But they may be able to undermine the authority of government by demonstrating its inability

Table 1.3. Antisystem Parties

	Extreme Left	Extreme Right	Nationalists
	% votes, latest election		
Belgium	2.3*	0	11.9 (Flemish
Denmark	1.1*	0	0
France	1.3	0	0
Germany	0.2	0.2	0
Ireland	0	0	0
Italy	1.4	5.3	0.9
Luxembourg	5.8*	0	0
Netherlands	2.1*	0	0
United Kingdom	0.1	0.6	2.6

*Extra-system Communist Party vote.

Source: Richard Rose, "Elections and Electoral Pressures," in *Democracy and Elections,* ed. V. Bogdanor and D. Butler (Cambridge: Cambridge University Press, 1984), p. 30.

to maintain law and order or even guarantee the safety of leading figures (e.g., the murder of Aldo Moro in Italy in 1978). But they may also provoke the government into taking extreme repressive measures and abandoning democratic procedures. The mass trials of terrorists in Italy, trials of suspected terrorists without juries in Ulster, the refusal of the British government to allow elected Sinn Fein spokesmen access to the broadcast media or the mainland, and the Stern antiterrorist legislation in West Germany are all examples of how regimes may feel they have to compromise liberal standards in face of terrorism.

The postwar period has seen societies in the region achieve rapid increases in living standards and virtually every state has had its version of an economic "miracle." Economic strength and widening affluence have undoubtedly contributed to the legitimacy of the democratic regimes. But in the mid-1970s the dramatic increase in oil prices and the slowdown in Western economies signaled the end of the long postwar economic "boom." There was a simultaneous increase in levels of unemployment and prices, and the resulting "stagflation" has produced strains for the welfare consensus as governments everywhere found it difficult to finance programs. Policies of increasing taxation, growing public expenditure, and new programs appeared to command less acceptance at the ballot box. The success in California of Proposition 13 in 1978 was paralleled by similar tax backlash movements in Denmark and the swing to the right in Britain and Sweden.

Increasing levels of unemployment and inflation promoted disillusion with governments, which were more frequently turned out of office in the late 1970s. There is little evidence, however, that antisystem parties are attracting much support (Table 1.3). Democracy does not need economic success to survive. Everywhere the growing costs of welfare have been a target for economy-minded governments in the 1980s. This has coincided with a swing to the political right in Western Europe in the elections over the same period. Even where left-wing governments have been installed, as in Spain, Portugal, Greece, and France, right-wing social and economic policies were being pursued and priority accorded to the battle against inflation even at a time of high unemployment. By 1985 only Sweden was still pursuing a Keynesian style program of government spending to maintain high levels of unemployment. The ideas of deregulation, tax cuts, and budget reductions have been widely accepted.

Parties of the left have suffered with the steady decline of their natural social and economic bases, namely the manual working class and manufacturing industry. The economic recession has, on the whole, turned voters away from the free spending policies of the political left, yet there remains extensive public support for social welfare and economic policies that are credible and realistic. If anything, tax cutting may have reached its peak by 1985. In Norway and Denmark electoral support for tax policies declined and surveys in Britain (like the United States) showed that this was a minority cause.

With the exception of the Italian Communist party—and it is arguable that it is no longer an antisystem party—most antisystem parties perform miserably at the polls. Opinion surveys for the Euro-Baromètre, a Community-wide survey organization, show that nearly four-fifths of the Community's population is still satisfied with their living conditions and support the regime. The apparent security of political regimes in Western European states and the consolidation of the democratic process and competitive elections in Spain, Greece, and Portugal mark 1985 as a good year for democracy.

NOTES

1. Gabriel Almond, "Comparative Political Systems," *Journal of Politics* 18 (1956):391–409.

2. Arendt Lijphart, *Democracies* (New Haven, Conn.: Yale University Press, 1984), pp. 38–39.

3. Seymour Martin Lipset, *Political Man* (Garden City, NY: Doubleday, 1960), p. 34.

4. Lijphart, *Democracies,* pp. 21–36.

5. Richard Rose, "Elections and Electoral Pressures," in *Democracy and Elections,* ed. V. Bogdanor and D. Butler (Cambridge: Cambridge University Press, 1984), p. 29.

6. Ivor Crewe, "Electoral Participation," in *Dunleavy at the Polls,* ed. Butler et al. (Washington, DC: American Enterprise Institute, 1981).

7. D. Katsoudas, "Greece: A Politically Controlled State Monopoly Broadcasting System," in *West European Politics* 8, no. 2 (1985):150.

8. Samuel Finer, *Man on Horseback* (London: Pall Mall, 1962), pp. 25–26.

2   North America

Martin P. Wattenberg

The year 1985 saw the continuation of recent positive trends in the health of democracy in the United States. Public confidence in the government continued to show signs of recovery from the low point reached during the domestic and foreign policy crisis year of 1980. In 1985, for example, for the first time since Eisenhower, a president in his second term maintained a popularity level above 50 percent for an entire year. The U.S. Congress also enjoyed an historically high level of approval, thereby indicating a more general sense of public satisfaction with U.S. political institutions than had been seen for some time. A December 1985 Gallup Poll found that 51 percent of the U.S. public reported being satisfied with the way things are going in the nation compared to just 12 percent six years ago.

Together, the president and Congress were able to accomplish little in terms of public policy in 1985. Yet a good case can be made that this was pretty much what the 1984 electorate wanted. As Seymour Martin Lipset[1] has written, by a 54 percent to 39 percent margin voters in 1984 held the opinion that it would be better if Reagan were to face a Democratic-controlled Congress that would not pass everything he wanted.

Although they approved of the job Reagan had done in restoring economic growth, reducing inflation, and bolstering U.S. power abroad, there was nevertheless widespread disagreement with many of Reagan's policy stands. Indeed, a plethora of academic studies emerged in 1985 arguing that Reagan would have lost to Mondale

had voters cast their ballots solely on the basis of policy positions.[2]
This fact was taken into account by many politicians on both sides
of the political fence. For example, Richard Cheney, Republican
House Policy Committee chairman, was quoted in September 1985
as saying "It would be a mistake to fall into the trap that, because
he's so popular as a person, that this automatically translates into
support for his policies."[3]

Knowing that the House of Representatives would continue to
check the president was thus a comfort to many people who voted
for Reagan as an expression of approval of his performance but not
his policies. Without this substantial rein on presidential influence,
the people of the United States probably would not have been as
pleased as they were in 1985 with the federal government.

During crisis periods, when efficacious responses to policy
problems are urgently needed, presidential-congressional stalemates
are most likely to be seen as troublesome both by the public as well
as by scholars. The seeming inability of the government to take
action has frequently raised public dissatisfaction during such times.
However, in 1985 the public seemed satisfied to have the government
deadlocked and unable to accomplish anything of note. After two
decades of turmoil, conflict, and crisis Americans were happy to
settle for quiescence, and satisfaction with the government continued
to increase.

AN END TO THE CRISIS OF CONFIDENCE?

To fully appreciate the relative degree of satisfaction with the
functioning of U.S. democracy in 1985, one must take into account
that throughout the 1960s and 1970s leading scholars and political
pundits in the United States drew our attention to a variety of negative behavioral and institutional trends in U.S. politics. Although the
psychological recovery is far from complete, it nevertheless offers
more encouragement than has been seen in a long time.

In general, what could be characterized in the early 1960s as
an allegiant participatory democracy whose politics were dominated
and structured by a stable two-party system had by 1980 become an
alienated and apathetic polity with a decaying party system. A citizenry that once usually trusted its government to do what is right
most of the time had become cynical and lacking in confidence of

its leaders and institutions. An electorate that scholars in the early 1960s proudly labeled as the "civic culture" had seen voter turnout figures decline continuously for two decades to the point where the United States ranked among the lowest of the world's democracies in voting participation. And a party system that once anchored voters into relatively stable and predictable patterns of political behavior had been seriously weakened due to neglect and indifference, leaving voters to drift and thereby creating a rise in political volatility.

Related to all of this was a view widespread among scholars of U.S. politics that U.S. political institutions were no longer functioning properly. By the time Reagan entered the White House in 1981 the failure of recent past presidents to maintain a reasonable level of public approval and a cordial working relationship with the Congress was seen by many as symptomatic of the failure of the institutions as well as the leaders.

In 1979, President Jimmy Carter called national attention to this point of view when he made his famous speech on the "crisis of confidence." Carter argued that Americans' growing pessimism about the future threatened to "strike at the very heart and soul and spirit of our national will" and to "destroy the social and political fabric of America." President Carter's political opponents attempted to turn the tables by saying that the problem could better be described as a "crisis of competence," reflecting a lack of public faith in Carter's ability to deal with governmental problems rather than a more general dearth of confidence in the effectiveness of the American political system.

Such arguments were broadly familiar to scholars, who had been following the decline of trust in government in the United States since the early 1970s. In the first of two major articles on the subject, Arthur Miller[4] argued that the public's greater cynicism reflected a "widespread, basic discontent and political alienation," whereas Jack Citrin responded that it could be more properly interpreted as a statement of dissatisfaction with the recent performance of American political leadership. Citrin argued that a "modest 'winning streak' and perhaps, some new names in the [political] lineup may be sufficient to raise the level of trust in government."[5] Miller, in turn, countered that public discontent extended well beyond dissatisfaction with the current incumbents and predicted that "a replacement of political leaders with no subsequent improvement in the performance of the government may generate a new spiral of political distrust."[6]

As the presidency went from Nixon to Ford, and then Ford to Carter, public trust in government continued to spiral downward despite the end of the Vietnam War and the Watergate scandal. Miller wrote in 1981 that

> Four administrations have come and gone since confidence began to decline. Simply replacing one set of incumbents with another political group is clearly not a solution to growing distrust. Institutional restructuring is obviously necessary.

But two years later data released from the National Election Studies conducted at the University of Michigan indicated that trust in government was on the rebound for the first time since such measurements began in the late 1950s.[7] Given the fact that this survey was conducted in late 1982—during the midst of the worst economic downturn since the Great Depression—this was clearly an expression of renewed confidence in the government.

One cannot deny that Reagan was able in 1981 to initiate the most important reversal in the direction of U.S. public policy in half a century. For once a candidate not only promised clear and dramatic changes but accomplished them as well. Reagan campaigned in 1980 on three major planks: cutting taxes, increasing military spending, and decreasing the rate of growth of federal spending on social services. If it can be said that the length and complexity of the Carter administration's agenda brought it to ruin, the Reagan administration was just the opposite. Having a clear and limited set of priorities in his first year in office proved to be a major advantage for Reagan in dealing with the Congress.

What made the Reagan agenda unique in twentieth century U.S. history though was that it called for a fundamental restructuring of federal policies without at the same time proposing a myriad of new programs. The Reagan years mark the longest period during which no major domestic spending programs have been proposed since the days of President Herbert Hoover. To Reagan, the federal government was more the problem on the domestic scene than the mechanism for solutions.

As a consequence, his budgetary proposals called for abolishment of many discretionary grant programs as well as for spending restrictions and cuts in social insurance programs. Had the Congress passed all of what Reagan asked for, federal spending on social services would have been reduced roughly 20 percent during his first term. In the end, the cuts amounted to about 10 percent—a major change in the course of public policy by any standard.

Yet it would be misleading to say that Reagan succeeded in cutting the growth of federal spending; rather he significantly redirected it from social service to military spending. While spending on social welfare was being curtailed, real defense outlays were being increased by 7 percent a year. These opposite trends resulted in defense spending increasing as a proportion of the federal budget from 26 percent in FY 1981 to 32 percent in FY 1985—the largest such increase ever in peacetime.

A final element of the Reagan program was the 1981 tax cut. While Reagan failed to reduce the overall size of government in terms of expenditures, he was successful in reducing the scope of federal revenue collection. The Reagan tax cuts resulted in a decline in the federal tax burden from 20.8 percent to 18.7 percent of the Gross National Product (GNP) from FY 1981 to FY 1985. Furthermore, by providing for the future indexing of federal taxes, Congress ensured that this would be a long-lasting change which would not be eroded by bracket-creep due to inflation.

All told, the implementation of the Reagan agenda produced the most significant changes in the course of American public policy in half a century. Such a demonstration that government in the United States can sometimes effectively implement policy goals was no doubt crucial to the small upturn in trust in government measured in 1982.

If the fact that a new president could increase public confidence in government by merely doing what he said he was going to do, it is reasonable to expect that any indication that the new program was working would produce further increases. When the 1984 National Election Study data were released in spring 1985, it became clear that this was indeed the case. Table 2.1 presents data on all the available questions regarding trust and efficacy for presidential election years from 1964 to 1984. From this it can be seen that the events of the first four years of the Reagan administration were sufficient to raise public confidence in the government back to approximately the pre-Watergate level.

For example, the most general question in the sequence asks people how often they can usually trust the government in Washington to do what is right: all the time, most of the time, some of the time. The proportion of the public who said "some of the time" or

Table 2.1. Trends in Trust in Government and Political Efficacy

	1964	1968	1972	1976	1980	1984
Trust government to do what's right some or none of the time	22	36	45	63	73	54
Government run for the benefit of a few special interests	29	40	53	66	70	55
Government wastes a lot of taxpayer's money	47	59	66	74	78	65
A lot of public officials are crooked	29	25	36	42	47	32

	1956	1960	1964	1968	1972	1976	1980	1984
People like me don't have any say about what the government does	28	27	29	41	40	41	39	32
I don't think public officials care about what people like me think	26	25	36	43	49	51	52	42

Note: Table entries are percent of the sample expressing each opinion.
Source: SRC/CPS National Election Studies.

volunteered the response "never" increased from 22 percent in 1964 to 73 percent in 1980. In late 1984 this figure was down to 54 percent.

Similarly, in spite of complaints about the unfairness of Reagan's program, the percentage who felt that the government is run for the benefit of a few special interests rather than all the people fell from 70 percent to 55 percent between 1980 and 1984. However, other data collected for the Harris poll shows that Americans are still widely dissatisfied with the distribution of income in the United States. In their 1985 poll on alienation, 76 percent agreed that "the rich get richer and the poor get poorer," about the same figure as has been seen for a dozen years and well above the 45 percent level when Harris first asked this question in 1966.

Another facet of growing distrust in government since 1964 has been the perception that government wastes a lot of the taxpayers' money. This has consistently been the item that people have been the most cynical on over the last 20 years, and 1984 was no exception in this respect. With the horror stories of Pentagon waste, such as $7,000 coffee makers, $659 ash trays, etc., coming out regularly over the course of the last two years, one might expect people to see the government as more wasteful than ever before. Yet, despite these scandals, Table 2.1 shows that the proportion of the public that believes that the government wastes a lot of money declined from 78 percent to 65 percent during Reagan's first term. Similarly, a *Washington Post*–ABC News poll conducted in July 1985 revealed that the average person thought the government wastes 42 cents of every tax dollar compared to a median estimate of 48 cents in a poll taken just before Reagan took office. Estimates of waste in the military budget were up significantly, as would be expected from the negative publicity, but these were more than counterbalanced by the lower degree of perceived waste in social service programs.

Most dramatic of the changes in trust in government evident in 1984, however, is the decline in the belief that public officials are crooked. Of the four trust-in-government items in Table 2.1, the results on the question about "crookedness" are the most similar in 1984 to those of two decades ago. Indeed, the difference between the 1964 and 1984 percentages is within sampling error. One possible explanation for this is that at the presidential level honesty has not been a problem since Nixon's resignation in 1974, whereas waste in government spending and the fairness of government have continued to be visible failings.

Finally, the last two items in Table 2.1 represent what social scientists have termed "political efficacy." Whereas trust refers to people's perceived need to influence the government, efficacy measures the perception of their ability to influence it. As with the trust items there is clear evidence of a long-term decline in political efficacy until the recent upsurge in the 1980s. From 1960 to 1980 the percentage of the electorate feeling that they didn't have any say about what the government does increased from 27 percent to 39 percent, but improved to 32 percent in 1984. Similarly, the percentage saying that public officials don't care what they think more than doubled from 1960 to 1980, but declined by 10 percent in 1984.

That the trends on trust and efficacy match one another over time is of no small consequence. The two concepts do not necessarily go hand in hand, and the combination of the two tells much about the character of democracy in a given country. In traditional deferential societies, the public trusts the government to do what is right despite their seeming powerlessness to direct it. Dissident societies, in contrast, are characterized by low levels of trust and high levels of efficacy, thereby providing both the perceived need and ability for antisystem activity. In the 1950s and early 1960s, with trust and efficacy both being relatively high, democracy in the United States could be fairly characterized as allegiant and participatory. As both measures declined the more appropriate description became alienated, and the government became increasingly deadlocked, as opposing factions lacked either the ability to further mobilize their own followers or to trust other factions.

The recent upsurge in both trust and efficacy is therefore an important indication that the United States is moving back toward a more allegiant democratic polity. The recovery is by no means complete, however, as the indicators are still well below where they were two decades ago. Furthermore, as will be elaborated below, electoral participation remains poor compared to other democracies and American political parties continue to be in decline.

THE U.S. TURNOUT ENIGMA

One of the most ironic and puzzling aspects about democracy in the United States is that although it is where populist democratic government began it nevertheless has long consistently ranked near the bottom of world democracies in turnout of eligible voters. Even the figures shown in Table 2.2 for the early 1960s, before turnout in the United States began its recent decline, fall well below those for Western European countries (presented by Dennis Kavanagh in this volume). For example, in the most recent French presidential election in 1981 the turnout rate for the second ballot was 88 percent compared to 53 percent for the 1984 U.S. presidential election. Or comparing parliamentary elections, the most recent turnout rate in Great Britain for elections to the House of Commons in 1983 was 73 percent whereas only 38 percent of the U.S. public voted in the 1982 elections for the House of Representatives.

Probably the most often cited reason for the low U.S. turnout is the unique U.S. requirement of voter registration. Whereas the governments of other democratic countries take on the responsi-

Table 2.2. Trends in Voter Turnout: 1960–1984

Presidential Elections		Congressional Elections	
1960	62.8		
		1962	45.4
1964	61.9		
		1966	45.4
1968	60.9		
		1970	43.5
1972	55.2		
		1974	35.9
1976	53.5		
		1978	34.9
1980	52.6		
		1982	37.7
1984	53.2		

Source: U.S. Census Bureau.

bility of seeing to it that all of their eligible citizens are on the voting lists, in the United States the responsibility for registration lies solely with the individual. The result of this is that one-quarter of the eligible electorate cannot vote at election time as the result of their failure to register. These disenfranchised individuals are disproportionally citizens with lower than average education, who are less likely to be able to overcome the bureaucratic hurdles involved in the voter registration process.

The institution of registration requirements in the early part of the twentieth century was part of the Progressive movement to provide for a more open and fairly run government. At the time, Progressive lawmakers were more concerned with the problems of voter fraud than they were with ensuring maximum voter participation. Cases such as West Virginia's 159,000 votes being cast by 147,000 eligible voters in 1888 were not much out of the ordinary. Today, voter fraud is largely a thing of the past. Yet its memory remains an important part of the American consciousness and is frequently cited by politicians as their major reason for opposing such reforms as postcard and election day registration.

It would probably be a mistake, however, to surmise that if European-style registration procedures were brought to the United States that turnout would rise to European levels. Registration in the 1980s is somewhat easier today than before the Voting Rights

Act of 1965, yet as Table 2.2 demonstrates overall turnout is actually lower than it was then. States such as North Dakota (which does
not have registration) and Minnesota (which allows election-day registration) do have above average turnout rates, but they are not equal
to those of most of Europe. Thus, the explanation for the comparatively low U.S. turnout no doubt goes much deeper than the simple
differences in registration.

While turnout in the United States is astonishingly low, the
average U.S. citizen nevertheless actually goes to the polls more
often than voters in other democracies. Ironically, one of the very
reasons that Americans are less likely to go in large percentages to
the polls at any given election is that they are called on to do so far
more often. While the typical European voter may be called upon to
cast two or three ballots in a four-year period, many Americans are
faced with a dozen or more separate elections in the space of four
years. Furthermore, U.S. citizens are expected to vote for a much
wider range of political offices, including president, senator, representative, governor, state senator, state representative, mayor, city
council, school board, sheriff, drain commissioner, and a host of
others, depending on the locality. With one elected official for every
442 citizens and elections held somewhere virtually every week, it is
no wonder that it is so difficult to get Americans to the polls. It is
probably no mere coincidence that the one European country that
has a comparable turnout rate—Switzerland—has also overwhelmed
its citizens with voting opportunities in recent years, calling 89
national elections in the period between 1947 and 1975.

Another possible reason for the low U.S. turnout rate is the
relative lack of major differences between competing political parties
in the United States compared to most other democratic countries.
When British, West German, Italian, or French voters go to the polls
in national elections they are deciding on whether or not their country will be run by parties with socialist goals or alternatively by conservative, and in some cases religion-based, parties. The consequences
of their vote for redistribution of income, government intervention
in the economy, and often foreign policy, are far deeper than the
ordinary U.S. voter can conceive of. This is because of the fact that
the United States stands virtually alone in the democratic world in
lacking a major left-wing socialist party. The political views of
Margaret Thatcher may largely parallel those of Ronald Reagan, for
instance, but there is no faction within the Democratic party that

resembles the British Labour party's stands for the nationalization of major industries, commitment to public housing, and unilateral nuclear disarmament. The result is that elections naturally matter somewhat less to Americans than to most Europeans and thus there is good reason to expect turnout to be lower.

It is also worth noting that the absence of a major left-wing party in the United States probably accounts for the unusual degree to which voting participation in the United States is skewed along class lines. One of the major functions socialist parties perform in other democracies is to mobilize the working classes. Without such a political party in the United States, there is a comparatively low degree of class-based politics, but the participatory system is nevertheless heavily class biased.

The importance of political parties in mobilizing the vote leads to a final reason for the low U.S. turnout rate, as well as its recent decline—the relative weakness of U.S. political parties. It is also interesting to note that, despite the genesis of many political party practices in the United States, parties play a uniquely weak role here. Unlike recently founded democracies such as West Germany or Israel, in which the political system was designed to be run via political parties, the U.S. constitutional structure was set up without any formal role for political parties and with the intention of minimizing their influence in practice. The Constitutional Convention of 1787 has often been described as a convention against parties, and politicians in the early years of the republic considered the formation of political parties to be at best a necessary evil. Today, U.S. ambivalence toward parties remains intact and politics in the United States is probably less channeled through parties than any other major democracy in the world. Unlike candidates for European parliaments, candidates for the U.S. Congress run largely on their own and often ignore the party position when it comes to voting on the issues of the day. With such weak levels of partisan behavior among the elite, it has been difficult throughout the twentieth century to mobilize the electorate on a partisan basis; the recent decline of party identification has only made the situation worse, and contributed to the drop in turnout shown in Table 2.2

REALIGNMENT AND DEALIGNMENT IN U.S. POLITICS

The decline of political parties in the United States has caused much alarm about the functioning of democracy in the United

States—not just for its contribution to the drop in turnout, but more importantly because of the crucial role that parties play in the U.S. system. In a system that is designed to fragment political power, parties have been held to be the one institution capable of providing a unifying centripetal force. With their decline in recent years, the United States now has a system that is capable of expressing a wide diversity of viewpoints but is rather poor at aggregating them. With parties increasingly less able to resolve conflicts, the tone of U.S. politics is becoming more negative and policy compromises are harder to come by. When decisions are reached they are now more likely to be made by ad hoc coalitions without relation to other policies, thereby greatly increasing the difficulty of governmental leadership. As Jimmy Carter found during his four years in office, governing without the continuous support of a political party is extremely hard.

The events following the 1980 election, however, provided as good an opportunity for party revitalization and realignment as had been seen in recent history. The major policy changes of Reagan's first term discussed above were accomplished with more unified party support than had been seen in Washington in decades. On the two key votes of 1981, for example—on the tax cut and the budget resolution—Reagan held all but one Republican vote in the House. Unlike recent presidents who have campaigned and governed largely on their own, staying relatively unencumbered by partisan ties or appeals, Reagan has exercised a substantial role as party leader. And on the other side, the Democrats have been forced into a far more unified stance than usual, much like Western settlers pulling their wagons into a circle to fend off attack. Wide differences over what the Democratic party stands for continue, but Reagan has given Democrats a clearer sense of what they are against.

The 1984 campaign offered increased signs that party revitalization was possible. For the first time since 1956 an incumbent president running for reelection was not challenged for his own party's nomination. Reagan's ability to gather unified party support exceeded even Eisenhower's; in 1956 Nixon, as Eisenhower's preference for vice-president, was challenged for his spot on the ticket, whereas Bush received no opposition. As for the Democrats, for the first time since 1968 a true party insider and loyalist was nominated for the presidency. Unlike George McGovern and Jimmy Carter before him, Walter Mondale clearly represented the traditional party mainstream. As the near-consensus choice of the party regulars, Mondale was the first Democrat in years to run with the party rather than against it.

Not only did Mondale provide continuity with the traditional Democratic mainstream, but also, as Carter's vice-president, he established a solid link to the most recent Democratic administration. Thus for once the choice for U.S. voters was not between the present and an uncertain alternative future. Rather, the Reagan-Mondale contest was one between the recent past and a present that had seen major changes. Such a choice was conducive not only to vote switching but to partisan switching as well.

As can be seen from Table 2.3 the ratio of Democrats to Republicans in the electorate reached its lowest point in 1984 since such measurements began in 1952. Whereas Democrats had historically outnumbered Republicans by an average of nearly 20 percent, the 1984 Democratic plurality was down to less than 10 percent. Furthermore, all the major commercial and journalistic polls showed that the Republican gains continued through 1985. At various points during the year some polling organizations even had Republicans ahead of the Democrats. Recent data from two *New York Times* polls in November 1985 show an edge for the Democrats of only 36 percent to 31 percent. If this is indeed the beginning of a partisan realignment, the consequences for the future of public policy in the United

Table 2.3. Party Identification: 1952–1984

	1952	1956	1960	1964	1968	1972	1976	1980	1984
Democrats	47.2	43.6	45.3	51.7	45.7	45.4	40.4	39.7	37.0
Independents	22.6	23.4	22.8	22.8	29.1	34.7	36.1	34.5	34.2
Republicans	27.2	29.1	29.4	24.5	24.2	23.4	23.2	22.4	27.1
Apoliticals	3.1	3.8	2.5	0.9	1.4	1.4	0.9	2.2	1.7
Democratic Plurality	20.0	14.5	15.9	27.2	21.2	17.0	16.5	18.4	9.9

Source: SRC/CPS National Election Studies.

States will be profound. As Burnham[8] has written, realignments are the United States' democratic substitute for revolution—overturning one pattern of political order in favor of another.

Yet there is justified skepticism as to whether the surge in Republican identification is anything more than another indicator of public approval of Ronald Reagan. Despite the fact that more people were calling themselves Republicans at the time of the 1984 election, the Republican party made only a limited gain of 14 seats in the House of Representatives and sustained a loss of two Senate seats. As of this writing, most knowledgeable observers expect a loss of seats in the House for the Republicans in 1986 and give the Democrats a good chance of regaining control of the Senate. In short, there was much ticket-splitting in 1984 and most observers see the impact of party identification on the vote as continuing to be relatively weak.

In this candidate-centered mass media age, the structure of U.S. politics is simply not conducive to strong political parties. On this score, it is important to note that although there was much evidence of realignment in 1984, the era of dealignment (i.e., lack of partisanship) remains firmly intact. Not only was split-ticket voting still high in 1984—so was the proportion of Independents in the electorate (see Table 2.3). Once the central guiding forces in American electoral behavior, parties have come to be perceived with almost complete indifference by a large percentage of the population. This decline in public affection for the parties has not been due to any greater negative feelings about the Democrats and Republicans but rather to an increasing sense that the parties just no longer matter much in the governmental process.[9]

For example, over a third of those interviewed in the 1984 National Election Study exhibited the following response pattern to a series of four open-ended questions about the political parties:

Q. What do you like about the Democratic party?
A. Nothing.

Q. What do you dislike about the Democratic party?
A. Nothing.

Q. What do you like about the Republican party?
A. Nothing.

Q. What do you dislike about the Republican party?
A. Nothing.

When these questions were first asked in 1952, only 10 percent of the sample responded this way—a figure that is still found in election studies in Britain. In the 1950s such indifference usually proved to be part of a more general sense of political apathy and a lack of political knowledge; by 1984 it was much more likely to be a specific indicator of apathy and lack of knowledge about the parties themselves.

It probably would have been better for the parties if the public had become more negative rather than more neutral toward them. Negative attitudes can easily be turned into positive attitudes by better performance or a change in politics. To get people to care about political parties once again is a much more difficult task in the current candidate-centered mass media age.

LEGISLATIVE–EXECUTIVE RELATIONS

The weakness of the U.S. political party system is nowhere more evident than in relations between the president and Congress. Even Reagan's relations with the Republican-controlled Senate in 1985 were quite shaky, with a major rift developing over the summer on the question of a freeze in social security benefits. With 22 of the 53 Republican senators up for reelection in 1986, Reagan was already finding their support hard to obtain on difficult political decisions that might not be popular for them at home. As Republican Senate leader Robert Dole said, Republicans would provide "strong support" for the president "when we can" but would also maintain "a certain amount of independence." The bottom line, he said, is that "We have a different problem, an election in 1986." And of course Reagan's relationship with the Democratic-controlled House continued to be one of conflict and frequent deadlock. Political battles between the House and the president have almost become commonplace in recent years, the two being controlled by different parties in all but four years since 1969.

The degree to which the government system of the United States fragments political power—as evident in the current conflict between the legislative and executive branches—is unique in the democratic world. Whether the U.S. emphasis on checks and balances, separation of powers, and federalism promotes or retards the progress of democratic government has been a matter of considerable debate ever since the founding of the Republic. The founders of the Constitution were undoubtedly more concerned with preventing a tyrannical government than they were with creating a system that would smoothly translate the popular will into political action. The result, as intended, is that it is much more difficult to achieve major political changes than to block them. The European parliamentary system is far more efficient in terms of fulfilling campaign promises, but most Americans would be wary of turning over such unchecked power to any political party or faction.

Nevertheless, there has been an active academic movement in the United States throughout the twentieth century advocating changes toward a more unitary, European-like form of government. This school of thought is generally known as the movement for a "more responsible party government" and traces its intellectual roots back to the writings of Woodrow Wilson. These scholars criticize the U.S. political system for rarely providing the electorate with a clear choice between different programs and blame the political parties for their frequent inability to exercise the internal discipline necessary to carry out even their firmest promises. Supporters of responsible party government desire parties that more regularly make policy commitments to the electorate and nominate candidates who will enact their programs.

To take a concrete example, if there had been responsible party government in 1985, the Reagan administration's major policy initiative of the year—the tax reform package—would no doubt have sailed through a Congress committed to passing Reagan's program into law. Instead, of course, the proposal got caught up in the usual maze of opposition from various interest groups. In December 1985, only with intense lobbying of his own partisans was President Reagan able to keep the proposal alive. Should some version of the bill eventually pass, it would no doubt be quite unlike the sweeping change that was first envisioned.

Another area where separation of powers resulted in a troubling and consequential policy deadlock in 1985 was on the crucial question of the budget. The Republican plan to mandate balanced budgets through across-the-board cuts in the future so sharply divided the House and the Senate that the federal government was faced with a pseudocrisis for weeks during which it was technically bankrupt. Once again, little progress was made toward reducing the massive federal deficit. The Gramm-Rudman budget bill of December 1985 may well force politically difficult budget cuts in its goal to balance the budget by 1991. Yet, many observers remain skeptical as to whether such across-the-board cuts in both defense and social programs can really be implemented.

EXECUTIVE–JUDICIAL RELATIONS

Relations between the U.S. Supreme Court and the executive branch were also stormy during 1985, largely due to outspoken remarks by the new attorney general, Edwin Meese. The political Right's dissatisfaction with the Supreme Court has been building for decades as the result of decisions such as those involving school prayer, criminal rights, and abortion. Yet, Meese's 1985 public criticisms went beyond such specifics to a more basic question of constitutional practice. He insisted that any constitutional decision not directed by the specific original intention of the framers of the Constitution is illegitimate. Any approach to constitutional interpretation other than a "jurisprudence of original intention" he warned must be "tainted by ideological predilection." Most shocking of his specific examples was his assertion that the 60-year process of "selective incorporation," by which most of the Bill of Rights' provisions have been applied to limit the power of the states, is wrong because it was the intention that the Bill of Rights should limit only the powers of the federal government.

What made this issue particularly noteworthy as one of executive-judicial conflict was the fact that it generated a rare public response from two Court members. Justice John Paul Stevens responded in a speech that Meese's view "overlooks the importance of subsequent events in the development in our law." In particular, he cited the 14th Amendment guaranteeing equal protection under the law, which has led the Court in recent years to uphold a number of specific individual rights that could not have been foreseen a century ago. Similarly Justice William J. Brennan, Jr. also criticized the views of the administration, as expressed by Meese. Without mentioning Meese by name, Brennan said that those advocating a return to the "original intent" of the framers reflected "arrogance cloaked as humility."

Ironically for the Reagan administration, perhaps the only real impact of this brouhaha was to further strengthen the resolve of many members of the Court to remain on until after Reagan's term. Having had only one change of membership over the past ten years, the Court is long overdue for an influx of younger members. Yet, Justices William Brennan (age 79), Lewis Powell (79), Thurgood Marshall (77), and Harry Blackmun (76) seem committed to outlasting President Reagan, if at all physically possible, in order to prevent him from appointing their successors.

One can never say with certainty how an individual will act once appointed to the Supreme Court, as President Dwight Eisenhower found, much to his dismay, in the cases of Justices Earl Warren and Brennan. Nevertheless, it seems quite likely that should Reagan receive the opportunity to appoint a couple of new justices that the Court will turn significantly away from interpretations extending civil and individual rights.

RECENT DEVELOPMENTS IN CANADA

Signs of stress in the Canadian confederation have been very troubling to Canadians over the past two decades. Although the existence of a democratic form of government was never in doubt, whether Canada would continue as a united country has been. Events in 1984 and 1985, however, have brightened the picture considerably.

Certainly the greatest threat to Canadian unity has been the presence of the separatist Parti Quebecois (PQ), which attained control of the provincial government of Quebec in 1976. In a political system less committed to democracy than Canada, the simple fact of a party coming to power dedicated to independence would probably have brought about either separation or civil war. Even the PQ's opponents readily acknowledge that they have pursued independence with caution and respect for democratic procedures. Indeed, the 1976 PQ platform contained a promise not to pursue independence without first obtaining specific support for it in the form of a referendum. This referendum was held in 1980 on the question of whether the provincial government should seek to negotiate an agreement with the rest of Canada based on the concept of political sovereignty in an economic association with the rest of Canada. Upon the failure of the referendum by a vote of roughly 60 to 40, the PQ respected the wishes of the people of Quebec without hesitation.

Following the referendum's defeat, the PQ nevertheless managed to win the next provincial election on the basis of support of those who approved of its governance as well as its natural constituency of separatists. Yet, while the party remained both in power and committed to pursuing the goal of independence, the momentum for separation clearly dissipated. By late 1984 Premier René Lévesque announced a retreat from the PQ's intention to fight the next election on the question of sovereignty-association. This led to the resignation of nearly one-quarter of Lévesque's cabinet over the period of the next several months, and split the party badly. Lévesque himself stepped down in 1985, and his party lost control of the provincial government in the December election to Robert Bourassa's Liberal party. (The PQ won only 39 percent of the vote compared to 56 percent for the liberals.) Thus, for the next five years at least, the movement for an independent Quebec is likely to be dormant.

A second problem that has troubled those concerned with Canadian unity in recent years has been the sharp degree to which Canadian voting behavior has been divided by region. Throughout the era of former Prime Minister Pierre Trudeau, the Progressive Conservatives were virtually unable to win any ridings (parliamentary constituencies) in Quebec while the Liberals were often shut out in the Western provinces of British Columbia, Alberta, and Saskatchewan. In a parliamentary system such as Canada's, where most political power resides in the majority party's cabinet, the result of a ruling party not being able to win more than a seat or two in a given region is that the region will be severely underrepresented at the highest echelon of decision making. (This problem was only partially overcome during the Trudeau and Joe Clark years by the addition of some members of the Senate to the cabinet.)

It is probably no mere coincidence that the regions (Quebec and the West) that went largely without cabinet representation for a period during the 1970s and 1980s are also those that have expressed the most discontent with the Canadian federal system. This problem was perceived as so serious by many that talk of instituting some sort of proportional representation—probably along the lines of the West German model—was quite prevalent among Canadian political scientists as well as some politicians. Yet ultimately the parties came to grips with the problem by trying to broaden their appeal to the regions where they were weakest.

The new leaders of the major parties—Brian Mulroney of the Progressive Conservatives and John Turner of the Liberals—were particularly good choices to try to appeal to the areas where the parties had been weakest. Mulroney, a Quebec native, sought election in 1984 in the riding of Manicouagan, on the north shore of the St. Lawrence River. Turner, raised in British Columbia, stood for election in the Vancouver Quadra riding. The result was a much less regionalized vote than had been seen for some time. In particular, the Conservatives swept 80 percent of the seats in Quebec. Considering that they held only one seat in Quebec prior to the 1984 election and had finished behind the fringe Rhinoceros party (a party specializing in slapstick politics) in two ridings in the previous election, this is quite astonishing. And with the greater geographic spread of seats, for the first time in recent years the cabinet contained members of each region in rough proportion to its population. Of the 40 members of the original Mulroney cabinet, 12 were from the West, 11 from Ontario, 11 from Quebec, 4 from the Atlantic, and 1 from the North.

CONCLUSION

In sum, both the United States and Canada have undergone much political stress in recent years. These problems, although not threatening to the well-entrenched North American traditions of democracy themselves, have called into question many aspects of democratic practice in the two countries. Recent events, however, have seen some significant reversals in these negative trends. Many problems remain but the health of the North American democracies appears to be on the upswing.

NOTES

1. Seymour Martin Lipset, "The Elections, the Economy and Public Opinion: 1984," *PS* 18 (1985):28–38.

2. Gerald Pomper et al., *The Elections of 1984* (Chatham, N.J.: Chatham House, 1985); Lipset, "The Elections, the Economy and Public Opinion: 1984," *PS* 18 (1985):28–38; and Herbert F. Weisberg, "The Electoral Kaleidoscope: Political Change in the Polarizing Election of 1984" Paper presented at the Annual Meeting of the American Political Science Association, Paris, July 1985.

3. Barry Sussman, "His Approval Rating and 50 Cents Will Get Reagan a Cup of Coffee," *Washington Post Weekly,* September 23, 1985, p. 37.

4. Arthur H. Miller, "Political Issues and Trust in Government: 1964–1970," *American Political Science Review* 68 (1974), pp. 951–72.

5. Jack Citrin, "Comment: The Political Relevance of Trust in Government," *American Political Science Review* 68 (1974), pp. 973–88.

6. Ibid., p. 1,001.

7. Arthur H. Miller, "Regaining Confidence: Challenge for Yet Another Administration," *National Forum* 61 (1981), pp. 30–32.

8. Walter Dean Burnham, *Critical Elections and the Mainsprings of American Politics* (New York: Norton, 1970), pp. 182–83.

9. Martin P. Wattenberg, *The Decline of American Political Parties: 1952–1980* (Cambridge, Mass.: Harvard University Press, 1984), pp. 125–26.

3

Latin America and the Caribbean

John D. Martz

Despite the historical fragility of democracy in Latin America and the Caribbean, the fortunes of democratic institutions prospered in 1985. Constitutional government remained solid in Venezuela, Colombia, and Costa Rica, despite formidable problems. Brazil, Uruguay, and Argentina had undertaken a transition from military to popularly elected governments. In Peru, Ecuador, and Bolivia, recently elected administrations struggled to deepen democratic practices. Many governments in the eastern Caribbean also continued the democratic traditions inherited from the legacy of Great Britain. While there remained long-standing authoritarian regimes in Chile, Paraguay, Haiti, and Cuba, the region as a whole has never before witnessed such extensive observance of democratic practices and institutions.

This was particularly striking because Latin America and the Caribbean, like other Third World areas, had become prone to constitutional irregularity, political upheaval, military interventionism, and demagogic caudillos. The violation of political liberties and civil rights has been common, while the chasm between the wealthy and the masses has stretched the capacities of democratic rule. Even where representative government exists, there frequently has been an abridgment of congressional authority, a politicization of the judiciary, and meddling with electoral procedures.[1]

At the same time, aspirations for a free society guided by democratic principles have never been erased. Even the most repressive regimes have regularly used the language of democracy. The pages of Latin American history are replete with both civilian and military strongmen who have rewritten constitutions and conducted expensive electoral charades in order to claim popular approval. Both domestic and international forces—the United States in particular— insistently urge the quest for electoral legitimacy. Venezuela's Rómulo Betancourt, one of the greatest twentieth century democrats, has aptly spoken of the "vocation for democracy." While attitudes and perspectives are inevitably different from those of Western Europe and the United States, this in no way denies the concept of democracy.

A cyclical process has been evident for some years. At the close of World War II, a number of dictatorships were swept aside by popular forces encouraged and stimulated by wartime advocacy of the Four Freedoms. Within a decade, however, a host of strongmen had seized power; among the more prominent were Cuba's Fulgencio Batista, Marcos Pérez Jiménez of Venezuela, and Manuel Odria of Peru. But by the close of the 1950s, many of these men had been ousted. There was talk of the "twilight of the tyrants" and, with the 1961 election of John F. Kennedy and the initiation of the Alliance for Progress, democratic reformism was on the rise.[2]

It did not last long, however. In 1964, the military took power in Brazil, and by the 1970s it was clear that the reformism of Social Democrats and Christian Democrats was no panacea for socioeconomic distress. Democrats were especially discouraged by the demise of presumably durable democracies when both Chile and Uruguay fell to military authoritarianism in 1973. With Argentina also dominated by the military, it appeared that democracy was a fragile flower, perhaps basically alien to the arid soil of Latin America.[3]

The gloom began to lift with the return to the barracks of Ecuador's armed forces in 1979, soon followed by those of Peru. The inauguration of Raul Alfonsín in Argentina in December 1983 heralded a strengthening of prodemocratic trends, which by 1985 had surged across the hemisphere. To be sure, the durability of democracies in the region cannot be assumed. The majority are tentative, partial, and uncertain, facing dire economic problems and social pressures such as those that led the military to withdraw from government. Even so, the advance of formal democracies and elected governments gives cause for optimism.

There are 33 sovereign states in the region. To cover all of these in a single essay requires arbitrary classifications. We will separate the countries into South America (12 countries), Mexico and Central America (8), and the Caribbean Islands (13). For each grouping, states will be categorized as stable democracies, insecure democracies, partial or emergent democracies, limited authoritarianisms, or absolutist or totalitarian regimes.[4]

SOUTH AMERICA

There are 12 countries in South America, ranging in population from Brazil with roughly 140,000,000 to Suriname with 400,000. It includes two of the few stable democracies in the hemisphere: Colombia and Venezuela. Insecure democracies are Argentina, Bolivia, Brazil, Ecuador, Peru, and Uruguay, all of which have returned from military rule in recent years, two of them in 1985. Five also conducted competitive national elections during the year. Four non-democracies, Chile, Guyana, Paraguay, and Suriname, continue under authoritarian rule, but none has the degree of state control to be called absolutist.

Stable Democracies

Two of the nations freed by the Liberator, Simón Bolívar, enjoy particular prominence. Although their historical experiences were quite different, since 1958 both Colombia and Venezuela have maintained democratic institutions and practices. For Colombia, military dictatorship and rural violence led to a power-sharing agreement in 1957 and 1958 between the traditional Conservative and Liberal parties. This stayed in place until 1974, but two-party domination has continued to the present. Conservative President Belisario Betancur, elected in 1982, undertook a program including domestic pacification, seeking to end the endemic guerrilla fighting and banditry in the countryside. Despite doubts from the military and the opposition of traditional economic elites, he negotiated a formal truce with three rebel organizations.

Signed on August 31, 1984, the truce extended amnesty to members of the M-19 group, the Communist party's Fuerzas Armadas Revolucionarias de Colombia (FARC), and the dissident Marxist Ejército Popular de Liberación (EPL). In exchange, participants were to cease armed hostilities. Next Betancur faced down traditionalistic congressmen who questioned reforms that would open all mayoralties to direct elections. The nation's worsening economic situation also threatened the limited pacification that the government had achieved, and the climate of partisan debate grew more heated toward the close of 1985, because of legislative and presidential elections scheduled for March and May 1986 respectively. By that time the truce was shattered and the president's policy lay in ruins.

The M-19 denounced the truce in June and, although badly divided over strategy, increased its activities. In November it seized control of the Palace of Justice in Bogotá. The army responded with a violent assault on the building that left 95 dead, including 11 Supreme Court justices and 35 M-19 members. The controversy over the action was still raging when the EPL rejected the truce agreement at the close of the month. Only the Communist party and the FARC, its military arm, remained moderately cooperative in the hopes of participating in 1986 elections.

Betancur sought to renew his peacemaking initiatives, but was undercut by the November attack in Bototá, while the nation's drug problem continued to sap the Colombian democracy. The industry was reaching into national politics through huge bribes and threats of physical attacks; despite the best efforts of the government, the power and insidious character of drug trafficking constituted a menacing challenge to democratic institutions and practices.

In Venezuela, the region's most vigorously competitive and participatory democracy continued to set an example for its neighbors. The government of Jaime Lusinchi, elected by a wide margin in December 1983, maintained the observance of personal freedoms and civil liberties. It also sought to alleviate economic pressures through a so-called Pacto Social—a tripartite collaboration of government, business, and organized labor. It was honored initially more in rhetoric than in fact, but in June of 1985 Lusinchi revitalized the effort to formulate and negotiate major policy agreements through committee discussions. Although Lusinchi's party, Acción Democrática (AD), had historically dominated the national labor federation, the president demonstrated that the interests of business would not be ignored.

Civil liberties were enhanced through a major reorganization and restaffing of Venezuela's multiple police and security forces. The interior and justice ministries—both headed by veteran AD leaders and associates of Lusinchi—collaborated in the reforms. The administration also worked closely with the United States in efforts to curb the burgeoning drug trade. While its effects were less severe than in Colombia, it had become a major problem. Individual rights continued to be honored both in theory and practice, despite periodic sensationalist press reports that in effect legitimized the system by leading the fight against potential violations of civil rights. The armed forces were acquiescent in their subordination to civilian authority.[5]

Insecure Democracies

The most significant event in 1985 was the restoration of elected civilian government in Brazil after 21 years of military authoritarianism. President João Figueiredo, the latest military president, hoped to move toward *abertura* (an opening toward civilian politics) without losing the ultimate veto power of the military. This produced a succession of ill-fated maneuvers in late 1984 and early 1985. A carefully crafted political system, with an electoral college naming the new head of state, was designed to maximize officialist control. However, Figueiredo and his associates underestimated public sentiment for full democratization.

The regime's Partido Demócrata Social (PDS) lost the intended advantage when the nomination was secured by former São Paulo Governor Paulo Maluf, who was widely regarded as unscrupulously manipulative in his quest for power. Maluf proved a contentious and unpopular candidate who split the PDS. This led to the defection of the Frente Liberal (FL), a sizable group joining with Vice-President Aureliano Chaves in endorsing the opposition. This in turn increased the momentum of the antigovernment Partido do Movimento Democrático Brasileiro (PMDB) and its candidate Tancredo Neves. A veteran of Brazil's political wars who had more recently served as governor of Minas Gerais, the septuagenarian Neves emerged in 1984 as the conscience of the opposition. By the time the electoral college met, the outcome was predetermined. Tancredo Neves won by a vote of 480 to 180.

Brazilian democratization was shadowed when Neves unexpectedly underwent surgery scant hours before his scheduled inauguration on March 15, 1985. His running mate José Sarney was sworn in as interim president as Figueiredo stepped down; however, Tancredo Neves died after a series of operations on April 21, 1985. The personification of democratic restoration, Neves could not be truly replaced. José Sarney succeeded to the presidency with a weak political base. A member of the government party until 1984, he was among the PDS dissidents who went to the new Frente Liberal. Neves had tapped him as a means of sealing the campaign coalition. Sarney was thus viewed by the PDS as a turncoat and by the PMDB as an opportunistic outsider not to be trusted.

In short order the Aliança Democrática (AD) coalition was verging on disintigration. Sarney sought to control the Neves- appointed cabinet, but there was drift and indecision in policy making. Intricate political maneuvering for partisan advantage revolved about anticipated 1986 elections for a Constituent Assembly. Aspiring presidential candidates sought to influence the timing of nominations and elections. While Sarney promised to serve no more than four (rather than the legal term of six) years, governmental authority was weakened. The municipal elections of November 15, 1985, while constituting another step toward an established democratic system, saw some fragmentation of the parties, mixed results for the governing PMDB, and the return of populist former president Jânio Quadros to office after more than 20 years.

Nothwithstanding Sarney's shaky position, 1985 stood out in having brought an end to more than two decades of military rule. The armed forces stayed in the background during Neves's illness and death. By August 1985 no fewer than 25 new parties had been legalized. The July release of a five-year study documenting torture by the military (especially for the 1969–74 period) encouraged human rights groups in their efforts in behalf of individual liberties, but it was politically impossible to prosecute violators of human rights under the military regime.

In Uruguay, after nearly a dozen years of rule, the armed forces called elections in 1984, to complete the movement begun when their carefully crafted constitutional referendum was resoundingly rejected in November 1980. They retreated with greater misgivings than their Brazilian counterparts, and unyielding restrictions were imposed on civilian parties and organizations. More than 2,000 political prisoners remained behind bars, and two prominent party leaders were barred from elections.

Wilson Ferrera Aldunate of the Partido Nacional (Blanco), who had been in forced exile for much of the decade, was forbidden to run. The Blancos named Alberto Sáenz Zumarán in his place. Liber

Seregnini, head of the leftist coalition Frente Amplio, was also denied paticipation. In his stead Juan José Crottognini, Seregnini's 1971 running mate, carried the banner. Julio María Sanguinetti was the Colorados' nominee. The campaign began in earnest in September 1984 under close military scrutiny. All three candidates were moderate in discussion of the armed forces and human rights violations. The military even negotiated an informal understanding that it believed would assure immunity from prosecution by a new government.

In the elections on November 25, 1984, Sanguinetti won a comfortable victory with 38 percent of the vote. Sáenz de Zumarán followed with 33 percent and Crottognini with 20 percent. The Colorados benefited by the fact that Sanguinetti's two principal rivals had been proscribed. The victors celebrated, and the losers pledged support for the new regime. When Sanguinetti took office, on March 1, 1985, he moved to secure legislation curbing the institutional authority of the military. While acting cautiously on this front, he promptly freed Uruguay's political prisoners, including long-incarcerated members of the Tupamaros group, the urban guerrilla movement of the early 1970s. He relegalized leftist parties and student groups previously outlawed by the armed forces. The threat of renewed military intervention was greater than in Uruguay's two populous neighbors, but the renewal of democratic principles and individual liberties was strongly supported.

Across the Río de la Plata, Argentina continued on its own rediscovered path. Raul Alfonsín proved a highly skilled politician, although few of the problems confronting his government at its December 1983 inception had been resolved. He renewed his popular mandate by calling a referendum on the Beagle Channel accord with Chile. On November 25, 1984, 70 percent of eligible voters went to the polls, with 81.1 percent favoring the agreement. The Peronist opposition at first was divided on the vote, then ordered an abstention. The vote consequently signified a defeat for it. On November 3, 1985, midterm congressional elections were held for the first time in 20 years. The Radicals dropped slightly but remained strong at 43 percent, winning 20 of 24 electoral districts. Reformers in the Peronist party, willing to work within the system, did better than old-line union leaders, which provided further encouragement.

The government meantime proceeded against military leaders accused of human rights violations. Nine former members of the juntas that ruled from 1976 to 1983 were tried. In December 1985 the courts found five officers guilty of the persecution and assassination of civilians, with two receiving life sentences. The others remained to be tried on charges produced by the disastrous Falklands/ Malvinas war of 1982. Still at issue was the question of some 300 officers at lower ranks who were widely regarded as also responsible for many human rights violations. Their fate was unclear, while President Alfonsín continued efforts to reorganize the military and to redefine their role in Argentine society. On May 1, 1985, he announced a host of "war economy" measures to cope with the huge foreign debt, rampant inflation, and slumping productivity. While Alfonsín's proposals generated support at the outset and proved remarkably successful in reducing astronomical inflation to a modest level and stabilizing the foreign exchange rate, it remained to be seen whether they could be sustained for more than a few months or long enough to be effective.

Even worse fiscal, economic, and security problems confronted Peru in 1985, although its emergent democracy succeeded in transferring presidential power by constitutional means. The youthful Alán García Pérez of the moderate leftist APRA party was the frontrunner from the beginning of the campaign, which started in late 1984. His personal charisma plus the unpopularity of the outgoing government gave García a resounding victory on April 12, 1985, with 48 percent of the vote. Second was Lima Mayor Alfonso Barrantes Lingán, head of the Marxist coalition Izquierda Unida (IU), at 24 percent. The conservative Luis Bedoya Reyes polled 15 percent, while Javier Alva Orlandini of the ruling Acción Popular (AP) won a mere 5 percent.

The APRA won over half the 180 seats in the Chamber and 32 of 60 Senate posts. The new president inherited a desperate economic situation, and proposed in his July 28, 1985, inaugural address that Peru drastically limit payments on its foreign debt (on which little had been paid for many months in any case). At the same time, the constitutional transfer of power between elected leaders could not obscure a worsening security situation. The Maoist insurgency of Sendero Luminoso continued in the southern Andes, as did the ruthless response of the military. After President Fernando Belaunde had turned over the counterguerrilla campaign to the armed forces, the level of violence escalated. Rebel groups other than Sendero Luminoso were also active in Lima and other cities, further testing the firmness of civil liberties and individual rights. The new García government promised to end terrorism through an amnesty for all political prisoners, removed officers responsible for atrocities, and promised that the corrupt judicial system would be overhauled. Prospects for improvement of public security were nonetheless poor, and García faced a situation less favorable to democracy than had Belaunde five years earlier.

Bolivia also underwent elections and a change of government. Historically unstable, the nation's leadership was perennially shaky. The elected government of Hernán Siles Zuazo was virtually powerless to deal with worsening economic problems. On November 19, 1984, Siles managed to preserve his presidency by promising to shorten his term from four to three years. This led to the elections of July 14, 1985. Retired General Hugo Bánzer Suárez, who had headed a dictatorship from 1971–78, narrowly outpolled Víctor Paz Estenssoro by 28.6 percent to 26.4 percent. However, the lack of an outright majority left the final choice to congress. The 77-year-old Paz, three times previously the chief of state, skillfully negotiated that vote, but he entered office without firm popular or legislative support.

Paz faced a four- or five-digit inflation rate plus a $4.8-billion foreign debt on which payments had stopped in early 1984. The powerful tin miners led demands for higher wages, and there were threats of further strikes by government workers and bank employees, among others. Neither the Siles government nor that of Paz was prone to systematic violations of individual liberties, but endemic violence among rival factions continued. The durability of elected government in Bolivia, as always, was much in question.

The fortunes of democracy were faring somewhat better in Ecuador. The return to elected government in 1979 had continued despite such disruptions as a border war with Peru and the death of President Jaime Roldós Aguilera in a plane crash. In August of 1984 Osvaldo Hurtado Larrea, who had succeeded Roldós, transferred the presidential sash to his elected successor, León Febres Cordero. The conservative Febres had won a narrow but undisputed victory over the Social Democratic candidate, Rodrigo Borja Cevallos, in the second round of presidential elections; but Ecuador's center-left had won control of the unicameral Chamber of Representatives. This assured bitter partisan conflict between the new president and the legislature.

During his first 18 months in power Febres progressively out-maneuvered and bullied his opponents into submission. A series of clashes over divergent constitutional interpretations invariably led to retreat by his congressional opponents. Over time the government also lured several legislators away from the opposition. By the close of his first year in August 1985, Febres was enjoying a narrow but workable majority in the chamber. The quality of political dialogue was harsh, and Febres was roughly vigorous in word and action. His critics charged him with authoritarian proclivities, as when Hurtado characterized Febres's first 100 days as a "quasi-dictatorship." Even so, the climate for democracy in Ecuador was less negative than in Peru and Bolivia.

Limited Authoritarianisms

The most notorious South American holdout from democracy and freedom is still Chile. The government headed by General Augusto Pinochet since 1973 remains an international pariah. A brief flurry of presumed liberalization in 1984 was first viewed as leading to 1986 or 1987 congressional elections. However, the government's chief architect of purported "dialogue," Sergio Onofre Jarpa, was dismissed from the cabinet. In February 1985 further shifts of personnel indicated a renewed hardening of official attitudes. General Pinochet himself stated that discussion of a possible apertura had been misconstrued as a sign of weakness, and insisted that he would remain at least until 1989. No election would occur in the meantime.

A state of siege imposed in November 1984 was extended in March 1985. External pressures for a relaxation of controls, especially from the United States and international banking interests, had little effect. In June the state of siege was redefined as a state of emergency, but the change was only cosmetic. Democratic political parties and labor leaders were harassed by officials while dividing on the form and tactics for opposition. Demonstrations and protests drew police retaliation, while other security forces operated outside the law. In mid-1985 a scandal over the killing of three communists brought the firing of the police chief. This did nothing to alter the scorn for individual liberties that remained a hallmark of the Pinochet government.

Paraguay was also in international disrepute. In May 1985, as General Alfredo Stroessner celebrated the thirty-first anniversary of his seizure of power, the government followed its practice of alternating restrictions and relaxations. Maneuvering inside the Colorado party was stimulated by competition for the succession. Stroessner's son, Gustavo, was among those aspiring to eventual power; but the general typically held himself aloof from such matters. Municipal elections on October 20, 1985, did little to alter the aging dictatorship or to clarify conditions were Stroessner to leave the scene.

On the northern coast of the continent, the countries that emerged from former British and Dutch Guiana constituted two additional nondemocracies. The former, Guyana, had been ruled by Forbes Burnham with increasingly autocratic control ever since independence in 1966. Burnham's self-styled "cooperative socialism" had veiled a personalistic regime in which his People's National Congress (PNC) maintained control through either fair or fraudulent elections. Opposition from the People's Progressive party (PPP) and the Working People's Alliance (WPA) was kept within manageable limits. A long-standing National Security Act aided the regime in denying justice to its critics.

With the economy slipping toward bankruptcy by 1984, Burnham cast about for solutions. A surprise visit to Cuba in September 1984 produced little, and efforts to co-opt PPP and WPA officials into government were fruitless. Announcement of an austerity budget in March 1985 produced disturbances and protests, while organized labor sought an enlarged role. Burnham shifted cabinet members to avoid the emergence of an obvious successor. However, the president died on August 6, 1985, during throat surgery. Prime Minister Hugh Desmond Hoyte was sworn in as Burnham's successor, while Vice-President Hamilton Green replaced Hoyte. General elections were unexpectedly called for December 9, some four months ahead of schedule. On election day both the PPP and WPA withdrew amid charges of fraud and intimidation. The government claimed to have received over 85 percent of the vote, capturing 42 of the 53 seats in Parliament. By all indications, the level of government intervention and manipulation was very high, and the PNC remained in charge of a virtual one-party state.

There was little uncertainty in neighboring Suriname. Colonel Desi Bouterse retained command of the military while his 25th of February movement dominated public affairs. Aid from the Netherlands remained suspended and, with the International Monetary Fund (IMF) also withholding assistance, the financial situation was grim. None of this led to democratization. Neither did it bring an end to the characteristic plotting and conspiracy that have marked the young country ever since independence in 1975.

MEXICO AND CENTRAL AMERICA

The Middle American isthmus between the United States and the South American continent contains roughly 80 million Mexicans and barely 150,000 residents of Belize, while the populations of the Central American states range from 2.5 to nearly 8 million. Distinctive characteristics notwithstanding, there is less subregional variability than in South America. Except in Costa Rica, democracy has been sporadic at best. The foreign debt, socioeconomic depression, guerrilla warfare, and the intrusion of the East-West conflict have contributed to the political problems.

Stable Democracy

With no break since 1948, Costa Rica has nurtured the longest established genuine democracy in the region. The absence of armed forces has been accompanied by consistent observation of individual liberties. A succession of competitive elections has seen power alternate between the Partido de Liberación Nacional (PLN) and an anti-PLN coalition. Since 1982 the PLN has held the reins of government under Luis Alberto Monge, at the same time enjoying a legislative majority. However, it inherited a burden of deficit spending, foreign debt, and declining productivity. An austerity program halted the rapid descent, but by 1985 the struggle to achieve economic stability was still unresolved. Only U.S. largesse—more economic aid per capita than even to El Salvador—and short-term emergency measures were keeping the country economically afloat.

At the same time, regional turbulence was further testing the limits of Costa Rican civility and domestic peace. San Jose followed its tradition of welcoming political exiles, but the presence of armed groups along the Nicaraguan border became increasingly troublesome. Just as Sandinistas before July 1979 had directed hit-and-run attacks against Somoza across the frontier from Costa Rican territory, anti-

Sandinistas adopted similar tactics. This inevitably provoked both diplomatic and military responses from Nicaragua, exacerbating the ill will between the two countries. On November 17, 1983, Monge proclaimed "perpetual, active, and unarmed neutrality," later proposing a constitutional amendment to this effect. Within the next 18 months, however, the temperature of domestic debate over foreign policy had risen dramatically.

Costa Rica was also pressured by the Reagan administration to adopt anti-Sandinista policies, and the importance of U.S. assistance gave a greater urgency to Costa Rican policy decisions. In the spring of 1985 Monge reversed himself and accepted North American Green Berets to provide training for Civil Guardsmen. Passions ran high over expanding U.S. military aid, which reached some $9 million in both fiscal 1984 and 1985. Meanwhile, partisan disputes among Costa Ricans continued to sharpen. The formation of rightist extremists into the Movement for a Free Costa Rica (MCRL) produced such atypical events as the stoning of the Nicaraguan embassy. By the close of 1985, the campaign leading to the elections of 1986, conducted with Costa Rica's usual democratic verve, had rendered the climate of discussion even more contentious.

Partial Democracies

The most important nation in the region, Mexico, resists easy categorization, although one-party control under the Partido Revolucionario Institucional (PRI) has entered its seventh decade. While President Miguel de la Madrid Hurtado grappled with an enormous array of economic problems, his intention of modernizing and democratizing the internal system was rejected by party bureaucrats. This was amply if crudely demonstrated in the July 7, 1985, state and local elections. Competition between the PRI and the Partido de Acción Nacional (PAN) in the northern states of Nuevo León and Sonora was hotly contested. However, the government announced its victory by above-average proportions even before the votes had been tallied. A wide array of obviously fraudulent activities were carried out in full view of both domestic and foreign observers, producing a major embarrassment to the government.

Democracy in the form of honest and open electoral competition thus remains nonexistent in Mexico. The 1985 record on public liberties was relatively better, although the state is willing to apply its power against individuals when necessary. A systemic constant remains *la mordida*—"the bite" of bribes and corruption at all levels. De la Madrid called for "moral renovation" when he took office. As an example, former Petróleos Mexicanos (PEMEX) director, Jorge Díaz Serrano, was imprisoned on charges of having embezzled at least $36 million. Past malfeasance was also dramatized by the two palatial estates constructed by a former Mexico City police chief, but little more was done, and the campaign was forgotten. Cynicism over the system of justice consequently remains deep-seated.

In Panama, democratic trappings mask undemocratic reality. The 1983 elections were in all probability stolen. Nicolás Ardito Barletta, the choice of the National Guard, was declared the victor by scarcely 1,000 votes over the octogenarian populist and former president Arnulfo Arias. Widespread protests, challenges, and the partisan composition of the electoral board all brought into question the announcement of the winner. Even if Arias was not in fact cheated by the count, public perceptions of presumed dishonesty weakened the moral and political standing of the administration from its inception.

Throughout 1984 and 1985 the discredited administration was dominated by the retitled National Defense Force (FND). Its commander, General Manuel Antonio Noriega, is the strongman of the nation. Barletta was a competent technocrat and international civil servant whose skills as a politician were limited. Efforts to cope with the foreign debt went awry. Intended reforms of the labor code in April 1984, cutting back on benefits decreed some years earlier by Omar Torrijos, produced major protests. At the same time Panamanian business had become vocally antigovernment, attacking administration efforts to restructure the economy while meeting its international obligations. Public demonstrations protested both IMF-inspired austerity and rampant official corruption. On September 28 General Noriega forced the resignation of Ardito Barletta, after he tried to have an investigation of the murder of a critic of Noriega. The successor was Eric Arturo del Valle. While constitutional forms had been nominally observed, it was clear that the National Defense Force effectively ruled Panama. Civil liberties are generally observed, but the trends in the conditions for democracy are far from promising.

Few countries have a more formalistic or precarious democracy than Honduras. Both international and domestic conditions are threatening. These include the presence of thousands of anti-Sandinistas, the "Contras," as well as Salvadoran guerrillas; there are also hordes of war refugees from both Nicaragua and El Salvador. Disapproval of the Nicaraguan regime has been tempered by anxiety over the presence of some 15,000 armed members of the Contra organization, the Fuerza Democrática Nicaraguense. Toward El Salvador hostilities from the 1969 Soccer War still simmer, and a final peace treaty remains to be signed.

The presence of thousands of U.S. servicemen and a succession of military maneuvers increased the influence of both Washington and of the Honduran military. President Roberto Suazo Córdoba saw his authority eclipsed by both U.S. Ambassador John Negroponte and armed forces commander Gustavo Alvarez Martínez for the first half of his term. However, when dissension within the military forced Alvarez's replacement by General Walter López, the ambassador's role was also diminished.

By 1985 Suazo Córdoba was exerting greater power, including efforts to handpick his successor. The resultant institutional and constitutional crisis occupied the political leadership for months. Early in 1985 Suazo Córdoba clashed with congress over the naming of supreme court justices, which affected control of the electoral board as well. Several judges and congressmen were jailed while the military maintained public silence; only in May was a compromise negotiated. A major provision stipulated that all aspiring presidential candidates would be listed on the ballot for November 24, 1985, elections. This meant that Suazo could not impose his preferred nominee on his badly divided Liberal party. In addition, the winning candidate for each party would receive the votes for all party nominees. This made elections both a party primary and a national vote for president.

When the elections took place on November 24, the electoral arrangement produced unusual results. The Liberal candidates outpolled those of the National party by some 80,000 votes, assuring victory for José Azcona Hoyo. Yet the leading National candidate, Rafael Leonardo Callejas, out-polled Azcona by more than 200,000 votes (some 41 percent to 27 percent). The verdict was accepted by Callejas after initial threats to challenge the constitutionality of the result. The fact remained, however, that the newly elected president was not the choice of the electorate, while the new congress would be controlled by an alliance of opposition parties. Human rights violations seemed unlikely to be reduced, given the continuing indifference of both government and armed forces.

In the case of El Salvador, status as a democracy was also shaky. The elections of 1984 and 1985 provide some basis for optimism, although significant groups were effectively proscribed from participation. The rebel forces of the FDR/FMLN, composed of both avowed Marxists and democratic reformers, would not and could not take part in these contests. Thus the solid May 1984 victory of José Napoleón Duarte was based on the political center and right. It nonetheless provided some legitimacy, strengthening Duarte's authority to the extent that he was able to hold peace talks with the revolutionaries at La Palma on October 15, 1984, and at Santa Tecla on November 30.

Contacts between government and insurgents have been infrequent and private since that time. Duarte improved his bargaining position as the result of March 31, 1985, congressional elections, in which Christian Democrats polled some 53 percent of the vote against a combined 37.4 percent fort the two major rightist parties, thus gaining for the first time a legislative majority with 33 seats. This improved Duarte's hand in efforts to establish a working relationship with the armed forces while curbing death squads of the extreme right. By the second half of 1985 the guerrillas had lost their initiative and were proclaiming the need for an extended struggle that included urban terrorism.

In rural areas, the guerrillas sought to intimidate or disrupt local rule through threats and killings or kidnappings of majors and police chiefs. While this indicated the difficulties in which the FDR/FMLN forces found themselves, it also led to a resurgence of violence from right-wing death squads. The abduction of Duarte's daughter in September and her release in return for freeing guerrilla prisoners weakened the president's position. By late 1985 the Ejército Secreto Anti-comunista (ESA) had renewed its activities, while a growing rift between the government and organized labor was producing public protests and work stoppages in urban centers.

Guatemala has remained a consistent violator of human rights, although elections late in the year offered cause for guarded hope. The de facto regime of General Humberto Mejía Victores labored for a new constitution and then for civilian government. On November 3, 1985, Christian Democratic candidate Marco Vinicio Cerezo Arévalo won the first round with 38.7 percent to 20.2 percent for runnerup Jorge Carpio Nicolle. The mandated runoff on December 8 provided Cerezo an easy victory with 1,133,517 votes and a margin of 68 percent to 32 percent. The president-elect indicated his determination to strengthen democratic rule, but also recognized that the armed forces could not be challenged.

The military had remained responsible for violence in both city and countryside. Urban killings had resumed around April after a brief respite; journalists, faculty and students, labor leaders, and party politicians were victimized. Private right-wing squads roved city streets while rural killings also continued. The lengthy insurgency by several Marxist groups also contributed to the intimidation of the Indians, while the military creation of strategic hamlets worsened conditions.

The newly independent country of Belize stands apart from its neighbors politically, historically, and ethnically. Belize received its independence from the British on September 21, 1982, and adopted a parliamentary system that was controlled by Prime Minister George Price and his People's United party (PUP). Dominant on the political scene since 1950, Price and the PUP met a startling defeat in the December 14, 1984, elections. The United Democratic party (UDP) won 21 of 28 seats, and Manuel Esquivel became the new prime minister. Price was among the PUP stalwarts to lose his own parliamentary seat.

Although Price remained respected, there was an evident desire for fresh leadership. Some voters had feared that he would pursue a hard line on the increasingly profitable production of marijuana, although Esquivel also promised to curb the traffic. The UDP's momentum carried over into municipal elections on March 22, 1985, winning five of the seven town boards. The fledgling parliamentary democracy was thus demonstrating vitality.

Limited Authoritarianism

Nicaragua moved in the direction of authoritarianism, with the control of the state increasingly penetrating society. Conditions worsened during the year following the elections of November 4, 1984, when over 70 percent of the electorate had voted. The Sandinistas polled 68 percent of the vote, winning a large majority in the National Assembly, which first met on January 9, 1984. Two days later Daniel Ortega Saavedra and Sergio Ramírez Mercado were sworn in as president and vice-president. The elections had included several antigovernment forces, although the most prominent opposition figure who might have run, Arturo Cruz, withdrew nearly two months before elections. On October 21, 1984, the Partido Liberal Independiente (PLI) and its leader Virgilio Godoy had given up campaigning and effectively quit the race.

Constraints on Nicaragua's domestic opposition stiffened during 1985. At the sixth anniversary of the Revolution on July 19, major Latin American leaders (excepting Fidel Castro) absented themselves. The opposition paper, *La Prensa,* published some criticisms, but censorship was increasingly severe. Individuals could denounce the government, but many opponents had fled the country. Faced with counterrevolutionary activities on both borders, the regime employed wartime controls that further abridged individual liberties. This helped to provoke a reshuffle of government structures in August 1985 that further concentrated power in the hands of a few individuals.

A significant human rights action was the government's decision to permit the return of the Miskito Indians to their traditional coastal environs from which they had been forcibly expelled early in the Revolution. Three years later Nicaragua began returning the first of the refugees; nearly 5,000 were back by the close of 1985. Others refused, however, as many of the original homes and villages had been razed. In the meantime Daniel Ortega in October announced a severe curtailment of constitutional rights and individual liberties, measures designed to restrict the rising currents of domestic criticisms. They further dimmed the prospects for democracy under the Sandinistas.

THE CARIBBEAN ISLANDS

Before the 1960s there were only three independent states on the islands: Cuba, the Dominican Republic, and Haiti. Today, however, there are numerous governments, leaders, and parties seeking to establish political traditions and electoral credentials. The larger islands that became independent in the 1960s are of greatest importance: Barbados, Jamaica, and Trinidad-Tobago. The others have secured sovereignty within the last few years and, in many cases, are only beginning the experience of democratic participation.

Of the relatively "senior" graduates from apprenticeship to the British, both Trinidad-Tobago and Barbados have fared reasonably well. The political history of the former, independent since 1962 and a republic within the Commonwealth since 1976, for years was the story of Eric Williams and his People's National movement (PNM). With Williams's death in March 1981, the succession by George Chambers reduced the personalistic character of government. Opposition parties have continued to contest elections and to work inside the labor movement, although the PNM remains dominant. Chambers, while gradually acquiring some seniority among leaders of island states, has generally followed quietly pro-U.S. views. Domestic affairs have focused on the need for housing, employment, and social services as the population has passed 1 million and steadily increases.

In Barbados, the adjustment from the generation of independence leaders has also proceeded. Grantley Adams was the first Barbadian premier in preindependence days and led the Barbados Labor party (BLP) both in power and in opposition. It was out of office when he died in 1972; his son, J. M. G. M. (Tom) Adams brought it back to power in 1976. He was a dominant figure in Eastern Caribbean affairs, and was a strong supporter of U.S. actions in Grenada. An ardent advocate of the Caribbean Community (CARICOM), he enjoyed subregional eminence at the time of his fatal heart attack in February 1985. He was succeeded by H. Bernard St. John, who had run the BLP and served as prime minister before Grantley Adams's 1971 victory. While enjoying a 17–10 parliamentary margin, St. John faced the necessity of calling elections no later than July 1986. Meanwhile, domestic politics unfolded without undue interruptions.

Insecure Democracies

The Dominican Republic has held elections at regular four-year intervals since 1966. The early domination of the U.S.-backed Joaquin Balaguer ended with his defeat in 1978. Four years later the Partido Revolucionario Dominicano (PRD) retained the presidency with the victory of Salvador Jorge Blanco over Balaguer by a margin of 46 percent to 36 percent. Even the suicide of outgoing president Antonio Guzman did not prevent the constitutional succession.

With elections for a new government set for May 16, 1986, political legitimacy has continued to grow. At the same time, imposing socioeconomic problems have impeded the deepening of democracy. The Dominican Republic was the first Latin American state to suffer major civic protests in response to IMF-dictated austerity. Blanco backed off for a time but ultimately felt required to pursue the policies being dictated by the IMF. Despite the pressures, the government continued to defend customary individual rights and freedoms.

The course of democracy was still rougher in Jamaica. The ruling Jamaica Labor party (JLP) under Edward Seaga had met only mixed success in dealing with the economic crisis left by Michael Manley and the People's National party (PNP). Notwithstanding approval from Ronald Reagan, priority treatment from the Caribbean Basin Initiative (CBI), and some improvement in foreign investment, the island still wallowed in economic distress. Having won office in October 1980, Seaga called new snap elections in December 1983. The PNP, awaiting a new electoral list that would incorporate at least 180,000 new voters, was caught off balance and boycotted the balloting. This left the JLP with all the parliamentary seats.

The government has not escaped economic pressures, while PNP attacks and criticisms are sharp. In January of 1985 a wave of riots created extensive turmoil in Kingston and dealt a serious blow to tourism. Local elections set for June 1985 were postponed by legalisms, but partisan rivalry was not diminished. With the political system limping, Jamaica saw extreme partisanship between the JLP and PNP breaking out into intermittent clashes and violence, especially in the cities. The sense of compromise and accommodation in the political system was minimal. The prospects for meaningful democracy in the near future were less promising for Jamaica than for the other major island states.

The newest Caribbean sovereign states have lacked the time necessary to establish strong democratic credentials, although basic impulses have been generally encouraging. In most cases the leaders of independence movements became the first to occupy government. Relationships with the opposition have been strained but usually civil. Economic difficulties are imposing; most ministates seek more tourism, while export products have limited promise for expansion. What is undeniable is the sense of nationalism and rising consciousness shared by the peoples and their governments.

Antigua and Barbuda, independent since November 1982, has been dominated by the Antigua Labor party (ALP) of Vere C. Bird and his son Lester, who have served respectively as prime minister and deputy prime minister. Political competition exists, although there has been little effective challenge to the septuagenarian Bird and his son. Antigua has fared less well than might have been expected from the Caribbean Basin Initiative, notwithstanding strong pro-U.S. sentiment, but thus far domestic politics have not been seriously affected.

In the Bahamas, democracy has been marred by graft and corruption at high levels. Prime Minister Lyden O. Pindling and the Progressive Liberal party (PLP) have been in power for more than a decade. Nonetheless, the 1985 arrest in Florida by U.S. officials of ranking Bahamian authorities has tainted the administration. A domestic investigation into alleged payoffs and the laundering of funds has also reduced the legitimacy of the Pindling government. Crime and urban violence were on the rise in 1985, although the PLP has confronted them with stern police action.

Dominica has been a relatively conservative, tough-minded state in the Eastern Caribbean, owing largely to Prime Minister Eugenia Charles. First elected to office in 1980 at the head of the Democratic Freedom party (DFP), Charles has faced down at least three coup attempts. A supporter of the United States who appeared at the White House with Ronald Reagan shortly after the launching of the October 1983 intervention in Grenada, Charles won reelection in July 1985 with a vocally anticommunist campaign. Her DFP saw its parliamentary majority reduced from 17 to 15 of 21 seats. The six opposition seats went to the Labour party under Michael Douglas. The balloting was generally fair and Eugenia Charles remained the recognized leader of Dominica, although the harshness of charges against the opposition was not conducive to compromise or accommodation.

Of particular interest in the Eastern Caribbean is Grenada. The process initiated after the U.S. invasion and the ouster of the Bishop government culminated in elections on December 3, 1984. Backed by the United States, a coalition known as the New National party (NNP) supported the leader of the Grenada National party (GNP), former prime minister Herbert Blaize. The election gave Blaize and his supporters all 15 seats in Parliament; in the popular vote the NNP received 58.4 percent to 36.1 percent for the Grenada United Labour party (GULP) of former prime minister Eric Gairy. The leftist Maurice Bishop Patriotic movement (MBPM) received 5 percent.

The enduring poverty of the island has left in doubt the extent to which democratic attitudes and procedures may be nourished, even as U.S. forces withdrew.

Fledgling elected governments have sought to meet popular demands and nurture democratic principles in St. Kitts–Nevis, St. Lucia, and St. Vincent and the Grenadines. St. Kitts–Nevis, which received independence on September 19, 1983, is headed by a coalition of the People's Action movement (PAM) and the Nevis Reformation party (NRP), with the former the senior partner. The opposition Labour party had controlled local affairs for nearly three decades before its defeat in 1980. The stability of Michael Powell's government was uncertain, especially given the NRP desire for the separation of Nevis. Meanwhile, St. Lucia continued to be led by John Compton of the United Workers' party (UWP), which returned to office after a three-year hiatus in elections in May 1982. Compton has continued in power while playing an influential role in Eastern Caribbean affairs—more so than James Mitchell of St. Vincent and the Grenadines, who was elected prime minister in September 1984. Proliferating parties in these island republics testify to the nascent quality of democracy as they move through the early independence years.

Absolutism

It would be difficult to find more starkly contrasting political systems than Cuba and Haiti, although both show a commitment to authoritarian rule and the denial of individual liberties. Despite economic shortcomings, Marxist Cuba can boast of positive accomplishments in health, education, and social services. In political terms, however, the authoritarianism of Marxist rule is blended with the demagogic *caudillismo* personified by Fidel Castro. Despite the institutionalization of the Revolution, he remains the dominant figure on the island. The state of individual rights and liberties changed little in 1985. In January of the year Castro reshuffled the highest ranks of party officials, but this was of little significance to the everyday life of the Cuban citizen.

The state of individual rights in Haiti remained among the most abject in the hemisphere. President-for-Life Jean-Claude Duvalier, who succeeded his father in 1971, hinted at a softening of government controls in 1984. The following year he proclaimed a publicly-heralded liberalization through a plebiscite vote held on July 22. The result was an overwhelming victory for Duvalier's proposition, which pledged a legalization of political parties so long as they promised fidelity to Duvalier. The 99.93 percent approval also anointed François Nicolas Jean Claude II as eventual successor to his father. This effort to give a slight touch of legitimacy to the dictatorship, in order to please the United States and attract development aid, did not contradict Haiti's status as the most depressed country in the region. After a series of civil disturbances, Jean-Claude fled Haiti on February 8, 1986.

On balance, 1985 was a positive year for democracy in Latin America and the Caribbean. In some countries constitutional governments strengthened their legitimacy, while elsewhere military dictatorships gave way to civilian rule. Only in a few cases, notably Nicaragua and Panama, were the developments for governmental democracy or individual liberties unfavorable. At the same time, most regimes also confronted fierce demands and staggering difficulties, like those leading to several of the military withdrawals from power. Whether or not civilian authorities would prove more effective was uncertain. Especially in Brazil, Argentina, Uruguay, Ecuador, Peru, and Bolivia the challenges were great. Even the maturer democracy of Colombia, Venezuela, and especially Costa Rica could ill afford to make comfortable assumptions about its permanence. Democracy is being called upon to provide practical solutions to excessively difficult public problems.[6]

NOTES

1. For fuller discussion, see John D. Martz, "Images, Interventions, and the Cause of Democracy" in *U.S. Policy in Latin America: Quarter-Century of Crisis and Challenge,* ed. John D. Martz (Lincoln, Nebraska: University of Nebraska Press, 1986).

2. A characteristic account is Tad Szulc, *Twilight of the Tyrants* (New York: Praeger, 1959).

3. This view was suggested by many writers of the decade. For a treatment drawn from the Argentine case, see the influential work of Guillermo A. O'Donnell, *Modernization and Bureaucratic-Authoritarianism: Studies in South American Politics* (Berkeley: Institute of International Studies, 1973), pp. 198–99.

4. A stimulating recent work is John A. Peeler, *Latin American Democracies* (Chapel Hill, N.C.: University of North Carolina Press, 1985).

5. The newest work on the evolution of the Venezuelan system is John D. Martz and David M. Myers, eds., *Venezuela: The Democratic Experience,* 2nd ed. (New York: Praeger, 1986).

6. For a statement of limited, formalistic democracy, see Alexander W. Wilde, "Conversations among Gentlemen: Oligarchical Democracy in Colombia," in *The Breakdown of Democratic Regimes: Latin America,* eds. Juan J. Linz and Alfred Stepan (Baltimore: The Johns Hopkins University Press, 1978), p. 29.

4

Sub-Saharan Africa

Larry Diamond

In 1985, various forms and degrees of authoritarianism continued to dominate most of the 44 states of sub-Saharan Africa, banning political opposition, restricting personal freedom, and often gravely violating human rights. Most of the states under discussion here have been cited by Amnesty International for serious and often widespread human rights abuses, such as detention without trial of political opponents, intimidation of political dissidents, torture, and political killings. Corrupt, absolutist, and highly personalistic dictatorships persisted in Zaire, Malawi, Gabon, and Togo, with little immediate prospect of liberalization or change. Highly centralized and autocratic ruling parties, again often dominated by authoritarian personal rulers, continued to hold sway in Benin, Burundi, Mali, Rwanda, and elsewhere. Neither was any progress toward political freedom or competition to be found in the Marxist-Leninist states of Ethiopia, Angola, Mozambique, and Congo-Brazzaville. In much of the rest of the continent, military regimes ruled in characteristic military fashion.

There were some glimmers of democratic progress, however. Military coups opened the way for greater political freedom and a possible transition to multiparty democracy in Nigeria and Guinea. Partial or tentative democracies were struggling to develop and mature in Botswana, Mauritius, Senegal, The Gambia, and—in increasingly trying circumstances—Zimbabwe. Liberalization was

73

apparent in Cameroon under a new and less domineering leader, and in Tanzania and Sierra Leone, the voluntary retirement of longtime personal rulers opened possibilities for greater pluralism in economics and politics. In the Ivory Coast and especially Kenya, some degree of political competition and pluralism continued within a single-party framework.

There were also several instances of authoritarian regress and political decay. The promised transition to democracy in Liberia was subverted with increasing blatantness as its military leader maneuvered to eliminate opposition and retain power behind the facade of a democratic constitution. In Uganda, a military coup once again overthrew a regime that was constitutional in name only, having failed not only to govern democratically but to extricate the nation from years of anarchy and brutality. And in South Africa, the possibility of constructing a multiracial democracy was being eroded by waves of mass violence, official repression, and significant but now clearly inadequate reforms.

Following a brief analysis of the demise of postcolonial constitutional regimes, this political review begins with developments in those few African regimes that can be classified as insecure, maturing, partial democracies. This grouping is limited to regimes that permit genuine competition between political parties. Recognizing that some significant political competition and freedom may exist within the framework of a one-party state, we review next what may be termed "one-party, partially competitive regimes." While these countries are classified as "limited authoritarian" in this annual survey, they are more democratic than other one-party or military regimes. Following this we review cases of recent democratic progress and then of authoritarian regress; absolutist regimes (non-Marxist and Marxist); and finally, other limited authoritarianisms.

There is no clear line separating the absolutist regimes from the more limited authoritarianisms, and regimes that may be considered Marxist-Leninist adhere to the model in varying degrees.

Since very few African nations even come close to filling the ordinary qualifications of democracy—fair political contestation, freedom of expression, and so forth—there is a temptation among sympathetic observers to apply different standards of democracy to the study of African politics; to accept as variants of an underlying ideal the various "people's democracies," "guided democracies," and so on that greatly outnumber the few truly liberal democracies or to take rhetorical and constitutional commitments at face value. Such cultural relativism not only precludes assessments of the kind in this book but also demeans African people and cultures, for it implies that political freedom is somehow less important to them and organized political competition beyond their capacity to manage. By contrast, this general survey assumes that the essence of liberal democracy—freedom of political expression and choice—encompasses panhuman values.

At the same time, because liberal democracy is so rare and repression so pervasive in Africa, an assessment of progress and regress must reach for subtle and sensitive indicators of even modest change. Changes in the level of political and civil liberties and in the breadth and autonomy of associational life may have important implications for the possibility of democratic development, even if they have little immediate impact on the distribution of political power. Certainly, one cannot expect that all the features and foundations of democracy will suddenly and simultaneously appear. As Richard Sklar has noted in an important essay, "Democracy comes to every country in fragments or parts; each fragment becomes an incentive for the addition of another."[1]

HISTORICAL BACKGROUND

Prior to colonial rule, many traditional African societies had limited, in some cases quite extensive, democratic features. This sometimes included insignificant limits on the authority of the king or chief, and even some competition and participation in his selection. Many smaller, less centralized societies institutionalized broad participation in decision making and individual rights of expression within the community. Nowhere, however, did democratic institutions exist on anything like the scale of the modern states constructed by colonial regimes, and certainly no traditional society confronted the challenge of developing democratic institutions to govern the heterogeneous multinational states carved out of Africa by the European powers. From the start, the democratic governments of the newly independent African states were gravely disadvantaged by the problematic character of their nationhood and the conflict and distrust between competing ethnic groups desperate for the expanding but scarce resources of the modern economy and state.

The lack of experience with modern democratic institutions was hardly filled during colonial rule, which was more or less authoritarian, and permitted little in the way of democratic participation. Only in the final stage of colonial rule, with the process of decolonization, were democratic institutions constructed (save in the case of the Portuguese territories, which were governed autocratically throughout and liberated by revolution). In most of Africa, "the colonies were transformed constitutionally into African democracies equipped with institutions modelled on those of the metropole." The process was most elaborate in the case of the British, "less pragmatic and painstaking in French and Belgian Africa," but almost everywhere it was hurried and rested on a shallow consensus: a "vindication" and "political expedient" for colonial powers, a matter of "dignity and equality" for African nationalists.[2] Lacking in virtually every case was a deep commitment to liberal democracy among the nationalist elite, whose main concern was power, and a broad understanding of it among the illiterate and politically excluded populations.

Because democratization was hurried, there was little time for institutions to develop. Political parties were largely reflections of ethnic and regional interests, or of individual politicians. Legislatures and judiciaries had little chance to build up experience and independence. Bureaucracies were similarly limited, and many countries that sought quickly to end their dependence on European expatriates suffered precipitous declines in state capacity and integrity. As Jackson and Rosberg have argued, in the absence of established and effective political institutions—of rules and structures to regulate political behavior—politics degenerated into a free-wheeling and often violent struggle for power. Elections and constitutions were replaced, first in practice and then often literally, by clientelism, factionalism, coups, purges, succession crises, and civil wars. The institutional void has been filled not by democracy but by authoritarianism, typically dominated by one or another type of "personal ruler."[3]

The weakness of democratic institutions, values, and restraints, and the depth of cultural divisions, were magnified by the huge stakes in the political arenas of newly independent African countries. Colonialism bequeathed modern states that were overdeveloped in relation to the economy and society. Most of the opportunities for upward class mobility and most of the resources for dominant class formation depended on control of, or at least access to, the state, and to this day in Africa "class relations, at bottom, are determined by relations of power, not production."[4] Against a background of pervasive poverty and underdevelopment, and weak or nonexistent institutional barriers to political corruption, the swollen state has sharply intensified the struggle for power in Africa, frequently making it an all-or-nothing contest. With the premium on political power so enormous, ruling parties were unwilling to tolerate serious opposition, and arbitrarily altered or flagrantly violated constitutional provisions to maintain themselves in power.[5]

Finally, the low level of economic development also stiffened the odds against democratic success. Extreme poverty tends to dispose people to a more desperate view of politics, reducing inhibitions against violent and extremist methods. This effect was heightened in a context where the state was the main source of progress for individuals and communities. Moreover, nationalist mobilization frequently generated extravagant claims and expectations for rapid development progress after independence, but limited state capacities and economic bases made these difficult to fulfill, and economic growth often suffocated in the grip of corruption, mismanagement, and rigid socialist or statist ideology. Also, because of their low level of socioeconomic development, the newly independent nations had little in the way of autonomous social and economic interest groups—such as business, labor, and professional associations—capable of limiting state power and of crosscutting, and so tempering, ethnic ties.

Unfortunately, two decades and more of independence have eased such problems little in many countries, and have accentuated some of them in others.

MATURING, INSECURE, AND PARTIAL DEMOCRACIES

No African country has a fully mature and stable democracy, and few are the African countries that have even a tentative democracy. Of these few, Botswana may have the most functional democratic system. Government is in the hands of an elected National Assembly, which in turn selects an executive president. Although the national dominance of the ruling Botswana Democratic party (BDP) has not been seriously threatened since independence in 1966, opposition parties are free to organize and compete. There is an increasingly vigorous system of democracy at the local level, and in the most recent elections, on September 8, 1984, the opposition parties won control of 5 of the 14 local councils, including those of the two largest cities. Although the BDP won 28 of the 34 parliamentary constituencies, its loss of the local council in the capital, Gabarone, was particularly striking. And at the national level as well, several prominent BDP candidates were defeated. This fourth general election since independence was, like the previous ones, impressively free of the intimidation, violence, and fraud that characterize elections in most African nations. And in one constituency where evidence of irregularities was presented, the High Court ordered new elections.[6]

Although Botswana is substantially democratic and politically stable—at least relative to most African countries—there are some qualifications. The ruling elite manifests "a paternalistic style of leadership which presumes that the public is not ready to govern itself."[7] While there is universal suffrage, the ability to run for office is limited to a rather narrow elite, excluding government employees and those illiterate in English. The government occasionally prosecutes political opponents for controversial statements, but the courts have frequently acquitted them. Botswana has no political prisoners, and in general there is a high level of civil and political liberty, protected by an independent judiciary.[8] Although newspapers are legally free to criticize the government, the precarious financial position of opposition newspapers limits the practical reality of press freedom. Nevertheless, the government-owned newspaper "impartially covered the statements of opposition parties and aired the views of opposition candidates" during the 1984 election campaign.[9]

The stability of the democratic system—evidenced by two decades of uninterrupted functioning of the independence constitution—has been underpinned by high rates of economic growth, deriving from mineral wealth, prudent planning, and competent, honest administration. Moreover, economic benefits have been reasonably well distributed, and a prosperous commercial cattle ranching sector provides the political elite a base of income and wealth outside the state.[10] However, the very lack of serious crises raises questions about the underlying stability of the system. A serious challenge to BDP rule in the future, possibly deriving from growing ethnic or class conflict, might provide a more telling indication of the degree to which democracy in Botswana is being institutionalized.

Excepting Zimbabwe (which has been independent for a much shorter time) only Botswana, Mauritius, and The Gambia have maintained their democratic systems without interruption since independence. (Interestingly, all three have populations of 1 million or less.) Although it lies in the Indian Ocean, more than 1,000 miles from the African continent, Mauritius may be considered the freest and most democratic African country. Since independence in 1968, free and fair elections, supervised by an autonomous electoral commission, have occurred at regular intervals. In 1982, Mauritius made history by becoming the first (and still the only) African country to transfer power to the political opposition through a democratic election, and in the elections of August 1983 executive power changed hands again. Mauritius has a Westminster parliamentary democracy with a unicameral legislature, and its legal system is also based on the British model. Individuals are free to speak and associate, and political parties are free to organize and compete. As in Botswana, a high level of political and civil liberty is buttressed by strong constitutional guarantees and an independent judiciary. Political activity is vigorous and voter participation is high. Despite its extremely heterogeneous mix of racial, ethnic, and religious groups, and a densely populated territory, Mauritius has no political prisoners or political violence. Democracy in Mauritius is also buttressed by "one of the freest and most widespread trade union movements in Africa,"[11] and by an extraordinarily vigorous free press, which dates back more than two centuries. In 1984, the government was forced to amend a new law that required newspapers to pay large financial deposits, which had forced 20 publications out of business by July. After a series of protests by journalists and the opposition party, the government accepted the recommendations of its independent commission not to implement the act and not to prosecute 44 journalists who were arrested in the protests.[12]

Through its quarter-century of independence, The Gambia has maintained a multiparty democratic system and political stability under the continuous rule of its first elected president, Sir Dawda Jawara. However, pressures have been building in recent years, and the system has still not recovered from the trauma of a bloody coup attempt in 1981. While the ruling People's Progressive party continues to dominate the political scene—winning 35 of the 43 House seats in the most recent (1982) national election—opposition parties and independent candidates are legally free to organize and contest.

But, complaining of persistent intimidation and harassment since the 1982 election (in which it won six House seats), the opposition National Convention party has maintained an electoral boycott, demanding that the state of public emergency be lifted. The state of emergency, imposed after the July 1981 coup attempt, gives the government wide powers of detention. More than 1,000 persons were detained immediately after the coup attempt, but most were released. Of the 188 who were brought to trial, 55 were acquitted; 63 were sentenced to death for treason, but these sentences have gradually been commuted by the president. Trials have observed due process of law and have been open to public and international observers.[13] The Gambia has not been accused of political killings, torture, or other grave abuses of human rights, but has detained critics and opponents of the regime for periods of weeks and in some cases months. Although press freedom is constitutionally guaranteed, and there is no censorship, in practice, "The Gambia, with its small, mainly rural, largely illiterate, and multilingual population, does not support an active press."[14] Criticism of the government appears to have been inhibited by the state of emergency. While civil and political liberties are substantial and the rule of law is institutionalized, the country cannot be classified as entirely free.

More problematic still is the level of freedom and the future of democracy in Zimbabwe. Constitutionally, Zimbabwe retains the parliamentary system established by the Lancaster House negotiations that led to independence in 1980, ending decades of racist white rule and a 15-year civil war. Despite the oft-expressed desire of the Marxist ruling party, the Zimbabwe African National Union-Patriotic Front (ZANU–PF), to establish a one-party state and a socialist economy, rights of property and multiparty competition have been preserved. Like the 1980 elections, the general elections of July 1985 were judged free and fair both by unofficial outside observers and by independent human rights groups in Zimbabwe.[15] Although ZANU increased its percentage of the vote from 64 percent to 77 percent and its share of the 100-seat Parliament from 57 to 64 (of the 80 Black seats), it continued to be shut out entirely in the ethnic minority area of Matabeleland, which has been the focus of political violence, repression, and instability over the past five years. Despite winning overwhelmingly among the various Shona-speaking groups (about 77 percent of the population), ZANU candidates (including several powerful party figures) again lost all 15 Ndebele seats to the opposition Zimbabwe African People's Union (ZAPU). ZAPU, however, lost its four other seats, becoming more clearly than ever a regionally limited opposition. Under the terms of the Lancaster House agreement, 20 House seats are reserved for whites (whose proportion of the population has dwindled to just over 1 percent), and 15 of these were won by the Conservative Alliance of former Rhodesian Prime Minister Ian Smith, a bitter enemy of Prime Minister (and ZANU president) Robert Mugabe.

The multiparty system has been badly battered by the violent rivalry between ZANU and ZAPU, which dates back to the civil war. The alliance between the two parties began disintegrating shortly after independence, and lost its last thread in November 1984, when Mugabe sacked two ZAPU ministers for their party's alleged support of dissidents who had murdered several senior ZANU officials. Over the past few years, Matabeleland has been the scene of armed dissidence by ZAPU supporters, claiming the lives of numerous ZANU officials and other civilians. In retaliation, government repression has been severe. It is believed that more than 1,000 people have disappeared or been killed by government forces. Countless hundreds have been detained, and there have been persistent, credible reports of torture and mistreatment of prisoners and suspects in Matabeleland.[16] Supporters of ZAPU (and other opposition parties) also complained of severe harassment during the 1985 election campaign, and of changes in election procedures that disadvantaged them. Pressure on the opposition escalated after ZANU's huge election victory. Homes of ZAPU supporters were ransacked; those of ZAPU leader Joshua Nkomo were raided repeatedly, and his passport was confiscated. In August, seven members of the town council of Bulawayo (the largest city in Matabeleland and second largest in the country) were imprisoned, and since the election six ZAPU members of Parliament (MPs) have been detained.[17]

ZAPU agreed to renew negotiations with ZANU on a possible merger of the two parties (previous talks had collapsed in 1983) but agreement was opposed by some ZANU leaders. The future of democracy in Zimbabwe depends on ending the political violence, which has justified continued renewal of the state of emergency in effect since 1960, providing the legal tools for detention of prominent government opponents and harassment of political opposition. An end to political violence and the state of emergency could enable democratic forces in the country to assert themselves more effectively.

There are strong pluralistic foundations to build upon. Throughout the past five years, a forceful, sophisticated judiciary, independent of government control, has played a crucial role in defense of human rights and the rule of law, frequently ruling against the government. A vigorous and pluralistic intelligentsia questions government authority, and there are many autonomous, private associations. Although the two daily newspapers are government-owned, they frequently air a variety of viewpoints, and weekly and monthly publications provide significant and widely read forums for political criticism and opposition. Church-based groups have led the way in monitoring and denouncing human rights violations. And despite the ruling party's socialist commitment, it has pragmatically preserved the autonomy of a dynamic class of capitalist producers in business and farming, who have been the mainstay of the country's continuing economic prosperity.[18] If pragmatism continues to prevail in ZANU, a merger with ZAPU might bring a one-party-dominant state without eclipsing political freedom or imposing legal restrictions on political party competition. But if the hardline ideologues prevail, Zimbabwe is likely to slip increasingly into the familiar authoritarian mold of African one-party states.

With the ambiguous exception of Madagascar (see below), the only other functioning multiparty system in Sub-Saharan Africa is that of Senegal. While most African political systems have become increasingly authoritarian, Senegal has made considerable democratic progress since 1976, when President Leopold Senghor permitted two opposition parties (and in 1978 a third) to contest alongside the ruling Socialist party (PS), under ideological labels approved by the government. Setting another important precedent in 1980, Senghor became the first of the generation of African independence leaders to relinquish executive power voluntarily and return to private life. In 1981, his successor, Abdou Diouf, removed the restrictions on the number and designation of political parties, giving birth to a vigorous multiparty system. Despite charges of electoral fraud, the 1983 elections were considered on the whole free and fair. Diouf decisively defeated four other presidential candidates, and the PS won 111 of 120 seats in the National Assembly. The Senegalese Democratic party (PDS) won eight seats, while most of the other six contesting parties failed to win any.[19]

Since 1983, however, the PS has tightened its grip on power. In the November 1984 local elections, the PS swept all 37 municipalities and 318 rural districts. Only two of the 14 opposition parties (neither of them significant) competed, as the others boycotted the elections in protest against "the absence of guarantees of impartiality."[20] Opposition parties have been badly organized and further weakened by their very number. But as the opposition parties have begun to draw together, government pressure on them has escalated. Shortly after the PDS joined with four Marxist parties to form the Democratic Senegalese Alliance (ADS) in July, 15 ADS supporters (including PDS leader Abdoulaye Wade) were arrested in a demonstration. On September 5, the ministry of interior prohibited ADS from all political activities until it declared itself and was recognized as a political party, stressing that political party alliances are illegal. President Diouf appears to have become nervous about popular unrest as the opposition parties have begun coordinating their attacks on his government's economic austerity policies, implemented as a condition of International Monetary Fund (IMF) assistance. Earlier in the year PDS supporters were arrested in an antigovernment demonstration, and in August the editor of a Senegalese periodical was arrested for publishing an interview with Wade alleging presidential involvement in corruption.[21] In October, a dissident union leader who joined the PDS and planned to form his own union was sentenced to a year in prison for illegal strike actions, along with more than 20 other union members.[22]

With the exception of its reported treatment of separatist dissidents in the Casamance region,[23] Senegal has maintained a relatively high degree of civil liberty. The French-style legal system, featuring an active, independent, and well-trained judiciary, has generally been effective in protecting constitutional rights. Although the major newspaper is controlled by the ruling party, it prints critical articles, and a wide range of other publications operate freely. There is also extensive academic freedom, and, despite some rise in harassment of late, considerable freedom of assembly. However, recent events raise questions about the degree to which the PS—which has ruled continuously since 1960—is willing to tolerate a serious political opposition.

ONE-PARTY, PARTIALLY COMPETITIVE REGIMES

Generally considered the most open and tolerant country in East Africa, Kenya is probably the best instance in Africa of a one-party system that allows a significant degree of political competition. Deeply divided along ethnic lines (with the largest group, the Kikuyu, accounting for just over a fifth of the population), Kenya has sought to avoid the ethnic polarization that might engulf political party competition, while at the same time fostering extensive local competition and participation for parliamentary seats and party offices. Although the only opposition party was banned in 1969, and the country became a *de jure* one-party state in 1982, parliamentary elections have been regular, vigorous, and "reasonably fair," repeatedly turning out of office numerous incumbents and established figures. In 1979, 45 percent of the incumbent members of parliament [MPs], including 7 ministers and 12 assistant ministers, were defeated. In the September 1983 election, 40 percent of the (non-appointed) MPs (five ministers and 12 assistant ministers) were defeated. More than 900 candidates competed for the 158 elective seats.[24] Not only do elections force MPs to be accountable and responsive to the demands of their constituents, but in addition, "the National Assembly has a higher degree of significant, independent constitutional authority than in any other sub-Saharan country."[25] Within the ruling party, the Kenya African National Union (KANU), electoral competition also opens up positions of party authority to popular participation and control. (As in the government, however, the presidency and vice-presidency of the party, held by incumbents of these positions in the government, are not open to competition.) In mid-1984, for the second time since 1976, KANU members (now roughly one out of every four Kenyans, or half the adult population), voted at the grassroots level for party leaders, followed by elections for provincial branch and then national officers. At the latter convention, several major party officials lost their jobs.

While competition is real in Kenya and human rights are not systematically abused, there are substantial constraints on political freedom, and these appear to have been growing in recent years, especially in the wake of a nearly successful coup attempt in August 1982. Since then, President Daniel Arap Moi has tightened his grip on the government and the ruling party, while at the same time strengthening the party's dominance over society. In the fall of 1984, 15 party members who had been associated with the purged former minister, Charles Njonjo, a powerful Moi rival who had been charged with corruption and treason, were expelled from KANU. These included several members of Parliament (previously KANU had expelled only two MPs in its entire 25-year history). After commuting the death sentences of hundreds of military personnel convicted of complicity in the 1982 coup attempt, 12 of the coup leaders were executed last year. Late in 1984 President Moi ordered all civil servants to join the ruling party by the end of the year, and widespread coercion was alleged in KANU's subsequent membership recruitment campaign. Late last year President Moi announced plans to restrict the number of candidates for Parliament (for the first time) in the 1988 elections. This might be an effort merely to rationalize the bewildering choices in some constituencies, but it could also represent an effort by the party leadership to impose more central control. While Moi is firmly in control now, he does not enjoy the ethnic power base or popular reverence of his predecessor, Jomo Kenyatta, the nationalist leader, presidential "monarch" and "patriarch of Kenya," who dominated national politics for more than two decades until his death in 1978.[26]

The insecurity of Moi's rule, especially after the coup, may help to explain restrictions on political freedom in Kenya. Relations with students and intellectuals have been tense, and the University of Nairobi has been plagued almost yearly by student demonstrations, closures, and numerous arrests. The practice of preventive detention was resumed in 1982, and since then a number of outspoken critics of the regime have been subjected to prolonged detention without trial. Such arrests have inhibited public debate, while the establishment of party daily newspapers has strengthened KANU's dominance of the print media. Television and films are subject to government censorship. And while torture is not sanctioned, the torture and killing of hundreds of ethnic Somalis in northeastern Kenya was reported in 1984.[27]

More limited political competition exists in some other one-party states, such as the Ivory Coast. For more than 20 years following the victory of his Democratic party of the Ivory Coast (PDCI) in national elections in 1956, the political dominance of President Félix Houphouët-Boigny was secured without serious challenge through impressive economic prosperity, a patronage-rich party machinery, skillful cooptation, tight press restrictions, and centralized control of the sole political party. Then in 1980, with the economy in sharp recession and the growing intellectual community increasingly restless with political stagnation, Houphouët-Boigny shook up his party structure and introduced significant electoral reforms, allowing for the first time multiple and non-party-sponsored candidacies for National Assembly seats and for municipal and local party posts. Those elections swept aside fully 53 of 80 incumbent National Assembly deputies, and seemed to produce significantly greater debate and responsiveness in the new body.[28] However, the party and its leader were unwilling to tolerate the degree of political independence and ethnic rivalry opened by the reform. In 1985, National Assembly candidates were screened for "moral criteria" by a party committee and troublesome individuals were screened out. Still, 575 candidates competed for the 175 contested seats in the November elections, and only 61 incumbent deputies were reelected. Competition for executive power is still ruled out completely. In October, the president won reelection to a sixth term with 100 percent of the vote (in a turnout of 99.8 percent).[29] Now close to 90 years old, Houphouët-Boigny appears determined to retain power until he dies. Given his continuing failure to fill the position of vice-president, that event will occasion a new presidential election, and possibly a severe crisis over the succession. Until then, the Ivory Coast figures to retain its limited political competition and its fine human rights record, while remaining "a highly centralised one-party state where dissenters are not welcome and where [individual candidates] generally have no policies or programmes to introduce, much less the power to implement them."[30]

A similar situation prevails in Zambia, where the sole legal party (the United National Independence party) conducts competitive primary elections to select a maximum of three candidates per constituency to contest for parliamentary seats. In 1983, 40 incumbents were defeated in 125 contests. As in the Ivory Coast, party and state power is concentrated in the hands of a president, Kenneth Kaunda, who has ruled since independence and shows no signs of quitting. In October 1983, Kaunda won election to his fifth five-year term with 94 percent approval, despite a backdrop of the worst economic crisis in Zambia's history and renewed friction with the country's powerful trade unions. Like Houphouët-Boigny, Kaunda is a savvy politician who has taken pains not to establish any clear successor. But as the economy has sunk into ruin over the past few years, exhausted by statist inefficiency and dependence on a sagging global copper market, Kaunda's rule has become increasingly repressive. Although there is limited freedom of expression and restraint in the use of sweeping presidential powers of detention (under the state of emergency in force since independence), critics are increasingly reluctant to express themselves in an atmosphere of growing surveillance by the Special Branch and imprisonment and alleged torture of some political opponents. The ideals of Kaunda's "participatory democracy" seem to be succumbing to "an undiluted developmental dictatorship."[31]

Idealism has fallen even harder in Tanzania, where President Julius Nyerere's socialist, egalitarian vision has given way to economic and political stagnation, while his "attempt at a planned socialist economy has spawned a bureaucracy as corrupt and inefficient as any in Africa."[32] Some electoral competition has been permitted under the umbrella of the sole legal party, the Chama Cha Mapinduzi, and parliamentary members have frequently been voted out of office. Limited freedom of expression and criticism is tolerated, and government policy forbids the use of torture (although it apparently occurs on occasion). But the primary political reality is the dominance of the ruling party at all levels of society. "Through its system of 10-family cells," whose leaders act as intermediaries between individuals and the government, the party "monitors even the most remote areas of the country."[33] Although Tanzania has been unusually successful in providing education, health care, and other social services to its predominantly rural population (achieving the highest literacy rate in Africa), its economy is bankrupt, despite massive foreign assistance, and the need for fundamental reform is increasingly manifest. With the voluntary retirement of President Julius Nyerere late in 1985, after a quarter-century in office, political and economic liberalization may finally be possible. His successor, Ali Hassan Mwinyi, eased restrictions on private business and implemented a new, more liberal constitution during his brief tenure as president of Zanzibar (a semiautonomous part of Tanzania). But Nyerere remains party chairman (and probably the supreme authority) and an entrenched party machine and state bureaucracy can be expected to fight any effort to redistribute power in society.

Finally, among the most difficult systems to categorize is that of Madagascar, where elections at the local, regional, and national level are contested by the seven parties making up the National Front for the Defense of the Revolution. Four parties won seats in the 1983 National Popular Assembly elections. Although President Didier Ratsiraka's party, Arema, won 117 seats, it also lost some major districts. Government policies are vigorously debated in the

Assembly. The judiciary is independent of the administration and has ruled against it in crucial decisions, some involving charges of election fraud. On the other hand, civil and political rights are restricted. Although there is a range of ideological and policy views among the National Front parties, parties outside the Front cannot compete. Political activity by groups outside the Front is prohibited and dissenting political opinion is limited. Some privately owned newspapers exist, but they are subject to censorship. Those alleged to threaten state security may meet with arbitrary arrest and detention, or worse. On July 31, 1985, the army assaulted the national headquarters of the country's kung-fu clubs, which have been associated with opposition to the Arema government, killing between 20 and 200 people.[34] For these various reasons, Madagascar is classified here as a limited authoritarianism, even though it has many features of a partial democracy.

DEMOCRATIC PROGRESS

There was little in the way of significant democratic progress in Africa during 1985 (or the immediately preceding years). But in the most populous country in Africa, Nigeria, which had once been regarded as the best hope for liberal democracy on the continent, dramatic change did occur. On August 27, 1985, the authoritarian and increasingly repressive government of Major General Muhammadu Buhari was overthrown in a military coup organized by Army Chief of Staff Ibrahim Babangida and other high-ranking officers. The Buhari government had itself come to power in a coup 20 months previously, pledging to restore accountability to public life and to reinvigorate an economy that had been ravaged by the unprecedented corruption of the four-year-old Second Republic. General Buhari's overthrow of the venal democratic regime was at first enthusiastically welcomed by the population. But his regime's harsh suppression of interest-group representation and critical commentary grated bitterly against the pluralistic structure of Nigerian society and the deep attachment of its people to personal freedom. Particularly odious was the shackling of Nigeria's vigorously independent press by Decree Number 4, which forbade the publishing of anything that might bring government officials into ridicule or disrespect. Under this decree, several prominent journalists and editors were arrested. Two spent nearly a year in prison and were adopted as prisoners of conscience by Amnesty International, as was a leading intellectual critic of the regime who was imprisoned. Also bitterly resented was Decree Number 2, which provided for the detention of any citizen deemed to constitute a security risk. Under this measure, the Nigerian Security Organization (NSO) was given a virtual blank check to arrest critics and dissidents. A number of Nigeria's leading social commentators were imprisoned and others fell silent in a growing climate of fear. Toward the end, even discussion of the country's political future was banned. In addition, dozens of prisoners were executed after conviction by military tribunal with no right of appeal. After the coup, evidence of torture and inhumane conditions of imprisonment by the NSO was presented by the new regime.[35]

After the coup of August 27, all journalists in detention were released and Decree Number 4 was abrogated. Numerous former politicians who had been in prison 20 months without charge or trial were also released, many to heroes' welcomes. A thorough probe and reorganization of the NSO was undertaken, and its top leadership was dismissed. Recognizing that even a military government "needs the consent of the people" to govern effectively, the new president pledged in his inaugural address: "We do not intend to lead a country where individuals are under fear of expressing themselves." The recently reelected president of the Nigerian Bar Association, which had boycotted the Buhari regime's corruption trials because they had been conducted by military tribunal in secret, was named to be the new minister of justice.

Soon thereafter, Babangida threw open to vigorous public debate the controversial question of an International Monetary Fund (IMF) loan for Nigeria. Although he was rumored strongly to favor the loan—which would provide $2.5 billion to an economy deep in depression, international indebtedness, and a desperate shortage of foreign exchange—the president deferred to the overwhelming public sentiment expressed against it, announcing in December the cessation of negotiations with the IMF. The decision was hailed by the press, businessmen, organized labor, students, and many other interest groups.[36]

By the end of the year, Babangida had established himself as one of the most tolerant and popular leaders in Nigeria's 25-year history, and was talking of devising a plan to return the country to civilian democratic rule. Under the new regime, there is perhaps as much freedom of expression as anywhere in Africa. Moreover, a strong democratic infrastructure has survived the failures of the Second Republic and the Buhari dictatorship, in the form of an autonomous judiciary, an experienced and liberal-minded legal profession, numerous business, student, and professional associations, an extensive university system with a tradition of academic freedom, and probably the largest, most diverse, sophisticated, and aggressive press in Africa. But the success of any future democratic system will require the construction of new and original institutions for checking the corruption and abuse of power that have destroyed Nigeria's first two attempts at liberal democracy.[37]

On April 3, 1984, a military coup also opened the way for democratic progress in Guinea, one week after the death of President Ahmed Sékou Touré, a brutal dictator whose socialist idealism had degenerated over his 26-year rule into tyranny and economic ruin. Under Touré, imprisonment without trial and torture of political dissidents had been "commonplace and thousands simply disappeared."[38] Declaring these victims "martyrs" who would be rehabilitated, and pledging to protect internationally recognized human rights, the new military government of President Lansana Conté moved quickly to dismantle the apparatus of dictatorship. The ruling Democratic party of Guinea (PDG) and the dreaded secret police were abolished. Special political tribunals were also abolished, and a new, autonomous judicial system was set up. The trade union movement was reorganized to permit political autonomy, democratic elections, and voluntary membership. Freedom of speech, association, and travel were established, and political prisoners were released. At the same time, the governing Military Committee for National Recovery (CMRN) indicated its desire to transform the statist economy and revive economic growth by attacking corruption, reducing state ownership and employment, encouraging private enterprise, and decentralizing government functions.[39]

The transition to democratic government in Guinea is clouded by a number of problems, however. Chief among these has been political and ethnic rivalry within the new government, which spurred an unsuccessful but bloody coup attempt on July 4, led by former prime minister Diarra Traore (who had been ousted by President Conté the previous December) and others from among Sékou Touré's Malinke ethnic group. The failed coup is believed to have resulted in a number of executions. While Conté remains in power, his authority has been weakened, and the political future is now uncertain. A possible manifestation of this was the warning in November by a French humanitarian group of "new cases of torture" by the police and military.[40] Sustained political liberalization will be difficult to achieve without some measure of political stability. And economic liberalization, on which any transition to democratic government would seem to depend, faces serious political, administrative, and financial obstacles.

Finally, in Cameroon, a civilian president, Paul Biya, is struggling to reconcile growing democratic pressure with the harsh, authoritarian legacy of his predecessor, Ahmadu Ahidjo. Since assuming power after Ahidjo's resignation (purportedly for health reasons) in November 1982, President Biya has been trying to liberalize political life in Cameroon, but was constrained by Ahidjo's continuing control of the sole party. However, Biya emerged strengthened in the wake of an unsuccessful but bloody coup attempt on April 6, 1984, believed to be designed to return Ahidjo to power. The fourth ordinary congress of the ruling Cameroon National Union, in March 1985, marked a possible turning point in the country's political development. There, President Biya elaborated on earlier calls for political liberalization and greater freedom of choice (though not yet multiparty competition) in elections. This contrasted sharply with Ahidjo's intolerance for political opposition and dissent and opened the way for expression of growing democratic pressures. Congress delegates debated the country's political future openly and critically for the first time. Newspapers called for freedom of the press, a reorganization of the country's security apparatus, and decentralization of the ruling party. The number of newspapers has increased markedly since the lifting of the severe press restrictions from the Ahidjo era, although the scope of permissible criticism remains limited. In addition, the party's name was changed to the Cameroon People's Democratic movement in an effort to reach out to opposition elements.[41] Although Cameroon remains a one-party, authoritarian state, with inadequate protection for human rights,[42] the increased freedom of expression and the prospect of limited political competition within the ruling party raised the possibility that Cameroon might eventually negotiate the path of democratization followed by Senegal with the retirement of its longtime personal ruler. The first significant test was due early in 1986, with promised competitive elections for offices in the ruling party's organs and sections.

AUTHORITARIAN REGRESS

In Liberia an attempted military coup, seeking to put the country back on the track of democratic development, was narrowly defeated on November 12, 1985, when rebel forces failed fully to execute their seizure of power. The long-awaited coup attempt appeared to be the best hope of freeing Liberia from the deepening tyranny of General Samuel K. Doe, who came to power in a sergeant's coup in 1980, overthrowing the 133-year-old constitutional oligarchy of the Americo-Liberians (freed American and West Indian slaves whose monopoly of political and economic power had largely excluded the 95 percent of the population from indigenous ethnic groups). The 1985 coup attempt was led by General Thomas Quiwonkpa, a leader of the 1980 coup and former army commander, who broke with Doe in 1983 over the latter's increasing authoritarianism and went into exile. A broadcast announcement of the coup by the popular Quiwonkpa, promising "free and fair elections and a democratic society," brought jubilant people rejoicing onto the streets of the capital, but the euphoria was quickly crushed by Doe's troops. In addition to rebel soldiers killed in the fighting, it was reported that some 200 soldiers thought to be loyal to Quiwonkpa were summarily executed. Loyalist troops were also reported to have gunned down celebrating civilians on the streets of the capital and over 500 of Quiwonkpa's sympathizers in his native Nimba county.[43]

The final precipitant for the coup attempt appeared to be the massive rigging of the October elections, in which Samuel Doe and his National Democratic party of Liberia (NDPL) were reported to have won the presidential election with 50.9 percent of the vote, while also winning 44 of 56 House seats and 22 of 26 Senate seats. Although they were the first multiparty, universal-suffrage elections in the country's 138-year history, with an impressively high and orderly voter turnout, the elections were widely viewed as fraudulent and illegitimate. The vote count taken on election day, in the presence of opposition party observers, reportedly indicated a victory for the Liberian Action party (LAP) candidate, Jackson Doe (no relation to the president). President Samuel Doe emerged victorious only two weeks later, after appointing a committee (stacked with members of his party and ethnic group) to "recount" the ballots in private. During the second vote count, the Liberian media reported and provided evidence of fraud and irregularity "on almost a daily basis." The three opposition parties that had been allowed to compete denounced the conduct of the election and the irregular vote count, pledging to boycott the new Senate and House.

Before the voting, the opposition had been widely repressed. Numerous leaders and activists of various parties (registered and un-registered) were detained or intimidated by security forces. Those parties that were able to compete suffered crippling delays in their registration and persistent harassment and obstruction of their cam-paigns, while the NDPL freely used government funds for its cam-paign and pressured civil servants to join and contribute.[44]

The election rigging and brutal postcoup repression appear to mark the consolidation of an authoritarian trend that had been developing throughout 1984. The list of political prisoners grew to include not only opposition politicians but several journalists, students, and other critics of the regime. The military invaded the campus of the University of Liberia and killed or wounded scores of students. A decree made it a crime to spread "lies, rumours, and dis-information" damaging to any government official or to state securi-ty. Continuing repression seems likely to extinguish any hope of liberty and democracy in Liberia for years to come.

In Uganda, the quest for democratic government and the rule of law continued to drown in the tyranny and anarchy that have gripped the country since Idi Amin came to power in 1971. Although the military overthrow of President Milton Obote on July 27, 1985, raised hope for the restoration of unity, stability, and legal order in the strife-torn nation, the five-year-old guerrilla war continued through the end of the year, and with it, reports of killings and atro-cities. Hopes had also been high that the human rights situation would improve after the overthrow in 1979 of General Idi Amin, whose reign of terror claimed the lives of some 500,000 people.[45] However, the dubious victory, in the December 1980 election,[46] of former President Obote (whose authoritarian administration had been toppled by Amin's 1971 coup) did little to alter Amin's legacy of state violence, torture, ethnic strife, and military indiscipline. The number of Ugandans killed or deliberately starved to death during the second Obote regime has been estimated at between 100,000 and 200,000 by the U.S. assistant secretary of state for human rights, and as high as 300,000 to half a million by opposition leaders in the southern and western parts of the country, where the violence has been concentrated. In addition, an estimated half million persons have been forced from their land by the armed insurgency and military counterinsurgency in that region, while more than 2,000 persons (mainly political opponents and critics) were imprisoned without charge, and torture remained a frequent practice.[47]

The new military government of General Tito Okello attempted to reach out to the rebels by appointing as minister of the interior the leading southern politician and primary political opponent of Obote, Paul Ssemogerere. An outspoken critic of human rights abuses, Ssemogerere subsequently supervised the release on August 10 of 2,200 political prisoners who had been detained under Obote. But the rebel National Resistance Army (NRA), led by Yoweri Museveni, objected to the appointment of Obote's vice-president and defense minister, Paulo Muwanga (alleged to have sanctioned the torture and civilian massacres), as the new prime minister, and to the inclusion in the military council of forces loyal to Idi Amin. The NRA was also emboldened by its increasing military advantage over government troops.

The growing civil war embodied the longstanding tension in Uganda between the more populous northern ethnic groups, who have controlled the army and the political system since independence, and the more educationally and economically advanced southern groups, such as the Baganda. It has reflected not only deep-seated ethnic and regional conflict, but also the erosion of law and civility in Uganda over the past two decades.

SOUTH AFRICA

South Africa's political system defies categorization. For the almost five million white South Africans (about 16 percent of the population), the political system is an electoral democracy, which—despite significant authoritarian constraints—is more pluralistic and representative than most African political systems. Although it is constrained by legal restrictions and pragmatic self-censorship, the largely white-owned press has been vigorous in criticizing the racist policies of the regime and calling for reform. Several white and multiracial human rights groups operate to monitor and aid the victims of apartheid, the country's racist system of separate and unequal development. In Parliament, state president Pieter W. Botha's National party, which has ruled continuously since 1948, faces spirited (although numerically limited) opposition on the left from the Progressive Federal party, which seeks an end to apartheid, and on the right from the breakaway Conservative party, which opposes any racial reform. In fact, the vulnerability of the current government to a democratic backlash from the right (underscored by rightist gains in 1985 elections) may constitute the most serious obstacle to the dismantling of apartheid.

The system of apartheid denies South Africa's 24 million blacks, who constitute almost three-quarters of the population, any significant political rights. They are prohibited from voting in national elections or determining their own affairs, except as "citizens" of one of ten mostly unviable "homelands," four of which have been granted an "independence" recognized by no other nation in the world. The blacks are effectively forbidden to move or live where they want, to assemble freely, or to organize politically. Internal security laws give the regime sweeping powers of arbitrary arrest, imprisonment, and banning (effective political isolation) of black protest leaders and white critics and dissidents as well. Under the "Group Areas Act," South Africa's ten million urban blacks are confined to living in segregated townships, impoverished satellite developments with inferior amenities and social services. "Influx control" laws strictly regulate the right of blacks to live and visit in South Africa's cities. Their movements about the country are rigidly controlled by "pass laws," which require all blacks over age 16 to carry a reference book indicating where they may live and work. Hundreds of thousands have been arrested yearly for pass law violations. Since 1960, more than three million blacks have been uprooted from their established communities and resettled in "homelands" or townships. Most of these restrictions and social disadvantages apply as well to the almost 2.8 million colored (mixed race) and 900,000 Asian (mostly Indian) South Africans.[48]

Under increasing pressure both at home and abroad, the South African government has moved cautiously toward piecemeal reform of the apartheid system. In what it regarded as its most important gesture to date, the Botha government drafted a new constitution creating separate houses of parliament for coloreds and for Asians, elected from separate voter roles and responsible for legislation affecting their racial communities. While blacks remained excluded and the white chamber continued to have unequal and preeminent power, the reforms were presented as a step toward racial power sharing. That partial step was overwhelmingly and militantly rejected by the nonwhite majority of the country, however. In 1983, more than 600 community organizations formed the multiracial United Democratic front (UDF) to oppose the new constitution and work instead for the total abolition of apartheid. In the face of a vigorous UDF boycott, less than 30 percent of coloreds and 20 percent of Asians turned out to vote in the August 1984 elections for the new chambers.[49]

In September 1984, opposition to the new constitution converged with growing discontent among black students over educational grievances (which had given rise to a protracted school boycott) and discontent in the townships over rent increases and other issues to ignite the most serious episode of racial unrest since World War II. Disturbances broke out first in the Eastern Cape and then in several townships south of Johannesburg, spreading subsequently to other areas of the country. The massive deployment of paramilitary police and in some cases troops produced hundreds of arrests and an estimated 170 deaths by the end of 1984 but could not quell the escalating unrest. As violent disruptions continued throughout 1985, government repression stiffened. On July 20, a state of emergency was imposed on parts of the country for the first time since the Sharpeville massacre in 1960. By the end of the year, more than 1,000 people (all but 20 of them nonwhite) had died in the 16 months of rioting, demonstrations, and repression. Although most blacks were killed by the security forces, a considerable number were killed in intrablack violence, as an angry new generation of militants and hooligans vented its frustration on suspected collaborators and innocent bystanders in the black community. More than 8,000 people were detained by security forces, and by the end of the year some 1,000 remained in prison, where, in some areas, torture and abusive treatment were common. In addition, more than 100 South Africans vanished, many of them suspected victims of clandestine elements within the state security apparatus.[50]

The Botha government has continued to resist fundamental change. While abolishing the laws prohibiting interracial marriage and sex and relaxing petty apartheid (by integrating many public facilities), Botha bitterly disappointed domestic and international opponents of apartheid by failing to announce major new reforms that had been promised. A growing segment of the business community sees the negotiation of an end to apartheid as a practical necessity for the revival and further development of the continent's most powerful and sophisticated economy, which now finds itself deep in depression and international financial crisis. In recognition of this reality, some of the country's most powerful white business-men met with leaders of the banned African National Congress (ANC) in Lusaka, Zambia in September. Recently, several party and government officials, including Botha, have warned with varying degrees of explicitness that the current white monopoly of power is untenable. In November, Botha announced vague plans for a new constitution incorporating the homelands and conferring South African citizenship on all blacks, an essential condition of any political settlement.

The outlines of a possible political settlement are not difficult to discern. As numerous foreign observers and moderate black and white South Africans have recognized, a multiracial democracy could only come about if there were solid guarantees of power and autono-my for the white minority, such that they could not be simply and predictably overridden on matters of fundamental concern. In part, this would involve a federal system with considerable local and regional autonomy. But it would probably also require other features of what has been termed "consociational democracy"—such as pro-portional representation, coalition government, and mutual veto power for the major racial groups over certain types of issues. Such a system would require political leaders sufficiently strong within their groups and moderate in outlook to "act as brokers to limit conflict and to reach accommodation."[51] While it would differ from absolute majority rule, it would be no less democratic (as evidenced by several European examples) and probably far more stable, produc-ing complex ethnic and racial coalitions.

By the time the Nationalist government is ready to negotiate, there could be no one left to negotiate with. The moderate genera-tion of black leaders is aging and losing touch with a new generation that has suffered the brutalising effects of arrests, street battles and police beatings. The longer the violence and repression continue, the more alienated and uncompromising this new generation will be-come, and the stronger will be the position of young black militants who insist that change can only come through massive violence. Such violence, which figures to remain sporadic and poorly organized, can-not topple the South African military machine, by far the most powerful and efficient on the continent. But it could polarize the society to the point where, as in Ireland and Lebanon, the chance for reconciliation drowns in an unending stream of blood.[52]

ABSOLUTIST AUTHORITARIAN REGIMES

Of the authoritarian regimes that predominate in Africa, a number may be distinguished as "absolutist" for their lack of any effective legal or constitutional check on government authority. Some of these absolutisms center around a personal dictator, others are based on a Marxist-Leninist ruling party. The archetypical case of personal absolutism is Zaire, where the regime of Mobutu Sese Seko has come to symbolize the venality and despotism of unaccountable government in Africa. During his 20 years of rule, Mobutu has dramatically centralized and personalized state authority, using the security apparatus and a patrimonial bureaucracy to control all key societal groups and intermediary authorities.[53] The sole legal party has become his personal instrument of domination and the national budget his personal account. Opposition is brutally repressed and the regime has been repeatedly cited for what Amnesty International terms "a consistent pattern of gross violations" of human rights. Victimized by rapacious officials at every level of the bureaucracy and military, the general population has "resigned to political apathy" and has "been reduced to living under conditions of servility and fear."[54] More than 1,000 political prisoners are believed to be held and numerous reports of torture have been confirmed. In 1982 and 1983, more than 100 prisoners were reportedly executed without trial.[55] There were a few signs in 1984 and 1985 of an easing of the repression and some reconciliation with the political opposition. The most dramatic of these was the return on June 30, 1985, of former prime minister Nguza Karl I Bond, a leader of the exiled opposition to Mobutu who had given graphic testimony of the regime's corruption and brutality to the U.S. Congress. But attempts of the banned Union for Democracy and Social Progress to organize political opposition continue to be brutally repressed, along with recurrent student protests. Reports of atrocities and mass killings indicate there is little prospect of change in the absolutist and repressive character of the regime.

In a similar fashion, the one-party state in Togo has been organized around the glorification and enrichment of President

Gnassingbe Eyadema, whose figure adorns the lapels of all government officials. Since seizing power in 1967, Eyadema has destroyed virtually all his adversaries. The two major opposition forces—the military-led National liberation Front of Togo and the civilian Togolese Democratic movement—are exiled, and internal opposition is ruthlessly repressed. In 1984, a former vice-president, Idrisso Meatchi, died after two years of imprisonment without trial. Numerous other political prisoners, dissidents, and potential rivals for power have died or disappeared mysteriously, including most recently the army chief of staff. Detention without trial of political opponents is widespread, as is the torture and ill-treatment of detainees. In 1985, Eyadema launched a new crackdown on critics and opposition elements after a series of bomb explosions in August highlighted the growing popular resistance to his repressive rule.[56]

Like Mobutu and Eyadema, President H. Kamuzu Banda completely dominates the public affairs of Malawi, tolerating no rivals and demanding total loyalty to himself and his ruling party. "His rule is absolute insofar as no important jurisdictions of law or policy—including the courts—are secure from his intervention or meddling."[57] Since independence in 1964, Banda, now 86, has ruled as a "paternalist despot," harshly repressing opposition and controlling all important government appointments and policies. The 18-year rule of President Omar Bongo in mineral-rich Gabon may be characterized in similar terms. Bongo totally controls the government and ruling party. No criticism of the president or one-party system is permitted, and opposition activity is harshly suppressed.

Although the line between absolutist and more limited authoritarianism is indistinct in practice, six other countries can be classified as absolutist: Benin, the Central African Republic, Equatorial Guinea, Guinea-Bissau (where the socialist one-party system bears some resemblance to a Marxist mobilizational regime), Niger (dominated by military dictator General Seyni Kountche), and Somalia (a one-party, socialist regime in which the president of 15 years, Mohammed Siad Barre, continues to depend on the military for his ultimate authority). Both the Central African Republic and Equatorial Guinea were decimated during the 1970s by the atrocities and terror of two notoriously bloody tyrants, from which their societies have not yet recovered. In Benin, the government of President Mathieu Kerekou and his People's Revolutionary party had been allowing somewhat greater freedom in recent years as it veered away from a Marxist-

Leninist orientation, but the growing economic crisis and its attendant unrest have precipitated a reassertion of absolutist control, as evidenced in the brutal suppression of student demonstrations in April and May 1985.[58]

MARXIST REGIMES

Like the nonideological absolutist regimes, Marxist-Leninist African regimes tolerate no organized political opposition and permit no criticism of government policies or officials. The media are owned and operated entirely by the government, and subject to censorship. Judicial autonomy is absent. In contrast to the personalistic dictatorships, it is the ruling party that is the supreme political authority; power, though highly concentrated, is not so nearly monopolized by a single individual. As with more deeply institutionalized Marxist-Leninist regimes, the ruling parties of the "Afro-Marxist" regimes are "Leninist in conception: . . . theoretically manned by a revolutionary vanguard" and standing over the state. However, Afro-Marxist regimes depart from the Leninist model, in part because of their origins in military coups or national liberation movements, which have left the armed forces in a far more central role.[59]

Of the five regimes that may be classified as Marxist, Ethiopia comes the closest to the totalitarian mobilizational state of the more established communist regimes, even though it has only recently established a Marxist-Leninist party. Since seizing power in 1974, Marxist military officers, led by Mengistu Haile Mariam, have ruled through the Derg (military coordinating committee). However, seeking to deepen and extend its control over the population, the regime formally established a Marxist-Leninist party, the Workers party of Ethiopia, on September 6, 1984, with Mengistu as secretary-general and other current and former military officers in prominent party positions. Through the new party and existing state structures, the regime "maintains complete control over the media, labor, education, internal and external movements of Ethiopian citizens, and all political processes."[60] Marxist-Leninist ideology is imposed in the press, the schools, and the network of urban neighborhood associations (*kebele*) and rural dwellers' associations. Officials of these local groups closely monitor the people and have powers of arrest. Failure to attend political or kebele meetings, criticism of the government, and suspicion of antigovernment actions or sentiments are grounds for arrest and detention without trial. While precise figures are unavailable, political prisoners number in the thousands and many have been held for years without charge. Torture of detainees appears to be routine and widespread, and summary executions reportedly continue, though not at the pace of the "red-terror" of the late 1970s. Grave human rights abuses have also occurred within the context of civil war and famine. More than a million people have fled their homes or been forcibly resettled. Recently, the Mengistu government appears to have used starvation as a weapon of war against liberation movements and political resistance in the provinces of Tigre, Eritrea, and Wollo. Callous indifference has further impeded famine relief: in 1984, the regime spent a reported $200 million to celebrate the 10th anniversary of its seizure of power while peasants starved.

Continuing insurgencies (backed by South Africa) have also been a factor motivating human rights abuses in Angola and Mozambique, but in neither country is state control over society as total or repression as ruthless as in Ethiopia. In Angola, 1–2,000 people or more are imprisoned for political crimes, most of them for opposing the government but some simply for criticizing or ridiculing government officials. Many have been in prison for years without trial, and allegations of torture and mistreatment of detainees persist. Hundreds of thousands have fled the country to escape the fighting between the government of the Marxist Popular movement for the Liberation of Angola (MPLA) and its chief armed rival, UNITA, which controls about a third of the country. Where the MPLA rules (with the backing of some 30,000 Cuban troops), political activity is limited to participation in it or one of its controlled and sanctioned organizations.

Although the ruling Front for the Liberation of Mozambique (FRELIMO) has control of more of the country in Mozambique, fighting between it and the National Resistance movement increased during 1984, with both sides committing atrocities and the insurgents exercising particularly "brutal violence" against civilians. The government holds several thousand members of armed opposition groups and a number of other political prisoners as well. Detention without charge or trial is common, and a number of detainees were reported to have been tortured or badly beaten. However, there were modest signs of improvement in the human rights situation in

1984, with the release of dozens of long-term detainees, a decline in the number of new political incarcerations, and the launching of a "Legality Offensive" to prevent abuses of detainees and ensure greater respect for the law. Although it is a Marxist, one-party state, with policies and initiatives determined from above by a small cadre of senior party officials, "at the local level, especially in the rural areas, there is considerable openness for the people to express their views on prevailing conditions," and the media have some scope to report on abuses and flaws within the system.[61]

Congo (or Congo-Brazzaville) was the first African country to declare itself a Marxist-Leninist state, in 1969. Since that time, the Congolese Labor party has controlled the government and media and been the sole outlet for political involvement, but military officers continue to occupy powerful political positions. There is persistent concern about the long-term detention and torture of political prisoners, but the recent trend has been toward a more open society. While not politically free, the Congolese go about their daily affairs with minimal government or police interference. A pragmatic administration tolerates a flourishing private sector and has distributed the country's oil wealth better than is typical in Africa.[62]

The tiny island nation of São Tomé and Principe is not officially Marxist-Leninist, but the government draws heavily on these principles in dominating its 100,000 people.

OTHER AUTHORITARIAN REGIMES

Although they vary considerably in their level of repression, the remaining 13 states are grouped among the "limited authoritarianisms" because they dominate their societies less completely and monolithically than the absolutist regimes. While political opposition is suppressed, often very harshly, there is at least some pluralism in associational life, modest scope for the expression of critical views, and in some cases, limited judicial autonomy and due process. The latter qualification, for example, is evident in the one-party states of Rwanda, where the independence of the judiciary has been strengthened somewhat in recent years as part of a modest liberalization, and Burundi, where there is also increasingly active debate in the National Assembly and some limited electoral competition within the ruling party. (However, religious practice is severely restricted in Burundi and Christian clergy and laity are victimized.) In Swaziland, the authority of the ruling monarchy is limited not only by an independent judiciary, but by traditional rights and responsibilities and modern politicians and technocrats. Such checks are lacking, however, in Mali, a highly centralized one-party state, and also in Chad, where political institutions have almost completely disintegrated during 20 years of continuous civil strife. The ministates of Cape Verde, the Comoros, Djibouti, and Seychelles are all one-party regimes that ban political opposition and restrict civil liberties. In the Comoros, however, legislative elections are freely contested within the ruling party.

Changes of leadership occurred in two other countries. In Sierra Leone, one of the more liberal one-party regimes in Africa, President Siaka Stevens became the fourth major African ruler to step down from power voluntarily, leaving office on November 28, 1985, after 17 years. (Like Nyerere however, Stevens is expected to retain indirect control for some time.) Although he declared a one-party state in 1978 and extended his term of office for another seven years, Stevens did not rule repressively. Contested elections were permitted for the one-party Parliament in 1982, when multiple candidates (up to three, chosen by the party) competed in about two-thirds of the constituencies. Although the Parliament is subservient to the president, the judiciary has maintained its independence and earned a reputation for providing fair, public trials. The press, which includes several private newspapers, is permitted considerable (though not full) freedom, and academic freedom is unabridged. While these factors might offer some promise for the resurrection of a multiparty democracy, Stevens's selection of the military commander, Major General Joseph Saidu Momoh, as his successor would seem to offer little hope of further liberalization. After a brief campaign to rally popular support, Momoh was elected president on October 1 with the reported approval of 99 percent of registered voters.

In the kingdom of Lesotho, Prime Minister Leabua Jonathan, who suspended the democratic constitution in 1970, presided over a one-party system. Although the independence of the judiciary and considerable freedom of expression were preserved, there were violations of human rights, and Jonathan became increasingly unpopular during his two decades of rule.

In Ghana and Burkina Faso, populist military regimes have emphasized the transitional and corrective character of their rule.

In Ghana, Flight Lieutenant Jerry Rawlings has taken a more moderate course in the past two years, seeking to rein in the militant Committees for the Defense of the Revolution while implementing an extremely austere economic reform program to regenerate Ghana's ravaged economy. Since seizing power for the second time in 1981, overthrowing Ghana's fragile Third Republic, Rawlings had sought radical reform of endemic corruption through new, populist committees and tribunals. This brought harsh punishments of corrupt former officials, but at the price of widespread human rights violations and severe damage to the judiciary, the one political institution in Ghana "that had maintained a semblance of autonomy through the years." While the human rights situation has improved somewhat in the past two years, the discovery of several coup plots has brought numerous new detentions and summary executions. A National Commission for Democracy is now studying how some type of more stable democratic government can be reinstituted, and has indicated that the new political order would be based on elective local government. In fact, with the disintegration of the state and the disengagement of society from the state over the past three decades, democracy has begun to reassert itself through informal, local structures. But if democratic government is to be reestablished, government authority and legitimacy must be reestablished in a country that is now "ungovernable."[63]

In Burkina Faso, the military president, Captain Thomas Sankara, who models his populist revolution on that of Rawlings in Ghana, tightened his grip on power in 1985. This was reflected in the growing power of the Committees for the Defense of the Revolution (CDR), over which Sankara exercises tight control. The CDRs have become ubiquitous in almost every phase of daily life. While they have won popular support through the success of their development programs, their disciplinary excesses and expanding surveillance have also generated increasing suspicion that they may be the instruments for the establishment of a repressive one-party state.[64]

CONCLUSION

The prospects for democratic government in sub-Saharan Africa are not encouraging. In most African countries, the conditions for democracy have hardly become more propitious since independence.

Aside from a small number of at least partially competitive and liberal systems, most countries lack any kind of institutional base— both political and social—for the development of democratic government. State structures have become even larger and more domineering; they have also become much more corrupt and inefficient. At the same time, the authority and capacity of the state has eroded in many nations, and utterly disintegrated in a few. Most African countries remain extremely impoverished, and their economies have been stagnant or contracting in recent years. In the face of sagging commodities markets, spreading deserts, disappearing forests, eroding soil, booming populations, and recurrent drought, they will be increasingly hard pressed to maintain even the current living standards, much less to create meaningful work for millions of new job-seekers. Where human survival itself is threatened, the prospect for democracy and liberty is grim.

In the immediate future, the prospect is grimmest in those absolutist regimes that have purged their societies of any social or political pluralism that could serve to limit state power and to articulate competing interests and ideas. In these countries, probably the most that can be hoped for in the near term is a reduction or cessation of human rights violations and the development of modest pluralism in the form of autonomous interest groups and partial freedom of expression—i.e., a transition from absolute to limited authoritarianism. Because African authoritarian regimes have generally been no more successful than competitive regimes in institutionalizing their rule, such a democratic opening may be conceivable in the event of the death or overthrow of the current personal dictators. A pluralist opening would in theory be less likely in the Marxist-Leninist states, but in Africa, these regimes show signs of being more flexible and less doctrinaire. In particular, a resolution of the civil wars in Angola and Mozambique and an increase in economic ties with the West might lead to a reduction in repression. However, it seems unlikely that parties with such a strong ideological mission and powerful doctrine of control will significantly ease their grip on government power.

Where some pluralism in social and political life already exists, in the one-party regimes, the most realistic hope would be for the development of genuine political competition within the framework of a single legal party, on the model of Kenya. Cameroon may well transit this path; Sierra Leone may or may not continue its hesitant progress in this direction under its new president. This is not to concede to the pessimistic assessment that "single-party democracy" may be the only form capable of enduring in African multiethnic states,[65] but simply to underscore that democratic progress in Africa is likely to be incremental (as it has been historically elsewhere in the world). Where there has been no tradition of political competition, open debate, free political organizations, judicial autonomy, and other checks on executive power, it is most unlikely that a multiparty democracy can suddenly emerge and endure. Of the limited military regimes, Nigeria and Ghana may both return again to democratic government by the end of the decade, and Guinea for the first time, but these prospects are clouded by the absence of any democratic tradition (and the legacy of tyranny) in Guinea, the weakness of state authority in Ghana, and the grave economic crisis in all three.

Where some political competition already exists, both in the one-party and multiparty systems, the key obstacle to further democratization in the near future is the reluctance of ruling groups to surrender their hold on state power. Too many interests within the ruling party machine have too much to lose, especially where the state is the dominant source of wealth and opportunity in the country. Although Senegal has shown that a one-party regime is capable of opening up the political system to competing parties, it has not shown that a long-ruling party is willing to tolerate a serious threat to its dominance. Indeed, recent developments in Senegal suggest that the emergence of a potentially triumphant political opposition would be more likely to induce an authoritarian response, in which cooptation, coercion, and fraud are employed to retain ruling party dominance indefinitely. Put another way, to the extent that multiparty competition is permitted in Africa, the systems are likely to look more like Mexico than Venezuela. After two decades and more of independence, only in Mauritius has a ruling party been removed from office in a free and fair election. Should the ruling parties in Botswana, Senegal, and The Gambia ever be faced with such a prospect, the future of their multiparty systems would be in serious question. In that event, two factors would be of crucial significance: the degree to which ruling party politicians have alternative professional and business avenues to accumulate wealth and prestige outside of politics, and the degree to which they value the democratic system over and above their own personal, political, and ideological goals. These factors will also weigh heavily in Zimbabwe, where the democratic system faces more imminent danger.

In the long run, the failure to institutionalize authoritarian rule and the continuing popular pressure for liberal and accountable government in many African countries may offer hope for democratic development. The spread of education tends to be particularly subversive of authoritarian constraints. But in the long run, democracy is not possible without development. Africa faces long-run economic and ecological crises of almost incomprehensible proportions. Per capita food production has been declining by 1 percent a year for a decade and a half. The populations of Nigeria, Kenya, and Zimbabwe (among others) will double in about 20 years or less. Africa's total population will triple in 35 years, at which time much of its existing forest cover may be gone. Unless urgent steps are taken to attack these catastrophic dangers, neither physical well-being nor political freedom will be possible.

APPENDIX: CLASSIFICATION OF NATIONS IN SUB-SAHARAN AFRICA

Insecure Democracies

Botswana
Mauritius

Partial Democracies

The Gambia
Senegal
Zimbabwe

Limited Authoritarianisms

Burkina Fasso (military)
Burundi (one party)
Cameroon (one party)
Cape Verde (one party)
Chad (one party)
Comoros (one party)
Djibouti (one party)
Ghana (military)
Guinea (military)

(Limited Authoritarianisms cont.)

Ivory Coast (one party, partially
    competitive)
Kenya (one party, partially
    competitive)
Lesotho (military)
Liberia (limited multiparty)
Madagascar (limited multiparty)
Mali (one party)
Nigeria (liberal military)
Rwanda (one party)
Seychelles (one party)
Sierra Leone (one party)
South Africa (apartheid)
Swaziland (monarchy)
Tanzania (one party, partially
    competitive)
Uganda (military)
Zambia (one party, partially
    competitive)

Absolutist (non-Marxist) Dictatorships	Marxist Dictatorships
Benin (one party)	Angola
Central African Republic (military)	Congo Brazzaville
	Ethiopia
Equatorial Guinea (military)	Mozambique
Gabon (one party)	São Tomé and Principe
Guinea-Bissau (one party)	
Malawi (one party)	
Niger (military)	
Somalia (one party)	
Togo (one party)	
Zaire (one party)	

NOTES

1. Richard L. Sklar, "Developmental Democracy" (Paper presented to the Annual Meeting of the American Political Science Association, Paris, June 15–20, 1985.

2. Robert H. Jackson and Carl G. Rosberg, "Popular Legitimacy in African Multi-Ethnic States," *Journal of Modern African Studies* 22 (1984):186.

3. Jackson and Rosberg, *Personal Rule in Black Africa* (Berkeley: University of California Press, 1982), pp. 1–26.

4. Richard L. Sklar, "The Nature of Class Domination in Africa," *Journal of Modern African Studies* 17 (1979):537. The emergence, character, and multiple dysfunctions of this phenomenon are also examined in Larry Diamond, "Class Formation in the Swollen African State" (Paper presented to the Annual Meeting of the American Political Science Association, Paris, June 15–20, 1985.)

5. Jackson and Rosberg, "Popular Legitimacy in African Multi-Ethnic States," p. 186. For an analysis of this effect in the Nigerian case, see Larry Diamond, "Class, Ethnicity and the Democratic State: Nigeria 1950–66," *Comparative Studies in Society and History* 25 (1983):457–89, and "Cleavage, Conflict and Anxiety in the Second Nigerian Republic," *Journal of Modern African Studies* 20 (1982).

6. *New African* (December 1984):39, and U.S. Department of State, *Country Reports on Human Rights Practices for 1984* (Washington: U.S. Government Printing Office, 1985), pp. 29–30.

7. John D. Holm, "The Development of Democracy in Botswana" (Paper presented to the Conference on Democracy in Developing Countries, Hoover Institution, December 1985), 42.

8. U.S. Department of State, *Country Reports,* pp. 26–30.

9. Ibid., p. 28.

10. *Africa Now* (September 1984):47; Holm, "The Development of Democracy in Botswana," pp. 25-9.

11. U.S. Department of State, *Country Reports,* p. 223.

12. *Africa Now* (August 1984):36.

13. U.S. Department of State, *Country Reports,* p. 127; Amnesty International, *Amnesty International Report* (1985):46.

14. U.S. Department of State, *Country Reports,* p. 129.

15. Masipula Sithole, "Zimbabwe in Search of a Stable Democracy" (Paper presented to the Conference on Democracy in Developing Countries, Hoover Institution, December 1985), 75; *West Africa,* 22 July 1985, p. 1,470.

16. *Africa Now* (August 1985):24; Amnesty International, 1985 Report, p. 116; *Africa Confidential* (December 11, 1985):6.

17. *Africa Confidential* (December 11, 1985):6; *New African* (November 1985):23; *Africa Report* (November–December 1985):50.

18. Richard L. Sklar, "Reds and Rights: Zimbabwe's Experiment," *Issue* 14 (1985); Sithole, "Zimbabwe in Search of a Stable Democracy"; U.S. Department of State, *Country Reports,* pp. 388-96.

19. Jackson and Rosberg, "Democracy in Tropical Africa," *Personal Rule in Black Africa* (Berkeley: University of California Press, 1982), p. 302; Richard L. Sklar, "Democracy in Africa," *African Studies Review* 26 (September–December 1983):13.

20. Paula Hirschoff, ed., "Update," *Africa Report* 30:1 (January–February 1985):38.

21. Foreign Broadcast Information Service, April 19, August 12, and October 7, 1985.

22. "Dateline Africa," *West Africa* (October 21, 1985):2,234.

23. A number of persons arrested for separatist agitation and violent disturbances in the Casamance region late in 1983 are alleged to have been tortured during prolonged pretrial detention (Amnesty International, *1985 Report,* p. 84).

24. Jackson and Rosberg, "Democracy in Tropical Africa," p. 304; and *Personal Rule in Black Africa* (Berkeley: University of California Press, 1982), p. 111.

25. Jackson and Rosberg, "Popular Legitimacy in African Multi-Ethnic States," p. 190.

26. For a study of Kenyatta's style of personal rule, see Jackson and Rosberg, *Personal Rule in Black Africa* (Berkeley: University of California Press, 1982), pp. 98–107.

27. U.S. Department of State, *Country Reports,* pp. 163-66; Amnesty International, *1985 Report,* pp. 55–56.

28. Howard French, "Ivory Coast: One-Party State at a Crossroads," *Africa Report* 30:4 (July–August 1985):14–17; U.S. Department of State, *Country Reports,* p. 160; Jackson and Rosberg, "Democracy in Tropical Africa," p. 304.

29. These were the officially reported figures. *Africa Confidential,* (October 30 and December 11, 1985); "Dateline Africa," *West Africa,* (3558 November 4, 1985). 2,325.

30. U.S. Department of State, *Country Reports,* pp. 156–59. The Ivory Coast is one of the few African countries for which Amnesty International reported no human rights concerns in 1984 and 1985, and it has a functioning Amnesty International chapter; "The Politics of Survival," *West Africa* 3559 (November 11, 1985):2349.

31. *Africa Report* 29:1 (January–February 1984):30, *Africa Confidential* (October 16, 1985):2; Amnesty International, *1985 Report,* pp. 113–14; U.S. Department of State, *Country Reports,* pp. 382–83; Sklar, "Democracy in Africa," p. 17.

32. *Africa Confidential* (November 27, 1985):5.

33. U.S. Department of State, *Country Reports,* pp. 341, 345; Amnesty International, *1985 Report,* 101–2.

34. U.S. Department of State, *Country Reports,* pp. 192–96; *Africa Confidential* (November 27, 1985):6–7.

35. Larry Diamond, "Nigeria Update," *Foreign Affairs* 64 (Winter 1985–86):326–30, and "High Stakes for Babangida," *Africa Report* 29:6 (November–December 1985):54–5; Amnesty International, *1985 Report,* pp. 78–81.

36. "Dateline Africa," *West Africa* 3565 (December 23, 30, 1985):2,716.

37. Larry Diamond, "Nigeria in Search of Democracy," *Foreign Affairs* 62 (Spring 1984):912–21, and "Nigeria Update," 333–35.

38. U.S. Department of State, *Country Reports,* p. 141; Amnesty International, *1985 Report,* pp. 50–53. The new regime also facilitated the efforts of Amnesty International and the national and international press to document and expose the sweeping human rights violations of the Touré dictatorship.

39. Richard Everett, "Guinea: A Tough Road Ahead," *Africa Report* (July–August 1985):19; Amnesty International, *1985 Report,* p. 50–51; U.S. Department of State, *Country Reports,* p. 141.

40. "Dateline Africa," *West Africa* 3561 (November 25, 1985):2498.

41. Frederick Scott, "Biya's New Deal," *Africa Report* 30:1 (July–August 1985):58–61.

42. Amnesty International, *1985 Report,* pp. 27–30; U.S. Department of State, *Country Reports,* pp. 49–56. It remains to be seen whether the most disturbing human rights violations reported—executions without due process and possible torture of detainees—are endemic to Biya's rule or a function (as seems plausible) of the insecure situation following the attempted coup.

43. "An Eyewitness Account," *West Africa* 3564 (December 16, 1985):7; *New African* (January 1986):25–26.

44. "Statesman or Dictator," *West Africa* 3529 (April 15, 1985):733.

45. Mary Anne Fitzgerald, "Uganda: What Prospects for Peace?" *Africa Report* 30:6 (November–December 1985):13.

46. In fact, the elections appear to have been marred by substantial irregularities. See *Africa Now* (August 1985):18, and *New African* (September 1985):18.

47. Amnesty International, *1985 Report,* pp. 105–7; U.S. Department of State, *Country Reports,* pp. 360–65; "Update," *Africa Report* 30:4 (July–August 1985):45. A special Amnesty International report released in June 1985 presented extensive evidence of torture and massacres on a massive scale, "Up-

date," *Africa Report* 30:5 (September–October 1985):38; *New African* (September 1985):18.

48. For an overview of the apartheid system, see for example, Report of the Study Commission on U.S. Policy toward Southern Africa, *South Africa: Time Running Out* (Berkeley: University of California Press, 1981). Also, U.S. Department of State, *Country Reports*, pp. 295–305.

49. U.S. Department of State, *Country Reports*, 303–4; Amnesty International, *1985 Report*, p. 90; Donald Horowitz, "After Apartheid: How Majority Rule Can Work," *The New Republic*, November 4, 1985, 20.

50. Sanford Ungar and Peter Vale, "Why Constructive Engagement Failed," *Foreign Affairs* 74 (Winter 1985–86):249.

51. Lewis Gann and Peter Duignan, *Why South Africa Will Survive* (New York: St. Martin's Press, 1981), pp. 298–300. On the role of proportional representation, see Donald Horowitz, "After Apartheid," p. 23. For a theoretical and comparative analysis of the consociational model, see Arend Lijphart, *Democracy in Plural Societies* (New Haven: Yale University Press, 1977).

52. Colin Legum, "South Africa on the Rocks," *New African* (December 1985):14–15; and "Reconciliation: Is It Still Possible?" *New African* (January 1986):15–16.

53. Thomas M. Callaghy, *The State-Society Struggle: Zaire in Comparative Perspective* (New York: Columbia University Press, 1984), p. 142.

54. Jackson and Rosberg, *Personal Rule in Black Africa* (Berkeley: University of California Press, 1984), p. 179.

55. Paul Wolfson, "What Governments Do to Blacks in the Rest of Africa," *Policy Review* 34 (Fall 1985):43.

56. Manfred Steinholtz, "Togo: West Africa's Middleman in a Pinch," *Africa Report* (July–August 1985):29; Amnesty International, *1985 Report*, pp. 102–4; *Africa Confidential* (October 30, 1985):5–6.

57. Jackson and Rosberg, *Personal Rule in Black Africa*, p. 160. See also, U.S. Department of State, *Country Reports*, pp. 199–203.

58. See the relevant sections of the U.S. Department of State, *Country Reports*, and also for Benin, *Africa Confidential* (July 3, 1985):7.

59. Crawford Young, *Ideology and Development in Africa* (New Haven: Yale University Press, 1982), pp. 27–8.

60. U.S. Department of State, *Country Reports*, p. 107.

61. U.S. Department of State, *Country Reports*, pp. 228–33; Amnesty International, *1985 Report*, pp. 69–73.

62. U.S. Department of State, *Country Reports*, pp. 87–91; Amnesty International, *1985 Report*, pp. 36–38; Young, *Ideology and Development in Africa*, pp. 32–36.

63. Naomi Chazan, "Democracy and Governance in Ghana: Problems and Prospects" (Paper presented to the Conference on Democracy in Developing Countries, Hoover Institution, December 1985), 42–43., 62–64.

64. *New African* (June 1985):27–28; (July 1985):24–25.

65. Jackson and Rosberg, "Popular Legitimacy in African Multi-Ethnic States," p. 191.

5

North Africa
and the Middle East

Glenn E. Perry

The Middle East, including North Africa, has known little democracy. Historically, the main exception was in simple societies, where an elected chieftain shared power with a tribal council (*majlis*). Early Islamic practice demonstrated quasi-democratic features, but Islamic ideals—an immutable sacred law that limited the ruler, the obligation of the ruler to engage in consultation (*shura*), and the theory (at least in Sunni Islam) of an "elected" ruler, as well as a pattern of toleration and autonomy (though not equality) for other religions—made way for highly autocratic and arbitrary government in practice. The region had no experience with representative assemblies or constitutions until such institutions were copied—with little impact in practice—from Europe in the nineteenth century. The tendency to call representative or quasi-representative bodies the Consultative Council (*Majlis al-Shura*) shows the need to legitimate modern practices in traditional terms.

A significant degree of democracy emerged during the post–World War I period in the Arab Middle East, especially in Egypt, and there was some development of parliaments in such other monarchies as Iraq and Transjordan and in French-ruled Syria and Lebanon. Systems that with some qualifications could be called democracies emerged in Israel, Lebanon, and Cyprus—and for short periods in Syria and the Sudan—during the post-1945 period. While Egypt's limited experience with free elections and parliamentary government

112

made way for a single-party regime after 1952, Turkey transformed itself from a single-party dictatorship into a two-party democracy by 1950, but this has since been several times interrupted by military intervention. Iran's constitution of 1906 gained effectiveness for almost the first time during and immediately after World War II only to make way for the restoration of monarchical supremacy in 1953.

In some circles in the Arab world during the post-1945 period democracy came to be regarded as inappropriate under current socio-economic conditions. Leaders all across the political spectrum tended to argue that landlords and such controlled the votes of the poor and thus inevitably caused democratic procedures to be perverted into oligarchy and exploitation. Proponents of radical regimes talked of the need for "real democracy," that is, a populist dictatorship representing the "masses."

"Real democracy" having lost its glamor in recent years, there is some evidence of a renewed sense of the importance of individual liberties and majority rule. One manifestation of this was a meeting of leading Arab intellectuals in Tunis in 1983 that deplored "the complete disappearance of democratic freedoms in the Arab world" and declared that democracy is both a fundamental goal in its own right and an essential means for achieving all other goals. A second meeting, held in Cyprus later in 1983, set up the Organization for the Protection of Human Rights in the Arab world.[1] According to some interpretations, growing Islamic fundamentalism represents a groping for an alternative to narrowly based undemocratic regimes—though one that sometimes demonstrates its own authoritarian or totalitarian features. Conversely, fear of populist theocracy may have caused many people to see the need for democracy as an alternative.[2]

OVERVIEW

The most democratic states in the Middle East are generally the ones that are the least Middle Eastern. Israel—established by Jewish immigrants from Europe, who are now outnumbered by those of Middle Eastern origin—is in many respects a model democracy. However, if the position of the Arabs under Israeli rule—particularly those in the areas occupied since 1967, which increasingly are being absorbed into Israel—is considered, this democracy takes on a discriminatory character similar in some respects to South Africa.

With its primarily Greek population, Cyprus also approximates the model of a democratic state. A major reservation in this instance is the fact that the northern part of the island is under Turkish occupation and that a separatist de facto state representing the island's ethnically Turkish population (solidified by the exodus of 200,000 Greek Cypriots) has been established there, now with its own seemingly democratic government (aside from its dependence on Turkey).

Turkey—which underwent massive, if superficial, Westernization after World War I and which long identified itself as a European country (and indeed is admitted to the circles of European states)—might be classified as a partial democracy, as the latest military junta, which took power in 1980, made way for a Third Turkish Republic two years later. However, the leader of the junta, General Kenan Evren, was designated as president until 1989 and the junta itself transformed into a Presidential Council. Most parties were banned from participating in the parliamentary elections of 1983, but the fact that the party favored by the military came in last testifies to the meaningfulness of the elections.

Lebanon was long a bastion of civil liberties and free parliamentary elections with a strong president chosen by the parliament. However, its democracy was marred by the predominance of "feudal" families and also by the failure to give the Muslim population representation proportionate to its growing majority. Today the state scarcely exists except on paper, having broken up into warring principalities and fiefs dominated by Syria and Israel.

Several essentially authoritarian countries have recently held parliamentary elections in which a limited range of opposition parties participated. In 1984, Egypt held its first relatively free elections in over 30 years. Power in Jordan is centered in the palace, but competitive parliamentary elections were held in 1984. Kuwait's emir and royal family also dominate that country's politics, but there is an elected parliament, which was restored in 1981 after a five-year hiatus; the most recent elections were held in February 1985. The early 1980s saw the legalization of opposition parties in Tunisia. Though real power is in the hands of the king, Morocco also has opposition parties, and relatively free parliamentary elections were held in 1984. In each case, some parties may be prevented from participating. The vote is usually not completely rigged, but there are varying degrees of governmental interference. The kings and presidents who wield real power are not subject to electoral contests, and it is doubtful that any of them would tolerate serious interference by an elected parliament. Incipient democratic practices may grow under the right circumstances in the future, but present economic and social strains in these countries provide little ground for optimism.

Revolutionary Iran demonstrates characteristics of a repressive theocratic totalitarianism. But intensely competitive electoral politics and a unique kind of separation of powers are important in some areas.

Afghanistan's communist regime, held up by Soviet troops, is at war with the bulk of the country's population, much of which has actually fled the country. The largely fundamentalist guerrillas thwart the government's attempts to control rural areas. Southern Yemen provides the only other example of a Marxist regime. It is run by the Leninist-style Yemeni Socialist party but has more authentic local roots.

Iraq has a highly repressive Ba'th party dictatorship, epitomized by the threat of imprisonment for anyone who has a typewriter without a special permit. Syria, also Ba'thist, is a personalistic military dictatorship, as is the conservative regime of North Yemen. Algeria, officially a single-party system, is ruled in an authoritarian fashion by a technocratic and military elite.

Despite a coup in December 1984, Mauritania remains a military dictatorship and disavows any intention to introduce democracy. By contrast, the leaders of Sudan's April 1985 coup have promised to restore democracy after one year, but the country's severe economic and political problems make it problematic.

Libya is supposedly the world's only direct democracy, with meetings of local citizens giving binding instructions to delegates in a hierarchy that culminates in the General People's Congress. Although this structure is not a rubber stamp, Colonel Muammar Qaddafi never fails to prevail on important issues.

No representative institutions exist in any of the monarchies of the Arabian peninsula except for Kuwait. Bahrayn held parliamentary elections in 1973, but the emir terminated this experiment two years later. Saudi Arabia has so far failed to follow up on announcements that it would establish an appointive Consultative Council. Another absolute monarchy, Oman, has had an appointive, purely advisory State Consultative Council since 1981. The United Arab

Emirates is a confederation of principalities each of which has a traditional authoritarian regime, without any elective features. Neither does Qatar have representative institutions. Most of these absolute monarchs are accessible to their people, but they can be called benevolent despotisms at best.

ALGERIA

Although Algerian president Chadli Benjedid has demonstrated a new kind of pragmatism in economic and foreign affairs since he took office in 1979, he governs the country in a highly authoritarian manner. The single party, the National Liberation Front (FLN), resembles the Leninist model but is essentially a facade for the military and technocratic elite.

Algerian voters are allowed to choose between two rival candidates of the FLN for each seat in local and provincial assemblies. There seems to be much authentic popular participation on these levels but mainly in relation to administrative matters. The FLN also gives the voters a choice among three candidates for each seat in the National People's Assembly, elections for which are held at five-year intervals (most recently in 1982); but the Assembly has no real power.

The president, the real center of the military and technocratic elite, is nominated by the FLN and elected by popular vote, but without opposition. Benjedid was elected to a second five-year term in 1984 with 95 percent of the vote.

A special FLN congress met in December 1985 to approve changes in the National Charter, which is the country's ideological statement. Although this followed a countrywide "national debate" called for by the president in February, no basic changes were expected.

In 1985 Benjedid made a pragmatic shift away from the country's previous rigid socialist orientation and also moved toward improved relations with the United States and the West generally, as exemplified by his visit to Washington in April 1985 and his country's permission to purchase American military equipment. In keeping with the more liberal trend since the beginning of Benjedid's presidency that resulted from increasing criticism of the cumbersome and inefficient bureaucracy and shortages of consumer goods, a five-year plan for 1985–89 provided encouragement for private investment and for a shift away from the former emphasis on heavy industry in favor of light industry, infrastructure, and agriculture. However, there is no outright rejection of socialism.[3]

Although the press has some room to maneuver, it is closely supervised by the government. Numerous cases of imprisonment without trial for political offenses have been reported. Several leaders of the newly formed Algerian League of Human Rights—including its secretary general, Ali Yahia—were arrested during 1985 because of their criticism of the regime's authoritarianism. Also, some Islamic fundamentalists, members of the Berber minority, and individuals who rioted in the old quarter of Algiers in April were sentenced to prison during the year.

In December 1985, two Algerian exiles in London, former president Ahmed Ben Bella and former prime minister Hocine Ait-Ahmed, issued a "Proclamation for the Founding of Democracy in Algeria." They announced that they were establishing an opposition movement called the Algerian Democratic Front. Presumably this group will operate abroad and clandestinely within the country. There is no indication of what it means by "democracy."

MAURITANIA

The bloodless coup of December 12, 1984, led by Colonel Maaouniya Ould Sidi Ahmad Taya, does not portent any basic changes in the military dictatorship. Reiterating an old theme, Colonel Taya dismissed the possibility of democracy until the people of his country become better educated. However, he emphasized the regime's commitment to human rights and stressed that the groundwork for future democracy is being laid by a process called the "Structure for the Education of the Masses," which involves locally elected committees that articulate complaints and promote literacy.[4] Of more immediate significance was the freeing of some political prisoners, although there were claims that arrests of other people on charges of corruption were politically motivated. Also, there were signs of greater respect for ethnic minorities, including the non-Arabic-speaking people of the south and the ex-slave caste known as *harratin.* Several of the latter have been promoted since the coup.

One of the world's most underdeveloped (and ethnically divided) countries, now devastated by drought and declining prices of its main export, iron ore, Mauritania is an unlikely candidate for democracy. Despite recurring attempts to outlaw it, slavery is still practiced but is being undermined by the current drought.

MOROCCO

Morocco is not far from an absolute monarchy. The power of other members of the elite is derived from their relationship with the king, who is a religious as well as a political leader and whose acts have been determined by the country's Supreme Court to be above the law.[5]

Yet the country has an elected 306-seat Chamber of Representatives (though sometimes disposed of in the past and still lacking real power) and both royalist and opposition parties that contest parliamentary and local elections. The press has a large degree of freedom, though at times there have been capricious crackdowns by the government. However deficient, the "Moroccan record" has been defended as "not bad by Third World standards."[6]

Town council elections held in June 1983 were contested by 14 political parties but were rigged by the government. Parliamentary elections that were originally scheduled for that year were delayed until September 1984. Again, there were charges of irregularities, but the consensus is that these were the country's most honest elections ever, as King Hassan II had promised, quite in contrast to the previous general elections (of 1977), in which "the Government privately parcelled out seats beforehand."[7] With a 67 percent voter turnout, most of the seats went to the proestablishment parties, with the Union Constitutionaliste (newly created, allegedly with royal encouragement, to undermine the older parties) getting about a fourth of the votes. The Rassemblement National des Indépendants, created in 1977 to support the king, got the second largest bloc of votes (17 percent), while a breakaway group, the Parti National Démocratique got 9 percent. The vote for the longstanding conservative Istiqlal (Independence) party declined from 21.6 percent in 1977 to 15 percent in 1984. The most important opposition party, the Union Socialiste des Forces Populaires (USFP)—whose leader, Abd al-Rahim Bouabid, reiterated that "The King is still our leader, and a democratic constitutional monarchy, even if it unfolds in several stages, is better than some colonel or a one-party-state"[8] —

got 36 seats, becoming the third largest group in the Chamber by virtue of the concentration of its vote (12 percent of the total) in urban districts. Additional members of the Chamber (one-third of the total) were chosen by local councils and professional associations in October 1984.

The king vacillates between repression and attempts at cooptation in his dealings with the opposition. Thus a man who had been imprisoned in 1981 was made minister without portfolio in 1983. Following the 1984 elections, the king delayed formation of a new government until April 1985 in the hopes of again giving the USFP a more important role, but its criticism of an International Monetary Fund (IMF)-recommended austerity program—and severe economic problems, including 25 percent unemployment and a $11-billion foreign debt—resulted in the party's exclusion.

Perhaps 100 people were killed in clashes with the police during massive riots in January 1984 resulting from price increases for staple foods. Larger numbers had been killed when security forces fired on crowds in similar circumstances in 1981. Since the 1984 riots, the licenses of several publications have been rescinded, while others have been harassed. The regime admits holding 150 political prisoners (fundamentalists and leftists). Sixteen members of the growing fundamentalist movement were sentenced to death in 1984 on charges of conspiring to overthrow the government. A religious reformer and publisher, Abd al-Salam Yasin, was sentenced to prison in 1985 for writing an article critical of the government.[9]

TUNISIA

Although supposedly committed in principle to liberalism, Habib Bourguiba (president for life since 1974) has in practice dominated an authoritarian single-party regime since the country's independence in 1957. An octogenarian in bad health (and senile), he has delegated more authority to his prime minister in recent years but remains ultimately in charge (though often manipulated by those around him, such as his wife Wassilah). The ruling Destorian (constitutional) Socialist party (DSP) once provided a meaningful framework for popular participation on a local level but has "atrophied" in recent years, with "grass-roots committees . . . controlled by local notables" and no longer "in touch with the masses."[10]

The other side of the story is one of limited political liberalization since Muhammad Mzali became prime minister in 1980. Certain opposition parties were permitted to participate in the 1981 general elections, but on last-minute presidential orders the minister of interior completely rigged the vote.[11] The range of legally permitted opposition parties includes the Mouvement des Démocrates Sociales of Ahmad Mestiri, a leading liberal voice in the ruling party before his expulsion in 1972; the so-called MUP-2 of Muhammad Bel Madj Amor, a breakaway faction of the banned leftist Mouvement d'Unité Populaire (MUP) of the exiled Ahmad Ben Salah; and the Tunisian Communist party (TCP).

The influential Union Général des Travailleurs Tunisiens (UGTT), which was formerly closely tied to the DSP but now is increasingly at odds with it, announced in 1985 that it will present its own list in the 1986 general elections. This could result in a meaningful opposition party for the first time, but there is speculation that the DSP's response will be to terminate the multiparty experiment. In fact, as the UGTT called for strikes in November 1985, its secretary general, Habib Achour, was put under house arrest. The UGTT newspaper, *al-Sha'ab,* was suspended in July after it strongly criticized the government. Other opposition groups, notably the burgeoning (especially among the youth) fundamentalist Mouvement de Tendance Islamique (MTI), are suppressed. However, with Prime Minister Mzali meeting with the MTI leader in October, the government seemed to be engaged in a process of accepting this group's role in the political system, partly to offset the UGTT and perhaps because of the boost given to fundamentalists by Israel's bombing of Tunis, which excited official fears of the growth of more extreme religious groups. Invoking Quranic stress on shura, the MTI calls for democracy, but there are doubts that it would follow through with this if it actually gained power.

Freedom of expression in Tunisia is high by North African standards, and many political prisoners have been released during the past few years. But dissatisfaction resulting from the increasing gap between rich and poor and from severe economic problems (and mostly taking an Islamic fundamentalist form) has evoked repression. Massive riots in January 1984 sparked by an announced increase in the price of bread were put down by the army, which charged into the crowds and killed perhaps 80 or more. With the regime thus dependent on the military to control the people, the classic prelude to a coup d'état may have emerged. A series of strikes and violent acts by students at the University of Tunis during the first half of 1985 provided manifestations of continuing unrest, as did anti-U.S. riots in October 1985 following President Ronald Reagan's initial condoning of the Israeli attack. Several newspapers were banned at least temporarily during 1984 and 1985.

The municipal elections of May 1985 demonstrated the limits of the multiparty system. All opposition parties decided that truly free elections were not in sight and refused to participate. They pointed specifically to confiscation of some opposition newspapers and the rejection of run-off elections as factors working against opposition parties. Also, this was the first time the UGTT refused to be represented on DSP electoral lists. Despite an attempt to obtain a popular boycott, the government reported an unusually high turnout of 92 percent (100 percent in some constituencies), a claim deemed by the opposition to be so incredible as to confirm their original suspicions.

LIBYA

Muammar al-Qaddafi's so-called Third Universal Theory enunciates radical political ideas reminiscent of Rousseau's, particularly in rejecting representation as a "fraud" and insisting on direct popular participation. In his Green Book, Qaddafi claims that he has finally discovered a way to implement what had previously been the utopian ideal of direct democracy. In his *jamahiriyyah*—a word he coined to mean something like "masses' state" as distinguished from a *jumhuriyyah* or republic—local citizens are organized in 189 Basic Peoples' Congresses, which deal with local matters and dictate the way their representatives in regional congresses and a General People's Congress will vote.

Some observers have reported meaningful deliberation in the local congresses.[12] However, Qaddafi, who has no formal role other than as "Leader of the Revolution," dominates the system. Demonstrations—apparently orchestrated by the regime—caused the Congress to reverse itself on at least one issue, leading to the conclusion that the popular political structure has "little real significance in establishing the true locus of power."[13] Since 1979, a network of secret Revolutionary Committees has overseen the congresses and meted out arbitrary punishments.

The regime has faced growing opposition of late. Though bolstering its support among the poor, economic leveling schemes implemented during the early 1980s have antagonized the middle classes. Declining oil revenues have posed serious problems. Several abortive coups and assassination attempts have occurred, including an army mutiny in August 1985. Hostile relations with several of his neighbors have added to Qaddafi's uneasiness, although his rapprochement with Morocco in 1984 and with the new regime in the Sudan in 1985 have provided some comfort. Qaddafi has responded to these threats by relying increasingly on members of his own tribe and East German security guards, as well as having several opponents assassinated abroad.

The most prominent opposition organization is called the National Front for the Salvation of Libya. It broadcasts messages from Cairo and claims credit for various assassination attempts. The Front calls for the overthrow of the present regime and establishment of a Western-style democracy. However, in November 1985, the Front strongly criticized reported United States plans to undermine the regime.

THE SUDAN

President Ja'far al-Numayri's dictatorship became increasingly oppressive during the early 1980s. His imposition of Islamic law in 1983—and particularly the brutal way it was implemented—antagonized many people. This was especially true of the non-Muslim south, where Numayri had previously been popular. The south was also antagonized by Numayri's arbitrary division of their region into three provinces in 1981. These and other grievances led to a Libyan- and Ethiopian-backed revolt organized by John Garang's Sudanese People's Liberation movement (SPLM). In the north too, Numayri antagonized nearly everybody with such actions as the hanging of a prominent modernist Muslim, Mahmud Taha, in January 1985 for criticizing the regime. Finally, the president broke with the fundamentalist Muslim Brethren by dismissing some of them from his government and arresting many others.

Opposition to the regime during the spring of 1985, particularly after increases in prices of necessities following adoption of economic austerity measures demanded by the IMF and the United States, increasingly looked like a revolution—a repetition of the popular overthrow of Sudanese military dictatorship and its replacement by democracy in 1964. Thousands were arrested during riots in late March 1985. Massive demonstrations followed in the early part of April. Professional associations and trade unions played a large role in the disorders.

These culminated in a coup d'état on April 6, led by former defense minister Siwar al-Dhahab while Numayri was out of the country. The 15-man Transitional Military Council (TMC), headed by Dhahab, promised to restore democratic government after a one-year period— a compromise between the 18 months originally favored by the military and the six-month limit at first demanded by the civilian leaders. Dhahab reiterated that "We have chosen democracy as our way of life in the Sudan"[14] and that elections to choose members of a constituent assembly would be held before April of 1986.[15] But by mid-1985 there were reports that political parties and trade unions were disillusioned by the slow progress toward democracy and particularly by the military's refusal to reinstate the 1956 constitution.

Despite the proclamation of martial law, the aftermath of the coup witnessed a remarkable upsurge in open, competitive political activity. Over 4,000 political prisoners were released, while 36 leaders of the former regime were jailed. Thousands of employees of Numayri's repressive apparatus lost their jobs. As many as 50 political parties emerged. With censorship gone, diverse views appeared in the press, while political rallies multiplied. Observers noted an unusual harmony of the various groups—a "lack of anarchy."[16] But a ban on street demonstrations announced in September following the outbreak of violence seemed to portend erosion of this freedom.

Whatever the intentions of the junta, the restoration of democracy faces serious obstacles. Disagreements within the TMC have been reported, evoking speculation about the possibility of another coup. Parts of the country are suffering from famine amidst an influx of starving refugees from adjoining countries. Virtually all foreign exchange earnings are required for servicing the $10-billion foreign debt. Precoup demands for an end to austerity measures remain unsatisfied, and the question of abolishing Islamic law—called for by all political parties except the Muslim Brethren—remains unresolved.

Most of all, the SPLM rebellion continues. Garang declares the new military government to be a mere continuation of Numayri's regime that has stolen real revolution from the people. Following the coup, he demanded the immediate restoration of democracy and refused to agree to a truce of more than one week. Not only is the war against the rebels a financial drain, but it prevents a resumption of the Jonglei Canal irrigation project and the exploitation of recently discovered oil in the south that had provided great economic promise. Unless the civil war is ended, elections are hardly possible, since they presumably could not be conducted without southern participation. However, a meeting of the civilian cabinet and the TMC late in December 1985 set April 1–12, 1986, as the date for general elections and restoration of democracy.

EGYPT

The former single-party system made way for the formation of opposition parties competing with the governing National Democratic party (NDP) under President Anwar al-Sadat's leadership during the 1970s. However, Sadat's "democracy" provided a mask for his "one-man show," especially as restrictions dealt blows to the opposition parties and finally as he arrested critics shortly before his assassination in 1981. His successor, Husni Mubarak, has permitted a more meaningful degree of democratization.

This was demonstrated in the most recent parliamentary elections (in May 1984), following the president's announcement that he wanted "genuine . . . democracy."[17] Five parties—the NDP, the center-right New Wafd party (NWP, a revival of the prerevolutionary Wafd party), the moderately leftist Socialist Labor party (SLP), the rightist Liberal party, and the leftist National Progressive Unionist party (NPUP)—contested the elections. With a low turnout, the NDP got 73 percent of the vote and 391 of the 448 elective seats, while the NWP, with 12.7 percent of the votes, won 57 seats. The other parties failed to meet the new requirement of 8 percent of the nationwide vote in order to win a seat. However, four SLP members were among the ten people the president appointed (in accordance with a constitutional provision that apparently is designed to ensure greater Coptic membership than produced by popular election).

It is difficult to determine how free the elections were. Fuad Serag al-Din, leader of the NWP, declared them to have been a "stage show." Khalid Muhyi al-Din, leader of the NPUP, argued that only "violence and forgery" could account for the NDP victory.[18] Several cases of vote tampering and even acts of violence by the members of the ruling party were reported, but such incidents did not seem to typify the overall conduct of the elections. It is true that religious and communist parties are not tolerated, but some members of the fundamentalist Muslim Brotherhood gained admission to the NWP's electoral list, while communists have some representation in the NPUP.

In any case, power in Egypt is centered in the presidency and more broadly in a military and bureaucratic elite. Following a unanimous vote for him in the People's Assembly, Mubarak was approved by a suspiciously overwhelming 98.5 percent of the voters for a six-year term in a referendum in 1981. There seems to be no likelihood of a seriously contested presidential election in the near future. Nor does it seem likely that a nondocile People's Assembly would be tolerated—or even allowed to be elected.

A state of emergency in effect since 1981 was extended by the People's Assembly for another 19 months in September 1984. This allows searches without warrants, prohibits strikes and demonstrations, and permits the holding of possible subversives without charges. Repeated arrests and cases of torture, especially of communists, have been reported. But Pope Shenoudah II of the Coptic Church, who was stripped of official recognition of his office during the last days of Sadat's rule and later exiled to a monastery in the desert, was restored to his rights on January 1, 1985.

Several recent events demonstrate some rule of law. The attempt of the government to prevent the reemergence of the NWP in 1984 was thwarted by a court decision. In May, the High Constitutional Court struck down a 1979 law limiting polygamy on the ground that it had been unconstitutionally issued by decree. (The People's Assembly later enacted much of the substance of the nullified act.) In June 1985, the State Security Court ordered the release of a fundamentalist religious leader whom it determined had been detained illegally. Another ruling later in the year permitted the formation of a Nasirite party, previously forbidden.

The press is relatively free. The government does not interfere much with the major newspapers, which it owns. The opposition-party press attacks government policies in strong terms, although some journalists still worry about the possibility of arrest. Perhaps the main limitation on journalists is a pervasive fear of antagonizing the increasingly popular theocratic movement. But some cases of censorship occurred during 1985—including a court's confiscation of copies of an edition of *The Thousand and One Nights* on grounds of obscenity. In October 1984, seven members of the NPUP were arrested for allegedly distributing antiregime materials.

The summer of 1985 witnessed a new campaign against religious fundamentalists. Shaykh Hafiz al-Salama, a leading religious figure, and several of his followers were arrested in July following the prevention of a demonstration during the previous month calling for complete implementation of Islamic law. A court had overruled the ban on this demonstration, but the government responded by invoking the emergency laws. Religious bumper stickers—which had provided mutual provocation for militants of both Muslim and Coptic persuasion—were banned, as Mubarak reiterated his intention to "continue to pursue democracy," but within "limits."[19]

LEBANON

Lebanon's constitutional system—democratic, though with some defects—remains formally in effect but has in reality been superseded by anarchy since 1975. The parliament still exists, although elections have not been held since 1972. The cabinet of "national unity" established in 1974 includes representatives of rival militias. The army tends to break up along sectarian lines when put to a test.

Lebanon is made up of numerous Christian and Muslim sects, none of which forms a majority or has much loyalty to the country as a whole. The Maronite Christian sect made up the bulk of the population in the smaller autonomous Lebanon that existed before World War I, but in 1920 the French created the present "Greater Lebanon" in which the various Christian groups then accounted for a small majority of the population. A pattern of confessional "balance" emerged that was in fact favorable to the Christians and to the Maronites in particular, with the presidency (the real center of power) guaranteed to the Maronites. The prime minister (appointed by the president but theoretically responsible to the parliament) is always a Sunni Muslim, while the speaker of the parliament is a Shiite Muslim. Parliamentary seats are divided among the various sects according to a ratio of six Christians and five Muslims. Each electoral district is assigned a quota of representatives from various sects, and rival lists with the required sectarian makeup are pitted against each other rather than allowing each group to choose its own delegates.

No census had been conducted since 1972, and Christians have resisted calls for a new one. However, it is understood that demographic changes have produced a Muslim majority—73 percent of the population according to one estimate.[20] In fact, the Shiites—the most deprived and until recently the least politicized group—have moved from third place to first (with a population of about a million and only 19 seats in the parliament), while the Maronites (with a population of only about 600,000 but with 30 seats) may be slightly outnumbered by the Sunnis (with 20 seats).[21]

The Israeli invasion of 1982 seemed to be part of the process of restoring Maronite hegemony in a more extreme form than before under the leadership of the rightist Phalangist party. The assassination of Phalangist president-elect Bashir Gemayel proved to be the first step in undoing the plan. His brother, Amin Gemayel, who was then elected president, is relatively moderate. Although he disappointed those non-Maronites who hoped he would restore order and give fairer representation to the different sects, the withdrawal of Israeli troops (except for a "security zone" in the extreme south) and victories of Druse and Shiite militias have left him under increasing Syrian hegemony, since Syrian troops are stationed in the eastern and northern parts of the country.

The goal of restoring order is inseparable from that of democratization since the former can presumably be achieved only by establishing a framework for the more equitable representation of the different communities. All attempts to find a solution, including the reconciliation talks among militia leaders in Switzerland in 1983–84, have failed.

Talks held in Damascus in the fall of 1985 involving representatives of the (Maronite) Lebanese Forces (under a leadership that asserted its independence from Phalangist political leadership in March 1985 and renounced ties with Israel in favor of working with Syria), the (Druse) Progressive Socialist party, the (Shiite) Amal militia, and Syrian vice-president Abd al-Halim Khaddam offered renewed hope. An accord announced in December—whose details have not been fully revealed—would allow for equal representation of Christians and Muslims in the government and the abolition after ten years of the sectarian distribution of offices in favor of a secular system. But implementation of the accord is problematic, as it evoked intra-Maronite violence and is opposed by the militant (Shiite) Party of God faction that has recently shown signs of eclipsing the more moderate Amal. The Sunni Muslims, whose military power has faded since 1982, were not represented in the talks at all.

JORDAN

Jordan has been under martial law since 1967, and, except for one session in 1976, its parliament did not meet between 1974 and 1984. Political parties have been banned since 1957. The National Consultative Council, or lower house, elected in 1967, was summoned to meet in January 1984 to approve a constitutional amendment allowing six deceased members representing occupied West Bank districts to be replaced by the chamber itself. There is an appointive Senate.

In March 1984, by-elections filled the seats of eight deceased members (two allotted to Christians and six to Muslims) from the East Bank, with 102 candidates in the running. The government apparently did not interfere with voting, and over 50 percent of the eligible voters participated. This was the first time women had the right to vote in Jordan. Largely because they were the best organized force in the absence of political parties and because of the absence of run-off elections, fundamentalists won half the Muslim seats. There has been no announcement of any plan for general elections.

Members of the parliament criticized the government on such issues as the ban on political parties and the continuation of martial law, but no one introduced bills on such topics. One deputy pointed out that the enactment of legislation unacceptable to the government would simply result in the dissolution of the legislative body.[22] In January 1985, seven members walked out of the chamber to protest the passage of a controversial passport law without hearing opposing views. Minister of Information Layla Sharif resigned during the same month because of the government's announcement of new restrictions on the press.[23]

The cabinet has become more representative in one sense by the inclusion of more Palestinians—who make up 60 percent of the country's population, not including the West Bank. The cabinet formed in January 1984 included nine Palestinians (compared with four previously) among 20 members, and this was increased to 11 in the new cabinet headed by Prime Minister Zaid al-Rifa'i in April 1985.

SYRIA

Electoral procedures in Syria have little to do with popular control. The People's Council (parliament) elected in 1981 is made up entirely of members of the Ba'th party and, to a lesser extent, its allies in the National Progressive Front. As for the Ba'th party structure, the party congress that met in January 1985 was controlled by President Hafiz al-Asad's "inner circle."[24] Asad was reelected—unopposed—for another seven-year term as president on February 10, 1985, allegedly by 99.97 percent of the voters. His real power is based on the military, particularly on officers from the formerly underprivileged Alawite sect (including his brother and other relatives), which makes up 11 percent of the population. The shows of force put on by military commanders when Asad was hospitalized during 1984 illustrates the real political dynamics of the regime.

Human rights violations occur on a large scale. Many opponents of the regime have been imprisoned without trial, tortured, and killed. Massive antiregime terrorism by the fundamentalist Muslim Brotherhool met equally massive repression in recent years, and much of the city of Hama was destroyed in 1982 in the process of suppressing a large-scale rebellion. However, President Asad offered amnesty to many members of this movement in January 1985.

IRAQ

Iraq under President Saddam Husayn has been described as "virtually a sealed society, secured by an organized party structure, an interlocking system of police, internal security and neighborhood organizations unusual in the Middle East."[25] Notwithstanding an offer of amnesty for his opponents in February 1985, the execution of opponents of his regime is commonplace. As a case in point, ten Shiite religious scholars belonging to one family were executed on March 6, 1985.[26] The execution of some leaders of the Ba'th party was also reported in 1985.

The regime's narrow base is indicated by the fact that, despite its secularism, it is overwhelmingly drawn from the Sunni Arab minority, although Shiite Arabs and Sunni Kurds together make up perhaps 75 percent of the population. In fact, much of the top leadership is drawn from one town, Tikrit.

An elective National Assembly has existed since 1980. Voters are given a choice among candidates approved by the Ba'th party, but 67 out of the 250 members elected in 1984 were at least technically non-Ba'thists. In any case, there is no indication that the National Assembly is much more than a decoration for the regime. There is also an elected Kurdish Legislative Council for an Autonomous Region in the north, but its meaningfulness is equally doubtful. The dictatorial president is chosen by the nonelective Revolutionary Command Council.

SAUDI ARABIA

Despite repeated promises going back to 1960, Saudi Arabia has no constitution or even a rudimentary representative system. The main limitation on the absolute power of the king is the influence of other members of the royal family (and related families). Important positions throughout the kingdom are filled from among the 3,000 to 5,000 princes, thus bolstering the family's collective rule.

In a December 1984 interview,[27] King Fahd outlined a plan to establish an appointive Consultative Council "within three or four months" and simultaneously to grant a written constitution to his realm. He indicated that after two years half the members would be elected by provincial *majlises* and that at least some members would be chosen by the people in the future. He said that the Consultative Council would facilitate popular "participation" in politics and would "supervise the execution of government policy." Although construction of a parliament building had already begun the month before, there have been no further moves to implement the announcement.

Expression of opinion is tightly restricted. There are reports of large-scale political arrests, as well as of frequent torture of prisoners. The regime's ultraorthodox brand of Islam is enforced by religious police. Non-Muslim foreigners can practice their religion, but not openly. Political parties are not permitted. The Shiite minority (in the eastern region) is subjected to much discrimination.

KUWAIT

Troubled by declining oil prices, pro-Iranian terrorism, the Iraq-Iran war, and the aftermath of its stock market crash (of 1982), oil-rich Kuwait continued to practice a degree of democracy. This was demonstrated by elections in February 1985 for the National Assembly, in which 231 candidates representing diverse views competed in 25 two-member constituencies and engaged in considerable public debate on issues ranging from the quality of health services to the country's position vis-à-vis the Iraq-Iran war. Although political parties are banned, clearly recognized informal factions participated, with the leftist Democratic group of Dr. Ahmad Khatib winning three seats, while two Islamic fundamentalist groups won several others. The defeat of some candidates closely associated with the ruling al-Sabah family (although conservative candidates close to the monarchy won most of the seats) was interpreted as a sign of dissatisfaction but was also an indication that the elections were relatively free.

Also, the meetings of the National Assembly were characterized by lively debate on important issues. Far from being a rubber stamp, the body forced the resignation of the minister of justice—a member of the ruling family—in May 1985 over the issue of his involvement in activities leading to the stock market crash. The parliament's legitimizing role is too important for the emir to dissolve it except as a last resort, and it has resisted efforts by the monarchy during the early 1980s to enact constitutional amendments transferring more law-making authority to the ruler. There is a great deal of freedom of expression.

However, the democratic features can easily be overstated. Districts are heavily gerrymandered to increase the representation of proloyalist Bedouins and to minimize the influence of such groups as the Shiite minority. And only those males over 21 years of age who have Kuwaiti ancestry going back to 1920 can vote; this amounts to 3.5 percent of the state's 1.7 million people. Growing demands for female suffrage continue to be rejected.[28]

CYPRUS

In 1985 expectations for a reunification of the island were dashed. Following separate talks with U.N. Secretary General Javier Pérez de Cuellar at the United Nations during the previous year, direct talks in January 1985 between Cypriot president Spyros Kyprianou and President Rauf Denktash of the de facto Turkish Republic of Northern Cyprus (whose independence was declared in 1983 but which is recognized only by Turkey) failed to agree on a formula to create a federal structure. Denktash accepted a draft agreement presented by the secretary general that provided for a federation with extensive autonomy for the constituent Turkish and Greek states and withdrawal of foreign troops in favor of international guarantees. But Kyprianou refused to accept the document as anything more than a basis for negotiations. Areas of agreement included a reduction of the Turkish-controlled part of the island from 37 percent to 29 percent, a provision for a Turkish vice president and a Greek president, and a seven-to-three ratio for the two communities in both the council of ministers and the lower house and equal representation in the Senate. But President Kyprianou refused to accept any plan that would allow a dispute between the two communities to end in deadlock. A renewed effort by Péres de Cuellar late in 1985 evoked pessimism from both Denktash and Kyprianou.

The two main political parties, the Communists (with 12 seats) and the conservative Democratic Rally (with 11 seats) joined forces in the parliament to censure Kyprianou and to demand that he either accept the draft agreement or call new presidential elections. (In December 1984, the president had renounced communist support, apparently in hopes of winning Democratic Rally backing.) Only Kyprianou's Democratic party (with nine seats) and the Socialists (with three seats) did not support the censure motion. But the president, whose five-year term does not expire until 1988, refused to succumb to this demand and warned of the dangers of deadlock between the legislative and executive branches.

The deadlock eventually led\the parliament on November 1 to dissolve itself and to call new elections for December 8 in the hope that a two-thirds vote could be obtained for a constitutional amendment allowing a majority vote to require the president to resign. But with the Communists dropping from first to third place in the elections, the Democratic party making major gains, and the Socialists also improving their showing (while the Democratic Rally made only small gains but enough to become the leading party), Kyprianou clearly thwarted his opponents' plan.

The Turkish Cypriots took steps to consolidate their own democracy during 1985. In a referendum on May 5, voters massively approved a new constitution. On June 9, Denktash was reelected president by a margin of more than 70 percent of the vote, despite the vigorous opposition of five other candidates, especially from two leftists who opposed the existence of a separate state. Parliamentary elections followed on June 23, with 350 candidates, representing seven parties, vying for the 50 seats. So far as appears, these elections were strictly democratic.

TURKEY

In 1980, following accelerating chaos, Turkey's third coup in 20 years inaugurated a period of rule by a military junta, the National Security Council (NSC), headed by General Kenan Evren. A new constitution was overwhelmingly approved in a plebiscite in 1982, thus creating the Third Republic. The military seems likely to allow civilian institutions to function unless the situation becomes intolerable from its point of view, as in 1980. But the new constitution also perpetuated a transitional military guardianship by providing that Evren would be president until 1989 and that the NSC would be transformed into a Presidential Council for the same period. The president was given extensive powers, though somewhat less than that of the French Fifth Republic that influenced the authors of the Turkish constitution. Political activity by former leaders was barred for a ten-year period; by former members of the Grand National Assembly (GNA, or parliament) for five years.

With all former political parties disbanded by the military regime, the formation of new parties was stringently regulated, and the NSC could veto candidates and party members. The narrow limits of the democratic process were demonstrated by the fact that only three parties got permission in time for the November 1983 general elections. Yet the authenticity of the elections was shown by the failure of the junta-favored Nationalist Democracy party (NDP), headed by retired general Turgut Sunalp, to win more than 25 percent of the votes and 70 seats in the 400-member GNA, trailing the left-of-center Populist party (which got 30 percent of the votes and 117 seats). The conservative Motherland party (MP), led by Turgut Ozal, won 45 percent of the votes and 212 seats (an absolute majority), and Ozal was duly designated prime minister.

Subsequent defeats have not put the failure of the NDP in doubt. The MP got 41.5 percent of the vote in local elections in March 1984, while the NDP's share fell to 7 percent. Three new parties had been approved in time for the elections; these included the left-of-center Social Democracy party (SDP), which came in second (with 22.9 percent of the votes) and the rightist True Path party (with 13.7 percent). But with the MP facing its "Watergate"— involving a parliamentary investigation of charges of corruption against a former minister and calls for resignation that the government was able to avert by virtue of its large majority in the GNA— elections that were seen as a bellwether in the town of Koycegiz resulted in a big victory for the True Path party. Sixty percent of the votes went to the two parties that had not been permitted to contest the parliamentary elections. In November 1985, Rahsan Ecevit, wife of former prime minister Bulent Ecevit (who is still banned from political activity) was elected leader of a newly established Democratic Left party.

Turkey's current record on human rights is more comparable to that of many authoritarian countries than to that of Western democracies. A report of Amnesty International in July 1985 put the number of political prisoners since 1980 at 180,000 and concluded that torture is "widespread and systematic."[29] While some observers stressed that improvements were being made, the overall thrust of this evaluation was not in dispute. Twenty-two Kurdish separatists were sentenced to death in February 1985.[30] However, in December 1985, five Western European governments dropped litigation before the European Commission of Human Rights when Turkey agreed to submit regular reports and to permit investigations, and representatives of some human rights organizations expressed renewed optimism.

Much of the country is still under martial law. But this was lifted in increasing numbers of provinces during 1984–85. Extensive curbs are imposed on the press and on speech. A press law of 1983 permits fines and imprisonment for publishing articles deemed to be a threat to national security, as well as closure of publications, confiscation of printing presses, and the seizure of issues of periodicals before publication. Numerous cases of arrests of writers and publishers and of banning magazines were reported during 1985. The deputy secretary general of the SDP, Nail Gurman, was detained in June 1985 after organizing a political rally. During the same month, the GNA debated a bill providing for extensive new powers for the police, which some Western diplomats said amounted to the creation of a police state.[31]

IRAN

Although, as in most authoritarian states, much of revolutionary Iran's constitution represents democratic ideals if taken at face value, Ayatollah Ruhullah Khomeini rejected the word "democratic" as part of the name of the country because it represented Western influence.[32] The constitution of the Islamic Republic indeed deviates from democratic principles by establishing the office of *Faqih* (Jurist), with Ayatollah Khomeini designated to fill this role during his lifetime. The Faqih has a vast number of functions enumerated in the constitution—corresponding to Khomeini's extraconstitutional charismatic authority. However, whether because of a lack of interest or as a pragmatic maneuver, Khomeini often chooses not to intervene in the otherwise relatively conventional governmental structure,[33] that is, an elective Islamic Consultative Assembly (parliament), a prime minister and a cabinet, and a relatively powerful elected president. According to the constitution, Khomeini may be succeeded by another single Jurist or by a collective Leadership Council as determined by a Council of Experts that was popularly elected in 1982. In November 1985 the Council of Experts decided in favor of Ayatollah Ali Montazeri, long known to be the choice of Khomeini, who will presumably continue to fill the position until his death.

Another limit on the majority-rule principle—but creating an element of institutional pluralism—is the constitutional provision for a Council of Guardians. This body, half of whose members are religious scholars appointed by the Jurist (or Leadership Council) and the other half elected by the Consultative Assembly after nomination by the High Council of the Judiciary (supreme court), has the authority to declare acts of the parliament to be *ultra vires* on grounds of incompatibility with Islamic law. The Council of Guardians has in fact emerged as a powerful institution whose economic conservatism has provided a brake for the regime's otherwise predominantly radical tendencies.

Elections are competitive within narrow limits. Most candidates are either members of or approved by the Islamic Republican party, which however is loosely organized and encompasses diverse opinions on some issues. The only other party that has not been totally banned is the liberal Freedom movement led by former prime minister Mehdi Bazargan, and this group is severely limited by having its newspaper closed down, press conferences banned, and regular access to the government denied, although Bazargan's criticisms of the regime's policies sometimes get published. During 1985, he addressed a letter to the Supreme Defense Council—and another such letter to Khomeini in 1984—criticizing the continuation of the war against Iraq now that Iranian soil has been liberated.

Bazargan's decision to contest the August 1985 presidential election offered the possibility of a real race, although it was assumed that his support would come from the numerically inferior middle and upper classes. But a majority of the members of the Council of Guardians—despite much apparent disagreement within the body—decided to reject his candidacy, citing wartime conditions. The candidacy of 46 others was also rejected, leaving only two unviable opponents for incumbent president Ali Khamanei. Information in President Jimmy Carter's memoirs revealing Bazargan's contacts with the United States was apparently an additional factor in the rejection of his candidacy. The election produced no surprises, as President Khamanei received 85.6 percent of the vote.

Parliamentary elections, including those held in April 1984, are hardly free. In fact, Bazargan protested the restrictions on him by boycotting the 1984 elections. However, parliamentary elections are vigorously contested by those candidates who are permitted to run. Debate in the parliament is equally vigorous. In August 1984, five cabinet members were given votes of no confidence, and debates in which the government was strongly criticized on some matters were broadcast by radio. Again demonstrating the nonmonolithic quality of their parliament, Prime Minister Mir Husayn Musavi was approved for a second term in October 1985 by a vote of 162 to 73 (with 26 members abstaining), and a Tehran newspaper opined that only Khomeini's support prevented Musavi's replacement.[34]

Perhaps the widest range of open, competitive, pluralistic politics centers on economic issues. The revolutionary regime's stress on its support for the *mustaz'afin* ("weak," "underprivileged") suggests a socialistic approach (even if such Western terminology is rejected), and this is borne out by the numerical predominance in the Consultative Assembly and the Islamic Republican party of those who favor radical redistribution of wealth. However, another tendency is represented by conservative clerics with close connections with the *bazaar* (old-style merchants and craftsmen). The more radical land reform legislation passed by the Consultative Assembly has been vetoed by the Council of Guardians,[35] as is also true of some of the articles of a bill nationalizing foreign trade, amid strong attacks on such legislation in the conservative press.

In several statements during the past two years, Khomeini has with seeming reluctance lent his support in varying degrees to free enterprise. Meeting with the new cabinet in October 1985, Khomeini advised it to allow "the committed merchants—those who want to serve the country"—to do so and not to "nationalize everything."[36] The ultraconservative Hojatiah faction even calls for denationalization of industries nationalized immediately after the revolution. A government bill providing for more progressive income taxes has evoked opposition from conservative members of the Consultative Council, as did the 1985–86 budget. One emigré Iranian scholar concludes that the revolution's "Economic Thermidor" is already in effect.[37] However, the Consultative Assembly passed a bill in May 1985 legalizing the large-scale de facto takeovers of land by peasants that occurred during the earlier phases of the revolution.[38]

During the early 1980s, Iran experienced a classic period of revolutionary "reign of terror" in which thousands were executed and 120,000 were allegedly held as political prisoners.[39] Khomeini's repeated intervention to stop excesses committed by revolutionary courts during the early 1980s culminated in an eight-point declaration of December 1982.[40] These tribunals have subsequently been brought under the control of the Supreme Judiciary Council, and the replacement of the head of Evin jail, who tortured and executed many persons, has brought some improvements.[41] Nevertheless, life is insecure for anyone suspected of threatening the regime. The Iranian ambassador to the United Nations recently replied to charges of human rights violations by declaring that only Islamic law—not human rights covenants—guides his government.[42] The Baha'i minority has been subjected to much discrimination, and there are allegations that some people have been executed solely because of membership in this sect.

ISRAEL

Since 1984, the democratic process has taken an unusual turn as the failure of each of the two major blocs in the Knesset (parliament) to win a majority in the general election made way for a shaky government of national "unity." Laborite prime minister Shimon Peres has gained increasing popularity despite his government's imposition (by emergency decree) of harsh austerity measures in July 1985 to confront the country's growing economic ills, and thus he would likely gain from a breakup of the coalition and resulting general elections. He is scheduled to be replaced by Likud leader Yitzhak Shamir in October 1986.

Israel has a highly democratic governmental structure. Each political party is represented in the 120-member Knesset in proportion to its percentage of the nationwide vote. Fifteen electoral lists won at least one seat in the last election. There are also other democratic institutions, notably the Histadrut Labor Federation, whose elections in May 1985—based on the same system of proportional representation—continued the perennial predominance of the Labor Alignment.

For the Jewish population, the level of civil rights is high, although the impact of relatively small religious parties that often are convenient coalition partners for the major parties results in the imposition of Orthodox rules that the nonpracticing Jewish majority find onerous. For example, marriages conducted by Reform rabbis are not recognized. The question of "Who is a Jew?" was again a heated issue during 1985 as the religious parties unsuccessfully pushed a bill in the Knesset that would, in effect, have denied the Jewishness of anyone converted by a Reform rabbi. The demand for a complete ban on pigs provided another heated issue in 1985. Aside from some censorship in matters related to national security, the press is quite free.

Some relatively subtle undemocratic features should be noted.[43] For example, Israeli parties are characterized by the "iron law of oligarchy" in an extreme form, particularly in light of the party leadership's control—especially in the Labor Alignment—over nominations and the positions of nominees on the party lists. However, the emergence of something resembling a two-party system since the 1970s provides the voters with a real alternative, in contrast to the previous seemingly permanent one-party hegemony.

In relation to the non-Jewish, that is Arab population, Israeli democracy fails the test. Considering the existence of a large Arab majority in pre–1948 Palestine, it was not easy to reconcile the Zionist goal of a Jewish state with the principle of democracy or the related concept of self-determination. The Jewish community in

Palestine developed highly democratic communal institutions but opposed the emergence of an overall representative structure that would have been dominated by the Arab majority. Even the territory that came under Israeli control in 1948–49 had contained an Arab majority, and—despite massive Jewish immigration—the new state was able to be both democratic and Jewish only by virtue of the flight or expulsion of the bulk of the Arab population.

The remaining Arab minority (now making up about 16 percent of the population) in principle enjoys full citizenship. But there is much discrimination in such matters as social services provided by the government, and expropriation of Arab-owned land is a major grievance. Also, one careful study of the Arabs' situation points to subtle means that are used to "control" them.[44] Arab nationalist political parties have never been permitted, although a joint Arab-Jewish list headed by an Arab, which initially was banned by the Central Election Commission, was permitted to participate in the 1984 election by virtue of a Supreme Court decision and thus to compete with the Communist party, support for which had previously been the only outlet for Arab protest. However, in October 1985 the Knesset deprived Muhammad Miari, the leader of the new party, of much of the immunity enjoyed by other members.

The 1.4 million Arabs in the occupied territories are a subject people lacking democratic rights. The occupation has increasingly brought a de facto kind of absorption of the territories that many observers believe can never be reversed. Yet the extension of citizenship and the suffrage to so many non-Jews is unthinkable from an Israeli point of view. The Israeli settlers in the territories constitute a clearly privileged—and armed—community subject to a different law from that which is applied to the natives. Already, according to a study conducted by Jerusalem's former deputy major, Meron Benvenisti, 52 percent of the land of the West Bank has been seized for exclusive Jewish settlement, with various ruses for acquiring the land described by Benvenisti as violations of the rule of law.[45] Democratic local elections were permitted in 1976, but most of the mayors have been removed (and in many cases expelled from Israeli-controlled territories) and town councils dissolved in favor of rule by military governors. Publications, films, and the theater are strictly censored, and universities are periodically closed down. Individuals are put under "town arrest." Various collective punishments are imposed, like demolishing the homes of people whose son is suspected of a terrorist act. Towns are sometimes put under curfew. The Geneva-based International Commission of Jurists recently concluded that Palestinian detainees are repeatedly tortured,[46] and Amnesty International made note of similar charges in criticizing Israel's human rights record in 1985.

In response to increasing violence between Arabs and Jewish settlers, the Israeli government decided in August 1985 to revive former policies that had previously fallen into disuse. These included admininstrative detention for renewable six-month periods without trial as well as expulsion of Arabs suspected of hostile activity and closing newspapers that violate military censorship.[47]

During 1985, the government took some measures giving Arabs greater protection of the law. After several years' delay, some prominent Jewish settlers who allegedly have connections to top military and political figures were arrested in 1984 on charges of terrorism against Arabs, and 15 of them were convicted in July 1985, although there were pressures on President Chaim Herzog for immediate amnesty—particularly from Foreign Minister Shamir, who declared the two convicted murderers to be "basically good boys."[48] Herzog reduced the sentences of three of the convicted individuals later in the year. An Israeli general was charged with excessive brutality against Arabs who had hijacked a bus, but he was found innocent. There were increased efforts by security forces to control armed Jewish settler vigilantes.

Perhaps confirming the prediction that one people cannot avoid erosion of its own democracy when it rules another people in an authoritarian fashion, there has recently been a perceptible growth of antidemocratic attitudes in Israel. In addition, growing tensions between the religious and secular elements and between European and Oriental Jews are putting strains on democracy, as are the country's severe economic problems, including growing economic inequality, that evoke increasing comparisons by Israelis with the experience of Weimar Germany. Polls have shown that one-third of the Israelis would like to have a nondemocratic government and that another one-sixth are indifferent on the matter. Among youths in particular, only one-third hold democratic views while another third hold consistently undemocratic views. Undemocratic views are even more prevalent among Orthodox and Oriental boys.[49]

The most obvious manifestation of the undemocratic trend is growing support for the Kach party of Rabbi Meir Kahane, who rejects the concept of a democratic state as inconsistent with its being Jewish, calls for a theocratic government, and demands the expulsion of all Arabs from Israel and the occupied territories. Among other indications of trends among the youth, a poll of Israeli high school students in April 1985 showed that 42 percent support Kahane's views; polls showed that Kahane's party could win more than ten seats in the 120-member Knesset.[50] Most of Kach's support is being drained from less extreme right-wing groups like the Likud. The Knesset has taken several actions against Kahane, such as limiting his parliamentary immunity in December 1984 in order to keep him from entering Arab villages to demand emigration and, in August 1985, banning parties (with Kach specifically in mind) that deny the country's democratic character and that incide racial hatred. But reversing the trend of public opinion can hardly be achieved by legislative fiat. In November 1985, the Supreme Court ruled that Kahane must be permitted to introduce bills banning the intermingling of Jews and others.[51]

AFGHANISTAN

The Afghan regime continues to exist only thanks to well over 100,000 Soviet troops. It has little popular backing and is unable to control most of the countryside. In an effort at legitimation, President Barbak Karmal called a People's Assembly in April 1985 (the first since 1964), made up of the representatives of various tribes. The delegates seem to have been handpicked by the regime. Local elections were conducted in August 1985, but the opponents of the regime called them a fraud.

Studies conducted by human rights groups point to massive violations. According to the United Nations Human Rights Commission, there is a "deliberate policy of bombing villages, slaughtering civilians, and executing political prisoners without trial."[52] Helsinki Watch pointed to "just about every conceivable human rights violation . . . and on an enormous scale."[53] At least a fifth of the population have taken refuge in Iran and Pakistan.

CONCLUSION

The above account reveals a Middle East and North Africa in which three countries may be called democracies, though with major qualifications in each case: Cyprus, whose territory is divided on a de facto basis into two states, one of which is occupied by Turkish troops; Turkey, whose recently restored representative system is engaged in a great deal of repression and operates under the shadow of a military guardianship; and Israel, whose democracy applies in theory more than in practice to the Arabs within its pre-1967 frontiers and not at all to those in the Gaza Strip and the West Bank. Another country, the Sudan, enjoyed many newly recovered freedoms during 1985 under the rule of a military junta that has promised to permit free elections in 1986. Aside from Lebanon's anarchy, all the other regimes are basically authoritarian, although the systems of Morocco, Tunisia, Egypt, Jordan, Kuwait, and Iran (in combination with elements of totalitarianism) contain at least some minor democratic features. Saudi Arabia and other Arab monarchies (except Kuwait), may be classified as absolutist, and Afghanistan as totalitarian.

There is little ground for optimism about the prospects for democracy in the near future. The people of each country tend to be too divided on fundamental issues, like national identity and the relationship between state and religion for any set of "rules of the game" to be workable, thus leaving repression and anarchy as likely alternatives. Many countries are divided into sectarian and/or linguistic groups that lack a strong overall identity, and even populations that are homogeneous are divided on issues of local identity versus various "pan" movements.

Several current socioeconomic trends work against political stability, especially of a democratic sort. The continuing massive influx of villagers has created cities with burgeoning slums whose populations are susceptible to messianic political movements. Also, there are recent economic pressures of various kinds, such as those caused by drought in some North African countries. Of broader relevance, the decline of revenues threatens to create a crisis not only for the oil-exporters but equally for those countries like Egypt and Jordan whose economies have come to depend on remittances from millions of their nationals who work in the oil-producing states.

In short, the political outlook is very cloudy, although there are encouraging signs of the appeal, even under adverse circumstances, of the ideals of freedom and democracy.

NOTES

1. See "The Hammamat Declaration" and Joe Stork's accompanying explanatory comments in *Merip Reports* (January 1984):23.

2. For a recent survey of elections through 1984 (but not including North Africa), see Dankwart A. Rustow, "Elections and Legitimacy in the Middle East," *Annals of the American Academy of Political and Social Science* (November 1985):122–46.

3. Robert A. Mortimer, "The Politics of Reassurance in Algeria," *Current History* 84 (May 1985):201–4, 228–29.

4. *New York Times*, February 28, 1985, p. 3.

5. Richard B. Parker, *North Africa: Regional Tensions and Strategic Concerns* (New York: Praeger, 1984), p. 21.

6. Ibid., p. 34.

7. *New York Times*, September 16, 1984, p. 13.

8. Ibid.

9. *Index on Censorship*, June 1985, p. 51.

10. Mark Tessler, "Tunisia at the Crossroads," *Current History* 84:502 (May 1985):230.

11. Richard B. Parker, *North Africa*, p. 55.

12. See John P. Mason, "Qadhdhafi's 'Revolution' and Change in a Libyan Oasis Community," *Middle East Journal* (Summer 1982):319–35.

13. George Henderson, "Redefining the Revolution," *Africa Report* 29:6 (November–December 1984):39.

14. *New York Times*, July 1985, p. 3.

15. Ibid., October 20, 1985.

16. See Eric Rouleau, "Sudan's Revolutionary Spring," *Merip Reports* (September 1985):3.

17. "Egypt: A Boring, Remarkable Event," *The Economist*, June 2, 1984, p. 29.

18. *Christian Science Monitor*, May 29, 1984, p. 9.

19. *New York Times*, July 7, 1985, p. 3.

20. Michael C. Hudson, "The Breakdown of Democracy," *Journal of International Affairs* (1985):281.

21. *New York Times*, October 2, 1983.

22. *The Middle East*, (August 1984):24–25.

23. *Index on Censorship*, June 1985, p. 51.

24. Yahya M. Sadowski, "Cadres, Guns, and Money: The Eighth Regional Congress of the Syrian Ba'th," *Merip Reports* (July/August 1985):3–8.

25. Elaine Sciolino, "The Big Brother: Iraq under Saddam Hussein," *New York Times Magazine,* February 3, 1985, p. 18.

26. *Index on Censorship,* June 1985, p. 51.

27. *Sunday Times,* London, December 2, 1984.

28. K. Celine, "Kuwait Living on Its Nerves," *Merip Reports* (February 1985):10–12, and Fred Lawson, "Class and State in Kuwait," *Merip Reports* 5:2 (May 1985):16–21, 32.

29. *New York Times,* July 24, 1985, p. 10.

30. *Index on Censorship,* June 1985, p. 53.

31. *New York Times,* June 11, 1985, p. 9.

32. Shaul Bakhash, *The Reign of the Ayatollahs: Iran and the Islamic Revolution* (New York: Basic Books, 1984), p. 73.

33. Ibid., p. 241.

34. *New York Times,* October 14, 1985, p. 7.

35. Bakhash, *The Reign of the Ayatollahs,* pp. 200–10.

36. *New York Times,* November 1,1985, p. 5.

37. Bakhash, *The Reign of the Ayatollahs,* p. 211.

38. *Middle East Monitor,* June 1, 1985.

39. *Index on Censorship,* June 1985, p. 50.

40. Bakhash, *The Reign of the Ayatollahs,* pp. 217ff.

41. *Christian Science Monitor,* August 16, 1985, p. 1.

42. *Index on Censorship,* April 1985, p. 54.

43. Asher Arian, "Israeli Democracy: 1984," *Journal of International Affairs* (1985):259–76.

44. Ian Lustick, *Arabs in the Jewish State* (Austin: University of Texas Press, 1980), passim.

45. *Jerusalem Post,* international edition, week ending April 13, 1985.

46. *Manchester Guardian Weekly,* February 10, 1985.

47. *New York Times,* August 9, 1985, p. 3.

48. *New York Times,* July 23, 1985, p. 4.

49. *Jerusalem Post,* international edition, March 17–April 1, 1983, and week ending June 8, 1985, and July 6, 1985.

50. *New York Times,* September 9, 1985, p. 3.

51. *Jerusalem Post,* international edition, week ending November 9, 1985.

52. *The Times,* London, March 1, 1985, p. 8.

53. *New York Times,* December 17, 1984, p. 14.

6

South Asia

Douglas C. Makeig

South Asia has seen little democracy until recently, as the history of the subcontinent has been one of despotic empires. India, however, had a number of republics in Buddhist times; Alexander the Great met some of them as he invaded the fringes of the subcontinent. There have also been institutions of traditional village democracy, leadership by elected elders. But more important for the present strength of democracy in the region is the fact that it was colonized from the eighteenth century by the British, who implanted legal institutions and elements of elected government. South Asia has consequently been the only part of the Afro-Asian world where democratic institutions have generally predominated since the achievement of independence after World War II.

For the purposes of this inquiry South Asia encompasses seven nations: India, Sri Lanka, Pakistan, Bangladesh, Nepal, Bhutan, and the Maldives. While many of the features of Westminster-style democracy are present in some form in all seven states of the region, only India can be classed as an organically evolving democracy. India (as until recently Sri Lanka) boasts an admirable record of free and fair elections observing the rule of law, an independent judiciary, protection of minority rights, and relative freedom of the press. However, the country's brush with authoritarianism during a brief period of Emergency rule (1975–77), the increased use of the army in domestic peacekeeping, and the selective imposition of virtual martial law in states experiencing violent disorders demonstrate the fragility of Indian democracy. Nonetheless, in 1985 India lived up to its image as the "world's largest democracy" by weathering a series of political storms. Under the able leadership of its newly chosen, 41-year-old prime minister, Rajiv Gandhi, India appears to have found renewed self-confidence in tackling its many problems within the framework of parliamentary democracy.

The erosion of democracy is striking in the case of Sri Lanka. Although Sri Lanka has, for most of its independent existence, followed India's lead in practicing as well as preaching democracy, the island's current difficulties in combating Tamil separatism have seriously undermined the constitutional process. The beleaguered government of President Junius Jayewardene remains committed, in principle at least, to restoring the island's communal harmony through dialogue and constitutional means.

The record of Pakistan and Bangladesh in forming and sustaining democratic institutions is poor. Both countries have been ruled for over half their independent existence by unpopular military regimes that came to power against a backdrop of domestic chaos and army plotting or a combination of both. Unlike in India, the British tradition of insulating the military from politics (and vice versa) gave way to a pattern of praetorian politics in both Pakistan and Bangladesh. Constitution making (as well as constitution breaking) proved a torturous process that, rather than uniting the population behind common ideals, served to divide the countries along ethnic, sectarian, and ideological lines. Although successive juntas in the two countries have imposed order without resorting to the gross violations of human rights that are common to other regions of the world, periods of relatively relaxed martial law have been interspersed by periods marked by strict press censorship, political detentions, the emasculation of civilian courts, and a ham-handed use of the army to put down dissent.

The Pakistani and Bangladeshi experience in elected civilian government has been almost as unfortunate. Pakistan's most recent period of civilian rule (1972–77) was marred by a systematic abuse of authority by Prime Minister Zulfiqar Ali Bhutto and his supporters. Similarly, Bangladesh's first experiment in democracy lasted only four years, ending when disgruntled army officers ousted the erratic and increasingly authoritarian government of the nation's founding father, Sheikh Mujibur Rahman. Numerous coups, counter-coups, and attempted coups have occurred in Bangladesh since Mujib's overthrow in 1975.

Martial law in Pakistan came to an end on December 31, 1985, and Bangladesh is also moving toward elected civilian government. But both states have yet to find a viable system of democratic government that can command broad popular support and offer a stable alternative to military rule. The transition to a modicum of civilian rule in Pakistan and Bangladesh is clearly at risk. Nevertheless, military officers and civilian politicians in both countries are in broad agreement that martial law is, at best, an interim arrangement designed to oversee the transition to a more legitimate political system. The question is not whether the army should return to the barracks but rather when and under what terms; but the armed forces of Pakistan and Bangladesh are so deeply engaged in politics that neither country is likely to revert to a political system in which the army does not have, at a minimum, veto power over the actions of civilian politicians. The loosening of martial law restraints and the holding of elections (however restricted) have unleashed popular expectations in both countries for an eventual return to democracy in some form. Whereas Pakistan is looking once again to Islam to provide the social and political cohesion for a return to democracy, Bangladesh appears more inclined to revert to a modified system of multiparty democracy.

Nepal, Bhutan, and the Maldives fall somewhere between the praetorianism of Pakistan and Bangladesh and the democratic blend of India and Sri Lanka. Even though none of these small states recognize organized political opposition, each country supports a relatively democratic system of government.

Nepal, the world's only Hindu state, is a constitutional monarchy in which King Birendra is responsible to a parliament elected on a nonparty basis. Opposition pressure is mounting in Nepal to introduce a freewheeling, Indian-style democracy. Events of the past year demonstrated that these pressures for change could take a violent turn if not met.

By contrast, the isolated kingdom of Bhutan is at a stage of political development comparable to Nepal in the 1950s. King Jigme Singye Wangchuck is, by all accounts, a capable leader who has promoted modernization. At the same time, the young king has been careful not to endanger the traditional social foundations of the secluded Buddhist kingdom.

The Maldives, an Indian Ocean microstate, achieved independence in 1965 when Britain completed the colonial disengagement process from the region. While the democratically elected government has made progress in developing the islands' precarious economy based on fishing and tourism, the cautious experiment in Islamic democracy is largely held together by the leadership of President Maumoon Abdul Gayoom.

From the standpoint of the extension or restoration of democratic institutions, the political trend in the region was, on balance, positive during 1985.

INDIA

In 1985, Indians observed two very different anniversaries that marked political watersheds in the nation's democratic experience. The first was the centenary of the founding of Asia's oldest democratic party, the Indian National Congress (or Congress-I in its current incarnation). Under the towering leadership of Mahatma Gandhi, Jawaharlal Nehru, and a generation of Western-educated nationalists, the Congress bequeathed to India a rich legacy of secular democracy and respect for individual freedom. The success of the Indian democratic experiment is, to a large measure, attributable to the Congress tradition. Since independence in 1947, India's democratic achievements have included eight national elections held at regular intervals, the orderly transfer of power to opposition hands after the elections of 1977 and 1980, and the growth of an ideologically diverse array of opposition parties that contest—and win—elections at every level of government. Moreover, a feature that is virtually unique when compared to other emerging nations is India's success in keeping a formidable military establishment that remains aloof from politics.

In 1985 there was also observed the tenth anniversary of Indira Gandhi's declaration of a state of emergency. Although the suspension of individual liberties lasted only two years and ended when the voters rejected Gandhi and her party in national elections, memories of the emergency provide a powerful reminder that India's survival as a stable democracy is not assured. Patently undemocratic practices such as the toppling of opposition state ministries on partisan political grounds, draconian internal security measures that negate constitutional guarantees of civil liberties, and the transformation of the Congress into a personal electoral machine of the prime minister are all legacies of the emergency that have become a seamy underside of Indian political life. These excesses and extraconstitutional devices are also a disquieting legacy of the leadership style of Indira Gandhi.

The election of Gandhi's son, Rajiv, in late December 1984 immediately after the assassination of his mother, served to renew the nation's faith in secular democracy. Campaigning on a platform of national unity against a deeply divided opposition, Rajiv secured an unprecedented three-fourth's parliamentary majority and garnered almost 50 percent of the popular vote. The Congress-I (for "Indira") electoral mandate not only signified the voters' preference for a continuity in national leadership against the unknowns of an opposition coalition government, but it also raised expectations that a new generation of Congress leaders would, in Rajiv's words, "propel the country into the twenty-first century."[1]

On the economic front, Rajiv has accelerated the liberalization process that was cautiously undertaken by his mother, and the central government has started to deregulate sections of the economy previously reserved for or dominated by bureaucrats. The resulting revitalized private sector has considerably expanded the Indian economy. At the same time, income taxes have been scaled back, import restrictions on capital goods have been eased, and Western investments have been actively encouraged. India is now an exporter of food, the country boasts a huge reserve of scientific manpower, and India's industrial infrastructure is among the most advanced in Asia. Economists who are critical of Rajiv's economic program note that economic liberalization carries with it the potential for crippling inflation as well as a further skewing of the nation's distribution of income. Despite these warnings, the Indian economy in general and the Indian private sector in particular are booming. India's economic expansion has occurred without running up a huge foreign debt, as was the case of comparably advanced economies such as Brazil.

While the Congress-I has clearly ensured its position as the dominant force in Indian politics, the party does not hold a monopoly of power. Besides the presence of a vocal (though greatly diminished) opposition in parliament, opposition parties control eight of India's 22 state ministries. One state (Karnataka) is ruled by the nationally based Janata party; five states (Jammu, Kashmir, Punjab, Assam, Tamil Nadu, and Andhra Pradesh) are governed by communal or regionally based parties; and two states (West Bengal and Tripura) are led by left-wing coalitions headed by the Bengali-dominated Communist party of India-Marxist. Unlike his mother, Rajiv has tolerated a healthy give-and-take with the opposition and has embraced the notion that the strength of Indian politics—as with India itself—lies in an accommodation between the ideal of national unity and the reality of regional diversity. Moreover, Rajiv has begun the long-overdue process of rejuvenating the Congress-I by decentralizing party decision making, promoting independent-minded leaders within the party ranks, and encouraging a return to intraparty democracy.[2]

Parliamentary by-elections and state assembly elections conducted in April and March, respectively, offered additional evidence of the independence of Indian voters. In both elections, opposition parties recouped some of their losses to Congress-I, though Rajiv's candidates fared well in the populous Hindi belt of northern India. Postelection analyses indicated that while Indian voters responded positively to Rajiv's appeal to preserve national unity by backing Congress-I at the national level, the same voters in state and local elections did not hesitate to elect opposition candidates who identified closely with local concerns. In critical state elections in the Punjab and Assam, voters decisively rejected Congress-I candidates. The Indian voters' ability to discriminate between national and local issues is a testament to the vitality of the Indian system.

Rajiv and his inner circle of Western-educated technocrats have fundamentally altered Indian politics by adapting the so-called "communications revolution" to the electoral process. Over 70 percent of India's population of 750 million now have access to television relayed by satellite, radio programs are broadcast in dozens of languages to every corner of the country, and rising literacy rates have created a huge domestic market for newspapers and books. Congress-I strategists took full advantage of these improved communications by skillfully advertising the party's election platform and utilizing sophisticated polling techniques. Although opposition candidates were at a disadvantage owing to their lack of financial and technical resources, the age of mass media politics has clearly arrived in India. In July, Prime Minister Gandhi conducted the first nationally televised news conference. Rajiv's polished and relaxed manner, reminiscent of President John Kennedy's mastery of the U.S. media in the 1960s, is ideally suited to television.

Rajiv's most pressing political challenge during his first year in office was in the fertile northwestern state of Punjab. Starting in 1981, sections of India's Sikh minority mounted large-scale demonstrations demanding political, economic, and religious concessions from New Delhi. The protests were overlaid with religious overtones, and control over the movement shifted from moderate Sikhs to a militant assortment of terrorists and religious zealots. In October 1983, Indira Gandhi dismissed the discredited Congress-I ministry in the state and assumed direct responsibility for maintaining order in the Punjab. The Sikh terrorist campaign that was based on the Golden Temple of Amritsar grew more violent and threatened communal harmony throughout India. In June 1984, Indira Gandhi ordered the army to take control of the Golden Temple and to crush the terrorist network. Over 1,000 civilians and at least 70 security personnel were killed in the ensuing battle. Sikh public opinion was deeply offended by the army's desecration of Sikhism's holiest shrine, and uncoordinated mutinies among Sikh army personnel occurred in several cantonments in the aftermath of the siege. Five months later, Indira Gandhi was assassinated by two of her Sikh bodyguards who sought to avenge the Golden Temple incident. In the troubled days after Gandhi's death, angry mobs—with some Congress-I operatives—roamed the streets of Delhi and several northern Indian cities, killing Sikhs and looting Sikh shops.

When Rajiv assumed office at a time of deep personal anguish, the situation in the Punjab was grim. Over 100,000 army troops were engaged in a tough counterterrorist operation, moderate Sikh leaders were either in jail or too embittered to deal with New Delhi, and Sikhs feared that the constitutional process was not a sufficient guarantee of the community's survival. Rajiv repeated his mother's pledge to apply the "healing touch," but because of continued unrest in the Punjab, the December 1984 national elections were deferred in the state. Of equal concern to the new government were the international implications of the Punjab turmoil. New Delhi charged that Pakistan was stoking communal flames in the state and that Britain, Canada, and the United States were turning a blind eye to the activities of expatriate Sikh radicals who operated within their borders.

The Gandhi government assigned top priority to the crisis. In July, after months of negotiations and an escalating cycle of Sikh terrorist outrages perpetrated across northern India, Gandhi obtained a political accord that addressed most of the outstanding issues in the dispute. Signing on behalf of the moderate Sikh leadership was Sant Harchand Singh Longowal, a factional leader in the major Sikh political party, the Akali Dal. The main provisions of the eleven point accord provided for:

- an equitable division of river water resources between the Punjab and neighboring states;
- the transfer of the city of Chandigarh to the Punjab;
- Akali control over Sikh temple revenues throughout India;
- a judicial inquiry into the anti-Sikh riots and financial compensation for the families of those killed since 1982;
- a pledge to treat some Sikh mutineers with leniency; and
- a dismantling of the more odious aspects of internal security legislation that had been brought to bear in the Punjab.

The negotiating breakthrough was hailed by most community spokesmen and political parties as an act of high statesmanship. Many of the Sikh political prisoners who had been languishing in jail under preventive detention were released, newsmen were allowed to enter the state for the first time in over a year, and state elections were called for September. The boundary changes under the accord increased the percentage of Sikhs in the Punjab, raising hopes that the Akalis could wrest control of the state government from the Hindu-dominated Congress-I state party apparatus. Fears that radical elements would attempt to sabotage the accord by mounting fresh terrorist attacks were realized when Longowal was murdered by Akali extremists less than a month after signing the agreement. If anything, Longowal's death served to promote the cause of communal reconciliation in a state that had grown weary of years of violence.

The election of an Akali Dal ministry on September 25 was hailed by the moderate majority of Sikhs and Hindus as a victory for democracy. Akali candidates campaigned on a platform that supported the Gandhi-Longowal accord. When the votes were tallied, the Akali Dal captured 73 of the 115 state assembly seats, enough to form a government without coalition partners. In the contests for the national parliament, Akali candidates won 7 of the 13 seats. In both contests, Congress-I ran a distant second. The acting Akali president, Surjit Singh Barnala, was elected chief minister of the new government. His selection virtually ensured that the moderate political heirs of Longowal would dominate the ministry. A minimum of campaign violence and a voter turnout of about 60 percent were widely interpreted as a rebuff to Sikh extremism. Most observers believe that the Akali victory has given the Sikh community a stake in electoral politics. Despite his party's stunning defeat at the polls, Rajiv Gandhi proclaimed "Democracy has won, non-violence has won, India has won!"

After achieving success in the Punjab, Prime Minister Gandhi turned his attention to the troubled northeastern state of Assam. Since 1979, Assamese students had been spearheading a broad-based campaign to expell Bangladeshi immigrants who had entered the state illegally. The growing immigrant presence threatened to upset the ethnic, linguistic, and religious balance in the state. As in the Punjab, the Assamese protests struck at the heart of India's existence as a multiethnic, secular democracy. Assam had witnessed numerous communal clashes over the years, necessitating the recurrent deployment of the army in the state and the imposition of extraordinary security measures. Various attempts to negotiate a political settlement had foundered because of New Delhi's reluctance to set constitutional precedents that could adversely affect the status of minorities throughout India. Some commentators also speculated that Indira Gandhi had personally contributed to the impasse by interpreting Assamese negotiating concessions as a sign of weakness and then pushing for a settlement more to her liking.

On August 15 (India's Independence Day), Rajiv announced that a negotiated settlement to the antiforeigner stir had been reached. Under its terms, all those who had arrived in Assam prior to 1966 were granted Indian citizenship and their names were retained on state voter rolls. Those who arrived between 1966 and 1971 were to be disenfranchised although they would be allowed to remain in the state and will be eligible to apply for citizenship after a waiting period of ten years. Those who arrived after 1971 will be liable to expulsion. An unwritten understanding was that the Congress-I state ministry—regarded by the protesters as unrepresentative because it was elected when Assamese voters staged an election boycott—would be dissolved and fresh elections would be scheduled. Although the possibility of renewed mob violence and the difficulty of separating foreigners by date of arrival could derail the political normalization process, the Assam accord offers fresh hope that democracy is the best remedy for India's complex political problems. By striking a balance between New Delhi's concern for national integration and Assamese demands for a more rigorous definition of citizenship, the accord symbolized another victory for Indian democracy.

Congress-I suffered a severe setback in statewide elections conducted in Assam on December 15. To everyone's relief, the presence of over 200,000 security personnel in the state prevented election day violence. The hastily formed coalition of Assamese ethnic groups, the Asom Gana Parishad ("Assam People's Council," AGP) secured 64 out of 125 state assembly seats. Rajiv's party managed to win only 21 seats. Probably the main reason the Congress-I lost the state was the emergence of a United Minorities Front that attracted the support of many non-Assamese voters who broke with Congress-I. To New Delhi's distress, the AGP state ministry promised to carry out the letter of the August accord by expelling non-Assamese residents of the state who arrived after 1971.

In the western state of Gujarat, battle lines drawn along caste lines led to sporadic rioting between high-caste Hindus and an amalgamation of political forces defending the interests of untouchables, tribesmen, and other classes at the bottom of the Indian social order. India supports the world's largest program of affirmative action, or "protective discrimination" in Indian parlance. Reflecting the Congress tradition of striving to eradicate untouchability, the Indian constitution reserves 31 percent of all government posts in the civil service, armed forces, and state-run schools for these depressed classes. Starting in 1981, high-caste applicants to Gujarat's highly competitive medical schools launched an "anti-reservation" movement. Under current regulations, almost 70 percent of the state's population is eligible for preferential treatment, leaving caste Hindus to compete among themselves for the remaining share of government spoils. The caste backlash against reservations is particularly nettlesome because of the political stakes involved.

Simmering caste tensions in Gujarat exploded in violence in March when the Congress-I chief minister of the state, Madhavsinh Solanki, attempted to woo the lower castes on the eve of a state election. Solanki announced an 18 percent increase in seat reservations in government schools. The antireservationists responded by mounting massive demonstrations that soon degenerated into bloody confrontations with police and rival demonstrators. Police discipline broke down; marauding gangs, many with ties to organized crime, gained control of the streets. When the protests began spreading to adjoining states, New Delhi dismissed the Solanki ministry and called in army and paramilitary forces to restore order. Over the course of the year as many as 200 persons were killed in the disorders. The violence also took a communal turn when Hindus and Muslims mounted organized attacks against each other.

By year's end, New Delhi's efforts to resolve the reservation issue proved futile, in part because the Congress-I stands to lose political support if any change is made in the status quo. If allowed to fester, however, the battle over reservations could threaten the national consensus that has evolved regarding the state's duty to correct age-old discrimination patterns. It is ironic that the focus of the agitation should be Gujarat, the home state of Mahatma Gandhi and the cradle of nonviolence.[3]

While India's commitment to democracy remains strong, efforts to safeguard national unity often involve hard choices between ensuring the domestic peace and remaining faithful to the letter and spirit of the constitution. Several trends in India suggest that the latter goal has suffered in recent years. A prime example is the passage of the 1985 Terrorist and Disruptive Activities (Prevention) Act. Enacted at a time when Sikh terrorists had initiated a bloody campaign of indiscriminate bombings in Delhi, the legislation calls for secret trials, lengthy periods of preventive detention, a minimum of judicial oversight, and the presumption of guilt on the part of suspected terrorists. India's small but vocal lobby of civil libertarians complained that the act was legally unnecessary as well as constitutionally repugnant. The central government retains a wide array of extraordinary powers, many of which date back to the colonial period, that can be implemented to contain violence. When simultaneously activated, these technically constitutional devices can amount to the imposition of another period of emergency rule at the state or local level.[4] Whether Rajiv uses his electoral mandate to press for political accommodations on the pattern of the Punjab and Assam accords, or resorts to an increasing use of extraordinary police powers to enforce order, will test Indian democracy. To judge from events of the past year, the outlook for India is promising.

SRI LANKA

Since the outbreak of vicious anti-Tamil riots in the summer of 1983, Tamil separatism has escalated from a low-level terrorist menace to a full-fledged insurgency that threatens the territorial integrity of the island state of 15 million. The response of the Colombo government to the spiraling violence has been ineffective and often brutal. Sri Lankan security personnel are poorly trained and unequipped for a protracted counterinsurgency, while the Tamil insurgents fighting from bases in the Jaffna peninsula and southern

India are not strong enough militarily to challenge Sri Lankan forces openly and have had to rely on hit-and-run tactics and terrorism.

As is often the case in brush wars of this kind, both sides have resorted to reprisals against civilians, the torture of prisoners, massacres, and assorted atrocities. The spreading violence has inflamed passions and frustrated efforts on the part of moderate Sinhalese and Tamil leaders to find a negotiated settlement.

The ferocious nature of the conflict was shown in May 1985 when army troops ran amok and massacred the inhabitants of Velvetturai, a Tamil fishing village on the west coast. Six days later, Tamil commandos retaliated by gunning down 150 Sinhalese pilgrims at the holy Buddhist shrine at Anuradhapura. With both sides exerting little or no control over combatants in the field, hardliners in both camps press for a military showdown. The spirit of communal accommodation as well as the democratic process itself has been seriously undermined in Sri Lanka.

The insurgents are loosely organized under the banner of approximately a dozen left-wing groups collectively known as the Tamil Tigers. The militants seek to carve out an independent state of Tamil Eelam from Tamil-majority areas in the north and east of the island. While a moderate political grouping, the Tamil United Liberation Front (TULF), has indicated a willingness to accept a constitutional solution that falls short of independence, the Tigers and their sympathizers have effectively employed terrorist tactics to silence Tamil as well as Sinhalese voices of moderation. The Tamil community is in broad agreement, however, that the communal chauvinism of the Sinhalese majority is responsible for forcing Tamils to take up arms in self-defense. Historically, Tamil grievances center around four issues: the role of the Tamil language in the affairs of the nation; Sinhalese settlement on traditionally Tamil lands; Tamil representation in government schools and services; and formulas for power-sharing or partition.

Since coming to power in 1977, the Sinhalese-dominated United National party (UNP) government of President Junius Jayewardene has instituted a series of legislative and constitutional measures that have tarnished the country's image as a representative democracy. In 1978, Jayewardene used his five-sixths parliamentary majority to transform the existing parliamentary system into a Gaullist presidential system. Under the revised constitution, the authority of the president is virtually immune from judicial or legislative challenge. Simultaneously, the president was given sweeping powers to arrest and detain suspected terrorists. In 1979, parliament passed the Prevention of Terrorism Act, which expanded the powers of security forces to detain suspects incommunicado for up to 18 months with a minimum of judicial oversight. Security personnel have been given virtually free rein to conduct counterterrorist operations in Tamil areas.

In 1982, Jayewardene again used his parliamentary majority to stage an extraordinary referendum in which voters prolonged the life of the existing parliament through 1989. This device allows the UNP to retain power without having to resort to the customary electoral process. Lastly, in 1983, parliament passed the sixth amendment to the constitution, which prevented all parties that advocated separatism from participating in the electoral process. The amendment effectively ousted the duly elected TULF opposition from parliament and drove the party underground into the company of the Tigers. Thus, while Sri Lanka retains the trappings of a parliamentary democracy, in reality Jayewardene heads a government that has almost no elected opposition and is not accountable to the electorate for at least another several years.

Relations between Colombo and New Delhi have deteriorated in recent years because of the presence of Tamil insurgent forces in the nearby Indian state of Tamil Nadu. In July, however, Indian prime minister Rajiv Gandhi broke the diplomatic deadlock and used his influence over the Tamils to arrange for a ceasefire, followed by negotiations. Although both the Tigers and the Colombo government had vowed never to negotiate under duress, the two sides convened a round of talks through Indian good offices at a neutral site in Thimpu, Bhutan. While several days of hard bargaining did not yield a breakthrough, the Thimpu talks offered some hope that the two sides can eventually agree to accord the Tamil minority a constitutional stake in a unified and democratic Sri Lanka.[5]

PAKISTAN

The martial law regime of President Mohammed Zia-ul Haq seized power in a bloodless coup in July 1977. Since arriving in power, Pakistan's ruling junta has been confronted with a classic dilemma: how to transfer power to a civilian government of the army's choosing without aggravating the country's deep political divisions that prompted the armed forces to step in and govern in the first place. National elections scheduled for July 1977 and November 1979 were both cancelled when it became apparent that the party ousted from power, the Pakistan People's party (PPP), stood a fair chance of winning or at least influencing the outcome of the election.

In the absence of a national consensus regarding the political and ideological character of the nation, Zia opted to mold Pakistan into a fundamentalist Islamic state. Owing to the country's repeated failure to adopt the institutions of Western-style, multiparty democracy, Zia and his supporters concluded that such a system is inherently divisive and unsuited to Pakistan's raison d'être as an Islamic homeland. In the place of parliamentary democracy, the Zia regime launched an ambitious campaign to Islamicize Pakistan's social system and political culture. Although opposition to the scheme runs deep among the country's Westernized intelligentsia, Zia pledged to use his coercive powers as Chief Martial Law Administrator (CMLA) until Nizam-i-mustafa ("Rule of the Prophet") becomes a self-sustaining system of government. To reach this goal, Zia began constructing the Islamic state "brick by brick" through a combination of reform, persuasion, and intimidation.

Islamic reforms have been applied piecemeal in several fields. A court system based on Islamic jurisprudence was instituted in 1979, although the British-style secular courts still operate alongside the new *shari'a* and martial law courts. Under the Hadood Ordinance of the same year, traditional Islamic punishments such as flogging, stoning, and amputation were introduced (though the latter punishment has yet to be carried out). Other reforms have included the imposition of Islamic tithes (*zakat* and *ushr*), a ban on alcoholic beverages, restrictions on women, and an experiment in interest-free Islamic banking. While there is no reason to doubt Zia's personal piety, many civilian politicians in Pakistan regard Zia's Islamicization program as an attempt to legitimize martial law through religion.

On the political front, the regime moved ahead with a program of restoring elected civilian government in stages, to culminate in a withdrawal of martial law by January 1, 1986. In November 1984, the regime ignored opposition pressures for a return to multiparty democracy by holding a national referendum that asked voters to approve Zia's plans to introduce an Islamic system of guided democracy. The measure passed by a huge majority and Zia interpreted the vote as a mandate to retain the presidency for another five years. Not only was the referendum worded so as to make a negative vote equivalent to a vote against Islam but it was flawed by an opposition boycott and widespread ballot-stuffing.

The next stage in the process occurred on February 25, 1985, when elections for the newly revived National Assembly (NA) were held. Originally proposed in August 1983, the elections were intended to create a parliament to replace the virtually powerless *majlis-i-shoora* (advisory council) that Zia appointed in 1981. Although the opposition again called for a boycott, the Assembly elections elicited some enthusiasm from a general public weary of almost eight years of martial law. Moreover, the opposition parties offered no coherent alternative to Zia's program other than a futile call for the army to relinquish power. Voting was brisk. Over 1,000 candidates running on a nonparty basis sought election to the 210 contested seats. A voter turnout of 53 percent and a general belief that the balloting was not tainted by electoral irregularities supported the regime's contention that Pakistan was rejoining the democratic fold.

The rules for the balloting were hardly conducive, however, to democracy. All candidates were screened to ensure that only "good Muslims" would be elected. Those who held office during the PPP years were disqualified from holding office for seven years. Despite these restrictions, identifiable supporters of the PPP managed to win 38 of the 210 contested seats, while the opposition Muslim League faction of Pir Pagaro secured 42 seats. Most surprising was the defeat of five of Zia's nine cabinet ministers, including Defense Minister Ali Ahmed Talpur. Jamaat-i-Islami, a conservative religious party that generally backs the regime, managed to win only nine seats. Zia cited these setbacks as proof that the elections were a legitimate expression of the people's will.

The NA is not exactly the "powerless debating club" the opposition contends it is, but neither is it an independent check on executive authority. The NA is dominated by landowners, whom the regime favors over the Westernized urban classes supporting the opposition. The Assembly's role in passing legislation and offering advice are clearly subordinate to Zia in his multiple roles as president, CMLA, and army chief. After the March election, Zia restored portions of the 1973 constitution and included new provisions that accorded the unelected president sole powers to appoint a prime minister, heads of the armed forces, provincial governors, and chief ministers. In addition, the president has the power to dissolve parliament, call new elections, return bills for reconsideration, hold referendums, and appoint cabinet ministers. More ominously, Zia hinted at the formation of a National Security Council (NSC) composed of handpicked appointees, presumably dominated by the military. It would have the power to overrule any action of the assembly. Zia withdrew the NSC proposal when members of parliament adamantly refused to grant the army an institutional role in overseeing the performance of future governments.

The NA convened its first session in a hopeful mood. Its first act was to reject Zia's candidate for speaker of the Assembly in favor of a candidate of its own choosing. Zia's selection for the largely ceremonial post of prime minister, however, was less contentious. Chosen for the part was Mohammed Khan Junejo, a mild-mannered Sindhi landowner connected with the old guard of the Muslim League. Two-third's of the technically nonpartisan NA is reportedly considered the "prime minister's party." Since appointing Junejo, Zia has shrewdly underplayed his own policy-making role and placed Junejo at the center of Pakistan's political stage. Consequently, Junejo has taken over many of the duties previously performed by the CMLA such as meeting with the voters and giving interviews to newsmen. Although NA debates are kept within the regime's threshold of tolerance, a number of parliamentarians have taken up controversial issues such as the defense budget, Afghan refugee policy, and the validity of martial law.

In order to protect the military from legal proceedings once martial law was lifted in 1986, Zia insisted that the NA pass an indemnification amendment to the 1973 constitution. Under terms of the act passed in October, all changes to the constitution decreed under martial law were declared valid and beyond legal challenge. The legislation also allowed Zia to retain both positions of president and army chief. Zia also insisted that the NA empower the regime to register political parties prior to all future elections. Under this device, Zia and the army leadership will continue to exert influence over the direction and pace of political change in Pakistan.

As Zia promised, martial law was formally lifted on December 30, 1985. Military tribunals were abolished and constitutional guarantees of basic freedoms were restored. It is still too early to tell, however, whether Pakistan's experiment in Islamic democracy can evolve into a genuinely representative government or whether it will serve as a cover for the perpetuation of army rule. There remains considerable opposition to the experiment in the minority provinces of Sind, Baluchistan, and the Northwest Frontier, as well as from the PPP-dominated political alliance known as the Movement for the Restoration of Democracy. The transition to democracy could also be sidetracked by a number of negative developments. These include a drop in workers' remittances from the Persian Gulf, a succession of crop failures, a breakdown in law and order, or a concerted campaign of political subversion mounted by communist elements from Soviet-occupied Afghanistan. Thus, while Pakistan is moving in the general direction of democracy, numerous obstacles lie ahead.

BANGLADESH

Like Pakistan, Bangladesh is an overwhelmingly Muslim country ruled by a martial law regime. Unlike Pakistan, however, the Bangladeshi regime is attempting to smooth the way for a return to democracy without Islamicizing the state or society. Bangladesh is not a fertile breeding ground for Islamic fundamentalism. Moreover, despite the country's abortive efforts in the past to fashion a working system of representative democracy, Bangladeshis of almost all political persuasions (including within the army) exhibit a pronounced preference for an open, multiparty system organized along secular lines.

Since coming to power in a bloodless coup in March 1982, Lieutenant General (and shortly thereafter president) Hussain Mohammed Ershad has tried to stage national elections three times. On each occasion, scheduled elections were called off at the eleventh hour when Ershad feared that an opposition boycott would render the polls meaningless. Because of the high degree of factionalism that characterizes Bangladeshi politics, Ershad's strategy has been to outflank the divided opposition by civilianizing his regime and eventually offering himself as a candidate to head a nominally democratic government. This strategy of taking off his uniform and leading the country in civilian clothes has precedents in Bangladesh's political history. Former president Ziaur Rahman achieved considerable success in governing after submitting the military's political program to the approval of the voters. During the Pakistan era of preindependence Bangladesh, Ayub Khan also made the transition from army commander to civilian head of state.

Within a year after overthrowing the inept government of Abdus Sattar, Ershad formed Janadal, a personal political vehicle composed largely of proregime opportunists, a smattering of opposition defectors, and, of course, the army. Another aspect of Ershad's strategy has been to woo the support of the rural masses by promoting grass-roots economic development, decentralizing the bureaucracy, and championing village democracy. Considering the immense challenges that would confront any regime ruling over a country of 100 million people with a per capita income of less than $150 per year, Ershad's performance in office has been respectable. The foreign aid lifeline has not been severed because of martial law, an economy oriented toward the free market has shown signs of growth, and martial law has been exercised with a degree of restraint. Nevertheless, most political observers doubt that the regime's performance is enough to generate broad popular support for Ershad, whose credentials as a political leader are uninspiring.

After rescheduling the December 1984 elections for April 1985, Ershad partially yielded to opposition pressure by appointing a nonpartisan government to oversee the transfer of power. Janadal members were dismissed from the cabinet in order to assure the opposition that the regime would not use its patronage powers to influence the electoral outcome. The opposition was unimpressed by the gesture and renewed the call for a complete withdrawal of martial law and the appointment of a neutral caretaker government as the price for their electoral participation. Ershad refused to take the risk, cancelled the April elections, and ordered the arrest of a number of opposition leaders. In March, Ershad called a referendum on his government's performance.[6]

The March 21 referendum bluntly asked: "Do you support the policies of President Ershad and do you want him to continue to run this administration until a civilian government is formed through elections?"[7] As in the case of Pakistan's referendum of the previous month, Ershad's initiative passed with a thumping 97 percent majority. Although this figure was undoubtedly inflated, most observers maintained that the oppositions's call for a boycott fell flat. The implications of the referendum were not clear to either the regime or the opposition. The balloting seemed to be a decisive defeat for the civilian political forces but a dubious victory for General Ershad. Undeterred by criticism, Ershad promised to go ahead with his controversial plans to stage *upazitta* (subdistrict) elections in May and national elections at some future date, though he has yet to announce officially that he will run as a presidential candidate.

Throughout the year, most of Bangladesh's 70-odd political parties were in the awkward position of blocking regime attempts to stage elections. The mainstream political parties in Bangladesh are grouped into two major alliances. The first is a 7-party, center-right coalition led by the Bangladesh National party (BNP). The central figure in the BNP-led combine is Begum Khaleda Zia, the widow of former president Ziaur Rahman. The second, more militant, alliance consists of 15 parties, most of which share a pronounced leftist orientation. The driving force behind the alliance is the Awami League (AL), probably the only political party in Bangladesh that maintains a grass-roots organization in most areas of the country. The AL is headed by Hasina Wajed, the daughter of the charismatic founding father of Bangladesh, Sheikh Muhibur Rahman, who was assassinated during a military coup in 1975.

The 7- and 15-party alliances differ on several basic issues. The 7-party alliance favors the resumption of the 1982 constitution, the retention of a presidential form of government, and a critical foreign policy line toward India and the Soviet Union. By contrast, the AL-led alliance favors the restoration of Mujib's 1972 constitution, the adoption of a Westminster form of parliamentary democracy, and accommodations with India and the Soviet Union. Despite these differences, the two groups have been generally successful in papering over their differences and forging a united opposition front against the Ershad regime. If national elections are ever staged, however, differences between the alliances and particularly within the center-left 15-party combine will be magnified. During the year, Ershad persuaded a number of opposition figures to join the government. The moderate BNP was particularly vulnerable to cooptation.

NEPAL

King Birendra Bir Bikram Shah Dev, Nepal's constitutional monarch, rules over a landlocked mountain kingdom where political parties have been banned since 1960. The 140-member Rashtriya Panchayat (national parliament) is dominated by the king's supporters, though factional infighting and palace intrigues are the salient features of Nepalese politics. Birendra exercises firm control over the direction and pace of change in the country.

In 1980, voters narrowly rejected a referendum that would have changed the political system to allow for a multiparty democracy in which the king's powers would have been circumscribed by a more assertive parliament. Since then political pressures to alter the system have been mounting in Nepal. The campaign to liberalize the political system is led by the Nepali Congress party, which has vowed to boycott general elections scheduled for 1986 if opposition parties are not legalized. Political violence is almost unheard of in Nepal, but in June 1985, terrorist bombs killed 18 persons outside the palace gates in Katmandu.[8] Should the ongoing political debate over the country's democratic future degenerate into violence, Birendra would be faced with difficult choices.

BHUTAN

King Jigme Singye Wangchuck has ruled the isolated kingdom of Bhutan since 1972. The Bhutanese system of government is a pyramidal structure of elected councils extending from the village level to the royal advisory council. Politics in Bhutan reflect the Buddhist and essentially feudal character of the country. Village elections are held every three years with each family unit casting one vote. As in Nepal, opposition parties are illegal in Bhutan.

THE MALDIVES

The strategically located, though little-known, state of Maldives consists of 1,200 sparsely inhabited coral atolls located southwest of India in the Indian Ocean. With a population of about 150,000 and a narrow economic base, the Maldives supports a quasi-democratic system of government. The 1968 constitution provides for a highly centralized form of government in which Islam plays a guiding role. The country has been ably led by its Cairo-educated president, Maumoon Abdul Gayoom, since 1978. The president is nominally responsible to a democratically elected *majlis* (council).

NOTES

1. Sumit Mitra, "Congress-I: Unexpected Setbacks," *India Today,* March 31, 1985, 31.

2. Charges of official complicity in the anti-Sikh riots are detailed in *People's Union for Democratic Rights, Who are the Guilty?* (New Delhi: Excellent Printing Services, 1984).

3. Shekhar Gupta, "Reservation Policy: The Caste Crunch," *India Today* (New Delhi), April 15, 1985, 52–61.

4. A. G. Noorani, "The Terrorist Act," *Economic and Political Weekly* (Bombay), June 8, 1985, 945.

5. Stuart Auerbach, "Sri Lanka's Tamil Rebels Travel to Crucial Talks." *Washington Post,* July 8, 1985, A19.

6. Hong Kong AFP (in English), March 20, 1985; Foreign Broadcast Information Service, *South Asia Report,* March 21, 1985, p. D1.

7. Ataus Samad, "Bangladesh's Military Leader Puts his Rule up for Vote March 21," *Christian Science Monitor,* March 20, 1985, p. 7.

8. Washington *Post,* January 21, 1985, p. A25.

7

Far East and Pacific

Edward A. Olsen

Democracy in the Far East and Pacific made minor gains in 1985, with no major setbacks. On balance, the forces for democratic pluralism made headway, while those for authoritarianism lost ground as they had to experiment with social and economic pluralism to compete with freer societies.[1]

The countries analyzed in this section range from the most sophisticated of past and contemporary societies to rudimentary stone age cultures. The phrase "Far East" encompasses East Asia (China, Japan, the two Koreas, Taiwan, Hong Kong, Macao, and Mongolia) and Southeast Asia (Burma, Thailand, Vietnam, Kampuchea, Laos, Malaysia, Singapore, Indonesia, the Philippines, and Brunei). For this book Mongolia, though an Asian state, is included in the Soviet section because the Ulan Bator government is a functional underling of Moscow. Southwest Pacific states are not Asian—Australia, New Zealand, and the small states of Oceania—are included because of their close ties to Asian-Pacific neighbors.

There is one major cultural zone, the Sinic realm: China and its neighbors—Japan, Korea, and Vietnam. There are also a less well-defined cultural zone (the Malay realm), a hybrid zone meshing Sinic and Indic influences that overlie parts of the Malay zone, and isolated pockets of aboriginal and Western cultures. Within these realms peoples and their values are the epitome of diversity. Similarly, the material development of the region runs the gamut from ultrarich and highly sophisticated to some of the most backward societies known.

166

Measured against that diversity, gauging the status of democracy presents manifest problems. Accordingly, each country study commences with an assessment of what "democracy" meant to that country throughout its history. Was there an indigenous democratic tradition prior to contact with Westerners? How did Western values influence perceptions of democracy, considering the less-than-democratic Western behavior within Western countries and by Westerners in Asia? How thoroughly does each country understand the theory and practice of democracy? Finally, for each country an attempt will be made to ascertain why the country in 1985 is becoming more (or less) pluralistic by assessing the domestic and external forces influencing the country's level of democracy.

RANKINGS

It is easiest to identify the most and least democratic. The area's clear examples of "stable democracies" are Japan, the most highly developed state, and Australia and New Zealand, two culturally Western states. All three are viable democracies, thriving in the hands of citizens who actively and enthusiastically practice democracy. At the other end of the spectrum are the "absolutist" communist states of the region: The People's Republic of China, the Democratic People's Republic of Korea, the Socialist Republic of Vietnam, the People's Republic of Kampuchea, and the People's Democratic Republic of Laos. Though there is increasing societal pluralism in contemporary China, politically it is nearly as absolutist as its smaller communist neighbors. North Korea, Vietnam, and Kampuchea remain firmly absolutist. Thinly populated Laos may be less heavy-handed, but it falls in this category.

Despite facades of democracy, and their people's aspirations for greater democratic pluralism, both the Republic of Korea (ROK) and the Republic of China (ROC) on Taiwan belong in the "partial democracies" category. Moreover, because of the military's strong role in South Korea and Taiwan, neither ranks in the upper portion of their category. The most democratic of the region's "partial democracies" are Malaysia and Singapore. Neither's commitment to democracy looks as good on paper, but each functions in a more democratic fashion than either Taiwan or South Korea. Somewhat lower than the ROC and ROK on the scale of "partial democracies" are Thailand

and Indonesia, where corruption and military cliques are overt influences inhibiting democracy. Lowest on the scale are Burma and the Philippines. Socialist Burma occupies this low rank because of its benign ineptness and inability to fulfill the desires of its people. The Philippines stands at the bottom because of the venality of its leaders, who frustrate the desires of its people, who have developed an appreciation for democracy. Papua New Guinea and Fiji also qualify for "partial democracy" status.

The category of "limited authoritarianism," includes two colonial "countries," Hong Kong and Macao. Hong Kong enjoys great societal pluralism along with its laissez-faire economy. Macao is a backwater anomaly. The third example of "limited authoritarianism" is Brunei, a Muslim monarchy whose paternalistic polity and oil wealth resemble a displaced Persian Gulf sheikdom. Its well-off citizens voice few complaints.

JAPAN

Many Westerners believe Japanese democracy is a post–World War II phenomenon, brought about by the enlightened policies of the U.S. occupation. This belief overlooks earlier roots of Japanese democracy. The most important go back to Japan's experiment with imported democratic structures during the late nineteenth- and early twentieth-century Meiji and Taisho eras. Though "Taisho Democracy" is often overrated, its impact on domestic opposition to imperialist policies in the 1930s and 1940s was a major legacy for the postwar era. Perhaps more profound, however, was Japan's Confucian legacy which showed ambiguity about democratic values.

The orthodox Confucianism that Japan imported early from China was a civil religion prescribing a hierarchical social order with well-defined classes. Its emphasis on hierarchy and subordination of the individual for the good of the group indicts Confucianism as an unegalitarian system contrary to individual rights or democracy. The Japanese significantly modified Confucianism by setting a military upper class at the top of the system, which made Japanese values even more hierarchical and authoritarian. However, the infusion of Japanese military values tended to underscore another element of Confucianism—the reciprocal obligations between leaders and followers. This produced greater societal cohesion, homogeneity, and groupthink than was found in China or other neighbors.

This outlook led Japan into fascism, but it also was the well-spring for a widespread appreciation of some facets of democracy. Within Japan's hierarchical social order and its thicket of intergroup relations, there is a predisposition toward consensual decision making in which virtually everyone's view is considered. When American authorities superimposed on that inclination a one man–one vote approach to democracy, most Japanese reluctantly accepted it. Japan's postwar leaders reassembled the facade of U.S.-style democracy on the foundation of traditional Japanese decision making.[2]

Neither American nor Western European patterns of democracy are entirely compatible with the Japanese way of thinking. The Japanese find adversarial politics raucous and repugnant. They consider up-or-down votes unfair to the losers. If forced by circumstances to such a vote, the winner frequently tries to salve the loser's feelings by compensating concessions. Western individualism in politics strikes many Japanese as egocentric and very un-Japanese, leading to accusations that Western Democracy is a "tyranny of the majority." The Japanese, viewing the turbulence of Western democracies and the failure of non-Western societies to copy closely Western models, believe they have struck a balance commensurate with their values.

One can criticize Japan's failure to be as democratic as other Western states. Japan in 1985 remained a hierarchical society with strongly authoritarian values and the structure of Western-style democracy might yet crack if Japanese society is strained internally by external pressures (i.e., over trade or security). Japanese democracy differs from that of the United States, Australia, or New Zealand, and, in a crisis, Japanese leaders probably will react in ways that might seem to threaten Western-style democracy. Yet no one should be unduly concerned because the Japanese ways of thinking about and implementing democracy are significantly different from those in the West.

This does not mean that foreigners should ignore Japan's unegalitarian attitudes toward its "untouchables" or its Korean ethnic minority. Nor should one ignore the persistent complaints of opposition party figures about the entrenched gerrymandering, payoffs, factional corruption, and feudal relationships that characterize Japanese politics. In many ways Japanese politics are reminiscent of U.S.-style ward-heeling politics. However, they add to the grass-roots' voice in decision making; in a perverse way, such abuses of democracy can play a democratic function.

During 1985 Japan's long-ruling Liberal Democratic party (LDP) remained firmly in control.[3] Because of the factional character of LDP politics and its grip on the Japanese political system, one should dismiss the criticism it receives in Japan as an undemocratic force in Japanese politics and focus on the internal politics of the LDP. In effect, the LDP factions act as de facto parties vying for power in coalitions that broker and balance competing interests against one another. The minority parties act as safety valves and, in the cases of the Democratic Socialists and Komeito, as external "factions" that could be brought into the LDP fold in an emergency. Interfactional rivalries are not particularly democratic, being semifeudal cliques run by leaders capable of raising and disbursing funds skillfully. Nonetheless, the factions need broad-based support with tentacles in the grass roots. Coupled with the necessity for consensus, intraparty politics must be judged democratic, albeit in a Japanese fashion.

Essentially Japanese democracy works well. Despite periodic violence by political radicals—such as the December 1985 sabotage of Tokyo and Isaka commuter rail lines[4]—which seems to threaten its stability, Japan's democracy is stable to the point of being akin to a game of musical chairs. There was some concern in 1985 that the unusual dynamism of Prime Minister Yasuhiro Nakasone has set the stage for increased political uncertainty because the contenders to succeed him in 1986 lack charisma. There is a chance that a return to a typically bland premier will adversely influence foreign impressions and encourage those in Japan who argue that more forceful leadership abilities will be required of future prime ministers. Though that logic is persuasive, few such candidates are in the wings, nor are they—or Nakasone—popular because of their egocentric behavior. On balance, such a shift should not be anticipated.[5] Instead, Japan will likely be led again by a series of reliable—if dull—prime ministers. Though this may portend problems in Japan's foreign relations, Japanese democracy is likely to remain healthy.

CHINA

The Chinese experience with democracy has been far less than Japan's. The Nationalist record on Taiwan is superior to that of the Chinese Communists, but neither have achieved the democracy Chinese idealists once sought. Unlike Japan's pragmatic approach to Western democracy—ingesting the theory and practice of democracy, digesting and adapting those portions deemed compatible, and discarding the rest—early Chinese would-be democrats tried to be selective from the start. China's smugness about the superiority of the Middle Kingdom's cultural legacy, and distrust of Western subversion of that legacy through proselytization of religious and civil values caused mid-nineteenth-century China to reject Western ideas about democracy. That rejection was supported by Confucian values, which denigrated the role of individual rights in favor of group cohesion, and by the need to reassert firm leadership over a weakened regime. The conservative elite had little interest in experimenting with democracy.

Even would-be successors to the last dynasty were encumbered by the Middle Kingdom's past greatness. Most could not bring themselves to look to the West for alternatives. They simply wanted to reform their system, borrowing a bit from the West but mainly looking to China's Golden Ages for guidance. Few considered radical reformation like the Japanese. The result was a halfhearted attempt to modernize, which produced only feudal warlordism and a quasi-colonial slicing of China into foreign zones of influence. In the absence of a central authority, China slipped further into disorder and corruption.

Beset by such problems, and influenced by Japan's emergence as the most aggressive foreign power, Chinese revolutionaries ultimately decided to fight Western fire with Western fire, using Western organizing principles in both politics and the military. By the 1930s and 1940s the two strains that emerged from this mix were the Nationalists and the Communists, one proclaiming democratic-capitalist values and the other asserting Marxist-Leninist political and economic values. Drawing sustenance from opposite ends of the West's intellectual menu, both positioned themselves as advocates of a progressive China that would be free of foreign domination. The communists emerged victorious, forming the People's Republic of China (PRC) in 1949 and forcing the Nationalists to Taiwan. Since then both regimes have pursued the same egalitarian and progressive goals, but neither has achieved them.

TAIWAN

The ROC has achieved many of the goals the nationalist Kuo Min Tang (KMT) once sought for all of China, but they have attained them only on their little island. Taipei's freedom from a two-front war and enhanced access to free-world trade facilitated their successes. However, the ROC's understandable garrison state mentality inhibits the democracy they proclaim. Thus, Taiwan in 1985 did not enjoy the freedom to which its people and leaders aspire. Political tensions are exacerbated by the domination of an aging mainland leadership cadre over the native Taiwanese and younger Chinese, and the heavy weight of hierarchical Chinese traditions. Taiwan's democratic activists want more democracy of the sort enjoyed in the modern West and Japan, but in a Chinese form that will not dilute their values.

Most of Taiwan's political tensions go unnoticed abroad because they are repressed and poorly reported overseas, and they pale into insignificance when juxtaposed with Taiwan's declining diplomatic status. Two major exceptions in 1984–85 cast the spotlight on Taiwan's less-than-democratic ways. In October 1984 a press critic of the KMT, Henry Liu, was killed in northern California by thugs working for the Taiwanese military. In September 1985, another press critic from California (Lee Ya-ping) was charged with sedition in Taiwan.[6]

The Taiwan government remains an authoritarian regime ruled by a small political clique in the KMT with the strong backing of the military. Given the precarious health of the current leader, Chiang Ching-kuo, a succession crisis is approaching. Rival factions are positioning themselves for that prospect. Given the ROC's Soviet-style political structures, deciphering the maneuvering behind the scenes of this ardently anticommunist state is ironically akin to Kremlin-watching. The odds are against a more pluralistic regime emerging. Instead, another generation of civil-military cronies is likely to take over and there is little chance that the constraints on Taiwanese democracy maintained through 1985 will be lifted. Instead, authorities in Taipei seemed preoccupied with preventing a crisis of legitimacy involving the succession issue, the gradual demise of the KMT's geriatric provincial representatives who embody the facade of a national government, and—most serious—uncertainties caused by the tendency of Taiwan's elites to hedge their bets over Taiwan's future by establishing financial and legal safety nets abroad. This tends to create the impression among the people who are excluded from power and lack the ability to hedge their bets that the very leaders who extoll them to persevere may be ready to desert the ship.

Although Taiwan is authoritarian, compared to China it is a soft authoritarian state, in which most people enjoy a reasonable degree of civil rights, economic freedom and security, and improving living standards. Most Taiwanese are not very agitated by the low level of democracy. They appear satisfied with their lot and accept the constraints imposed on their liberties as necessary for their security and in harmony with China's traditions. Thus, it will not be easy for Taiwanese advocates of democracy to generate support. Whether the ROC remains intact, or Taiwan enters the Chinese fold, democracy on Taiwan does not have a bright future.

PEOPLE'S REPUBLIC OF CHINA

To avoid pessimism about Taiwan, one must measure it against the dismal democracy of China. For its short history the People's Republic of China (PRC) has been a thoroughly totalitarian state. On a Stalinist model, Mao built a state that evolved from a rigidly authoritarian equality for the masses into a chaotic experiment with perpetually self-replicating revolutionary activity. It culminated in the disastrous Great Cultural Revolution, designed to throw off the debilitating legacy of China's past. The communists set out to create a new China, populated by an improved version of the Chinese. The Maoists assumed revolutionary fervor would simultaneously rid China of the old ways and reveal the alternatives leading China to a brighter future.

The results were devastating. Radical Maoists were destroying China's viability when Mao curbed Red Guard excesses and, in the mid-1970s reasserted a more moderate approach. Yet the Maoist "Gang of Four" who succeeded him attempted to return China to an extremist course. Cooler heads prevailed, however, enabling Deng Xiaoping to put China on a more pragmatic course by the late 1970s.

Throughout modern China's tumultuous efforts to create a more egalitarian society, democracy was judged an illusion that would distract the masses from creating a communist society. Such perceptions stem not only from Marxist dogma but from deep-seated Chinese cynicism about the efficacy of democracy. Even if it works elsewhere (and most Chinese communists were unwilling to accept that proposition in light of U.S. racial problems and British class conflicts), few thought it appropriate in China's circumstances. Because of past Chinese lapses, when egocentric corruption and cronyism overcame attempts to put the national commonwealth first, few Chinese leaders seemed prepared to experiment with democracy.

By the mid-1980s China, though still totalitarian, is experimenting with profit motives, free enterprise, and enhanced mobility.[7] Many foreign observers prematurely concluded that China is reverting to the China of old, succumbing to the blandishments of capitalism, and on the verge of abandoning its destructive course since 1949. Though there is truth in these observations, more accurately China should be seen as a dedicated communist state trying to adapt what it views as the best Marxist-Leninist virtues to the most useful techniques of Western capitalism. Deng Xiaoping, summing up a major 1985 Chinese Communist party conference, said, "only socialism can eliminate the greed, corruption, and injustice that are inherent in capitalism."

At long last, China is doing what Japan once did: adsorbing a great deal from abroad, experimenting to see what fits China's needs, and absorbing only what it can use. China may call the product "communism," but it will not be closely comparable with Soviet communism. If Deng succeeds, China is likely to see a refinement of the markedly pluralistic society emerging in 1985. The shakeup of party leaders in September 1985, in which 131 elderly officials were retired and 189 younger supporters of Deng's policies were appointed to senior posts,[8] provides reason to believe this pluralism will continue. China is becoming more tolerant of diversity, and some of its traditional "Golden Mean" pragmatism is again evident. This partial reversion to traditional ways has facilitated the PRC's remarkably rapid adjustment to very uncommunist economic reforms.

However, this display of flexibility should not be construed as sufficient tolerance for even a limited democratic renaissance. There is a delicate political balance at work in contemporary China that permits its leaders, who remain dedicated to the same long-term goals as Mao, to pursue those goals by means that differ radically from the Maoist approach. Maoism has been discredited, giving Deng some latitude for experimentation, but he does not have a clean slate upon which to design a new China. The China that seems to be taking shape today almost certainly will have to conform to Marxian expectations.[9] Should the Dengists falter, there will be ample critics ready to seize the opportunity.

Should Dengism ultimately meet the fate of Maoism, Chinese communism's viable options will be severely constrained if it is to retain any pretension of being "communist." To avoid that dilemma, China's leaders must retain their ideological credibility and legitimacy by—if possible—shunting aside nascent aspirations for political pluralism and—if necessary—supressing its advocates. One might assume that China's growing economic pluralism will help set the stage for democracy, but this is not necessarily true, because the rise of democracy would likely be regarded as an intolerable threat to China's party elites and their vision of China. Even if the Chinese communists could overcome their strong ideological opposition to democracy—and there is no sign of that—they would oppose it in practice as inappropriate for China's needs.

Democracy was anathema in 1985 China because it is too uncertain and subject to disruptive external influences. The expressions of Chinese popular political feelings on big character posters at Beijing's "democracy wall," or the protests in Tienanmen Square, especially between 1978–80, were snuffed out before they got out of hand. Such feelings resurfaced during 1985 when government-encouraged anti-Japanese demonstrations got out of control and shifted their focus to calls for democracy. By year's end, these student-led democratic protests had become a moderate challenge to the stability the Deng regime needs for its "Four Modernizations" program to succeed.[10] Consequently, these signs of Chinese desires for democracy face dim prospects. Most Chinese, like most Taiwanese, seem intent on staying out of trouble with political authorities. For both, pursuit of material opportunities outweighs the desire for democracy.

KOREA

Korea's experiences with democracy fall between those of Japan and China, but closer to China's.[11] When Korea's last dynasty was tottering, reformers were divided, as in China, between conservatives hoping to restore a decaying regime and progressives who looked overseas for inspiration. The most progressive admired Japan's modernization. In the course of the Sino-Japanese and Russo-Japanese wars, Korea succumbed to Japan's influence. Idealistic Koreans hoped that the United States might assert a corollary of its

Open Door Doctrine for Korea, but they were disappointed, and Japanese colonial policies in Korea were oppressive.

Koreans who supported self-determination looked to foreigners for sympathy. Despite earlier disappointments, many Koreans hoped for educational, political, and religious succor from the United States. U.S. support was tepid at best, but some Korean patriots found refuge in the United States. More important, American missionaries provided educational and intellectual opportunities that exposed Koreans to democracy. These factors were important for the development of the Republic of Korea, but Japanese suppression of Korean freedom fighters, especially communists, drove many leftist Koreans to the USSR or Chinese borders. Cynical about the ability of democracy or capitalism to rescue Korea from Japan, these Koreans heeded Moscow's calls for world revolution and Chinese communist appeals for help. After World War II, when the emerging Cold War led the United States and the Soviet Union to foster rival Korean states, Moscow was prepared to install a viable totalitarian regime, while Washington halfheartedly backed a democratic alternative with little more than good intentions.

REPUBLIC OF KOREA

South Korea's start in 1948 was not auspicious. U.S. officials on the scene had difficulty in finding authentically popular political figures among the numerous pretenders. The result was the selection of a group led by Syngman Rhee, who were compatible with Americans and anticommunist, but who were basically authoritarian. They admired the democracy they read about and saw practiced in the West, especially in the United States, but interpreted democratic theory and practice by infusing Confucian hierarchic ideas. The ROK's U.S. mentors were displeased by this version of democracy, but ascribed it to inexperience, happy that South Korea, with all its handicaps, maintained even a semblance of democracy.

South Korea's student activists were not so ready to condone flaws in the Rhee regime. Led by idealists who took ROK and U.S. promises of democracy at face value, the students demanded democratic reforms and an end to the cronyism plaguing the South Korean economy. The ROK military backed these demands, as did the United States, though less overtly. The Rhee regime fell in 1960. It was replaced by a transitory regime whose democratic reforms were undisciplined and seemed to the military to threaten anarchy. The 1961 Park Chung-hee coup ended that turmoil but ushered in military-backed governments under Park and, since 1980, Chun Doo-hwan.

Neither Park nor Chun, who replaced Park by a controversial power grab after Park's assassination in 1979, demonstrated great interest in democratic principles. Both wanted a disciplined government to guide South Korea toward material progress and strategic stability. They paid attention to "democracy" to mollify domestic pressures for a full-fledged democracy and satisfy U.S. desires that its ally demonstrate progress toward democratic goals.

Dissidents in the political, intellectual, student, clerical, and labor ranks appear intent on challenging Seoul until it allows true democracy. The government hopes periodic alterations in the trappings of democracy will maintain quiet at home and quell foreign pressures. But because of South Korea's greater aspirations for its economic and political future and the U.S. connection—still crucial to South Korea—the ROK cannot slough off external criticism or deny media access to its domestic politics. Consequently, South Korea's democratic flaws are regularly exposed.

The best known opposition figure is Kim Dae-jung, a skilled spokesman for democracy. His past trials, imprisonment, and exile to the United States were well publicized. His manhandling upon his February 1985 return to Korea, in the company of U.S. human rights activists, gave Seoul a public relations black eye. Also in 1985, a series of antigovernment student protests peaked in the May seizure of the U.S. Information Agency (USIA) Library in Seoul to denounce alleged U.S. complicity in Chun's takeover, his harsh suppression of the 1980 Kwangju uprising, and continuation or intensification of his authoritarian denial of democracy.

How accurate were the accusations?[12] The Park and Chun regimes were and are authoritarian, often restraining democracy severely on grounds that it can undercut national security by allowing North Korean agitation. Still, under U.S. pressures and a genuine appreciation of rising popular demands for greater democracy, Seoul has made a guarded commitment to political pluralism. A wide range of political parties are active in South Korea, even including minor socialist groups which the government sanctions to improve the ROK's worldwide relations.

Despite access to the political arena, political power rests in the hands of an ex-military and active-duty military elite with some business leaders and technocrats. Unmet democratic aspirations deflected toward a Japan-like system (dominated by a conservative elite while liberal activists dissipate their energies in meaningless party activities) identify South Korea as a soft authoritarian state. South Korea is "softer" than Taiwan and its prospects for achieving democracy are significantly greater. Demands for democracy are greater in South Korea than in Taiwan, and Seoul has made more explicit commitments for reform than has Taipei. However, the product of those commitments—South Korea's ruling and opposition parties—tend to be raucous. Their tendency to degenerate into factional clashes and strong-arm tactics—exemplified in the early December 1985 pandemonium in the National Assembly—diminishes popular respect for the limited democracy Seoul enjoys.

If the Chun government hews to its agenda, which it reaffirmed repeatedly in 1985, it will yield to a more civilian regime in 1988. That coincides with the Seoul-hosted international Olympics, an unsurpassed opportunity for democratic activists to press their case before the international media.

DEMOCRATIC PEOPLE'S REPUBLIC OF KOREA

While one could argue the quality of South Korea's democratic record, in North Korea's case there is no argument, for there is no democracy. North Korea, under Kim Il-sung, is probably the most rigid, repressive regime in the international system. Based on Stalinist principles of centralized rule, terrorism, and deceit, the Pyongyang regime lacks any democratic value.

North Korea's founders were Soviet functionaries who gathered a Korean cadre from the ranks of Soviet and Chinese communist forces. The Koreans who served in such positions were a mixed group. Few were attracted by a prior knowledge of Marxism. The majority were anti-Japanese patriots who fled to the nearest sources of succor. There they put their energies into the anticolonial struggle that helped oust Japan. They did not plan to become communists, but many did because of the milieu in which they worked. The process was aided by their contempt for weak foreign democracies that did not help Korea. Though many of those Koreans sought freedom and egalitarian goals, the trauma they experienced made them receptive to Marxism.

When World War II ended and these Koreans returned to their homeland, they found two liberators. Returnees to North Korea found a sympathetic protector. Those going to South Korea found their claims to leadership rejected by the U.S. liberators. As the Cold War intensified ideological divisions among Koreans, many leftists drifted north to a more hospitable political climate, producing struggles in North Korea among rivals for Moscow's blessing. Some sophisticated, articulate communists who held high positions were purged in the 1940s and 1950s as a lesser-known figure, Kim Il-sung, an obedient Stalinist, rose to the top. Egalitarian objectives fell by the wayside as a rigid North Korean regime established itself, fought an aggressive war, and regrouped after it failed.

Because of Korea-China cultural ties, North Korean gratitude for greater Chinese help in the war than was provided by the USSR, and Sino-Soviet tensions, Pyongyang gradually adjusted its position between Beijing and Moscow despite Kim's credentials as a Soviet creature. This put Pyongyang on a fence between its erstwhile backers, and created both opportunities and problems. Soviet post-Stalin upheavals did not sit well with Pyongyang, but the Kim regime was also unsettled by China's disorder under both Maoist extremists and de-Maoification. The cult of Kim, verging on deification as the secular god of an atheistic society, indicated a sense that North Korea's way was the true path to communism, and others were heretical. Kim apparently planned to create a dynasty by the succession of his son, Kim Jung-il.

By 1985, however, cracks appeared on that facade. After Pyongyang's disastrous attempt to destroy South Korea's core leadership in the 1983 Rangoon bombing of President Chun's touring entourage, North Korea shifted to a more moderate posture. On the economic front North Korea in 1984 edged closer to China's economic experimentation by praising China's "Four Modernizations," adopting the development zone concept, and opening to foreign investment. These efforts continued with marginal results in 1985. However, North Korea has not gone nearly as far down this experimental path. Similarly, North Korea's flirtation with Chinese economic flexibility stands even less chance of being converted to gains for political pluralism. Also in 1984–85, North Korea tried to compensate for its Rangoon blunder by making overtures to South Korea and its friends. These overtures peaked in a series of North-South talks ostensibly aimed at tension reduction.

Despite the benign face it tried to present in 1985, Pyongyang remains what it has been for decades: a hardline, Stalinist state with its obsessive drive to unify Korea on Kim Il-sung's terms and a paranoid fear of sinister forces supposedly threatening it.[13] By keeping its people at fever pitch and ready for war, Pyongyang enforces an automaton-like regimentation. Regardless of who succeeds Kim Il-sung, the legacy of Kimism will be an inhibiting force over North Korean freedom of thought and action for years.

VIETNAM

The other major state in the Sinic cultural realm, Vietnam, is in the Southeast Asian rather than East Asian geographic zone. This distinction is important because Vietnam shares the dominant legacies that shape both regions: very strong Confucian influences from its northern neighbor and the complex influences of Western colonialism. No other major part of the Sinic realm experienced long-term Western colonialism.

Vietnam's history is marked by its persistent efforts to remain free of foreign domination. Despite ethnic ties and centuries of Chinese suzerainty, the Vietnamese consistently stressed their own identity. Because this was more difficult for the Vietnamese than the Koreans, who are a distinct and different people, the Vietnamese have been ambiguous about China. Though proud of adapted Chinese values, they have long struggled against Chinese dominance. Vietnam's great historical heroes were anticolonial figures trying to throw off the Chinese yoke.

When French colonialists arrived, many Vietnamese learned to treat them as another wave of foreign oppressors. Vietnam's independence had been snatched from them again, this time by a nation which preached freedom, liberty, and equality while denying them to colonial subjects.

After World War II Vietnam's fate was precarious. French colonialists thought they had earned the right to return to their empire; but Vietnamese nationalists, heady with hopes of independence, were as adamant about keeping them out. There followed a long and bitter war between the French and the Viet Minh. It is arguable whether postwar Vietnamese nationalism might have avoided a marked shift to the far left had the French not reimposed themselves in Indochina. Nonetheless, the French reappeared and the Vietnamese reacted adversely. Vietnamese communists appealed for support as nationalists on the basis that the French were supported by other noncommunist states—especially the United States—trying to deny the Vietnamese what they proclaimed as a universal human right, namely freedom and democracy.

When the French were defeated, the Viet Minh had a pronounced Marxist identity. Nonetheless, not all Vietnam's nationalists were communists or antidemocratic. After France's ouster, Vietnam's politics was complicated by rivalries among the nationalists, supported by separate camps in the Cold War. Vietnam, like Korea, became a divided nation, and South Vietnam was vulnerable. Much as Saigon's leaders respected the democratic freedoms of the West and wanted to emulate some version of those values for Vietnam, they always had difficulty reconciling their nationalist aspirations for an independent and free Vietnam with the realities and appearances of growing, and ultimately massive, foreign influence over their policies. While Saigon's backers aspired to freedom and democracy, a new and worse round of war gradually forced South Vietnam to yield some of its independence to U.S. decision makers and constrain democracy in South Vietnam so that North Vietnamese could not disrupt southern society.

Since Saigon's fall, the few aspects of democracy formerly enjoyed in South Vietnam have been smothered by communist ideology, bureaucracy, and regimentation.[14] Those political and religious activists in South Vietnam who clamored for freedom and democracy and protested against South Vietnam and the United States for denying it to them, if they survived Hanoi's purges, or the hazards of being "boatpersons," were by 1985 either in Vietnamese prisons, or dwelling abroad as refugees.

Repression has been exacerbated by continuation of hostilities. Hanoi sought to control neighboring Kampuchea, then in the throes of a bloody restructuring of Khmer society. It also rid Vietnamese society of ethnic Chinese. This was part of an effort to put some distance between Vietnam and the PRC, which was displaying signs of expansionism. Vietnam received support from the Soviet Union and gave Moscow basing rights in former U.S. facilities. In 1985 it remained a heavily armed garrison state, sporadically fighting a two-front war, and playing host to a sizable Soviet presence.

It may be that Vietnam's leaders are capable of operating only in a war-oriented society, as they have been accustomed to for many years, and they run the civilian sector of their society on the principles developed for the military settings they know best. This may explain both the economic failures of Vietnam in the past decade and its inability to foster a more relaxed postwar atmosphere.

However, there are portents of change in Vietnam. Hanoi's independent-minded nationalism has raised frictions over the Soviet force presence that could spell future trouble. Similarly, Hanoi's mid-1980s foreign policy has an innovative strain, apparently hoping to improve political and economic relations with noncommunist states in the region and with the United States. Although Hanoi clearly is not emulating Beijing's example, it is pursuing some parallel experimentation with economic reforms. None of these steps would require domestic political liberalization, but they hint at greater societal flexibility and pluralism.[15] Further, the apparent inability of Hanoi's leaders to snuff out the spontaneity of the southern Vietnamese (compared to the more dour northern Vietnamese) provides the potential for more diversity. The experiments being conducted with private sector economic incentives—producing a marked shift toward economic pluralism—coupled with the Vietnamese people's passion for national independence, provide hope that in the long run the Vietnamese can achieve a degree of political pluralism within the constraints of their Marxism. In the face of the Soviet Union's evident ambitions in Southeast Asia that are pegged to bases in Vietnam,[16] Vietnam's historical struggle for freedom may make it a more likely candidate for relaxing its rigid ways than either China or North Korea.

MACAO

Hong Kong and Macao are two relics of the colonial era, remnants, respectively, of the British and Portuguese empires. Both are anachronisms that superficially appear embarrassments to China's leaders, who long have railed against colonialism and neocolonialism yet tolerated it on Chinese soil. China could have seized both of them, almost at will, for many years, yet did not do so. Moreover, the Portuguese would happily be rid of Macao. After Portugal's 1974 military coup, designed to reduce overseas burdens, Macao has been merely administered by the Portuguese. Mao's China was not anxious to have it back, nor is Deng's. Macao has been an entrepreneurial center, a window to the wider world, and a living reminder of China's maltreatment by imperialists. Macao is now only a pseudocolony, but its Portuguese officials still rule firmly, with the advice of an elected assembly (dissolved in 1984 after a dispute with the governor).

When Macao is returned (negotiations start in March 1986), China hopes the Portuguese will have been repatriated and the dwindling Macanese will have either departed or accepted Chinese identity. Because Macao has had little experience with freedom or democracy, and less hope of achieving either, eventual integration with China has generated little anxiety. This contrasts markedly with Hong Kong, which has experienced severe jitters.

HONG KONG

Hong Kong's anxiety does not stem from fear that its residents will lose the democracy they enjoy, for they do not participate in democratic self-rule. Its forte long has been a preoccupation with entrepreneurial economics and an almost apolitical internal ambiance as China was wracked by the trauma of weak governments, poverty, and violence. British colonial rule sheltered Hong Kong from China's storms. The benefits of political and economic stability trickled down to Chinese clustered in the enclave who appreciated life in a safe haven in the midst of China's turmoil.

Beijing chose not to take Hong Kong for a variety of reasons. It provided a social safety valve and link to the capitalist world, especially to countries which refused to accept China's communist rulers as legitimate. Though some Hong Kong Chinese held strong political views, most were emphatically apolitical to avoid antagonizing anyone and allow Hong Kong to go about its business—for the business of Hong Kong is business.

Hong Kong's preoccupation with entrepreneurship made it valuable to China, and enabled Britain to perpetuate a colonial administration with strong guidance by the prominent Chinese business and banking elites whose activities justify Hong Kong's existence. Freedom for Hong Kong is not a political question but an economic one. Democracy is not feasible for Hong Kong in the shadow of a totalitarian state.

PRC-British negotiations over Hong Kong's fate made the Hong Kong Chinese very nervous, but an agreement was reached in 1984 that will bring Hong Kong under Chinese rule in 1997. The agreement, reached under the diplomatic gun of a Chinese ultimatum to unilaterally return Hong Kong to China, was remarkably considerate of Hong Kong Chinese concerns over future economic freedoms, for it was based largely on Deng's idea of "one country, two systems."

This device, with its obvious implications for a reunification of Taiwan and China, sounds good in principle. However, Hong Kong Chinese harbor two main concerns. First, Deng's commitments may not mean much should China again turn leftward. Second, even if Dengists retain control, there is doubt that they can tolerate the laissez-faire experimentalism of Hong Kong and allow Hong Kong freedoms almost denied to China's internal enclaves.[17]

INDIC/SINIC REALM

Indochina implies the merger of Indian and Chinese influences. But Vietnam has only remnants of early Indic peoples absorbed into minority status over the centuries. The other two Indochinese states, Kampuchea and Laos, are products of merged political cultures, being partial spinoffs of India's very different political culture. Though neither Thailand nor Burma are normally identified as "Indochinese," they both fit the dual legacy mold. Consequently, these four states will be examined as a distinct subset.

KAMPUCHEA

Kampuchea is a small state with a long history of independence, often threatened by neighboring Vietnam and Thailand. The Khmers possess an ethnic and historical consciousness very different from the Thai or Vietnamese. Ancient Khmer kingdoms, derived from Indian political and religious traditions, left important legacies for the Khmer people.

When French colonialists seized power, the Cambodians succumbed with equanimity because these subordinate relations with a distant state enabled the Khmer to maintain their identity. As a result, the Khmers lived without fear of Vietnamese or Thai aggression.

In this milieu they cultivated an otherworldly religious orientation. Coupled with a fatalistic respect for secular authority inherited from Hindu traditions, this produced an apolitical passivity. This was inherently infertile soil for democracy. The French did nothing to develop democratic values in Khmer or other Indochinese societies, preferring to cultivate a Francophone elite as an intermediate layer between the French and the masses.

The Cambodian reaction to French efforts to reassert its colonial prerogatives after World War II was not as violent as the Vietnamese reaction. The Khmer—though sharing the same anticolonial boat as the Vietnamese—would not pull on the same set of oars. Led by Prince Norodom Sihanouk, whom the French had installed, Khmer patriots strove for an independent monarchy. As the Vietnamese sealed France's colonial fate in the region, Cambodia benefited by joining the decolonization process. Throughout the 1950s and 1960s, the Khmers kept the horrors of Vietnam's next round of war from encroaching on Cambodia's fragile tranquility. The ability to remain near, yet aloof from, Vietnamese hostility and Thailand's preparation for hostilities stemmed from Cambodia's apparently overwhelming popular support for an alternative route to peace and prosperity, namely reliance on traditional ways.

During this artificial isolation from the problems surrounding Cambodia, most Khmer lacked rights to participate in their own governance. "Democracy" was no more meaningful for most Khmer than "capitalism" or "communism." They seemed content with life free from the strife, intrigue, and devastation on their borders. However, a 1970 palace coup sought to preserve Cambodia by delivering it into the Western camp for protection. Instead of enhanced security, however, it emneshed Cambodia in the very conflicts it had tried to avoid. For the next five years Cambodia was wracked by the Indochina war. Previously minor leftist political forces in Cambodia were stimulated in opposition to the Lon Nol regime and its monarchist predecessors. Cambodia's leftists, less sophisticated than their Vietnamese counterparts, were nativist-anarchists marching under the banner of Marxism because it coincided with their aspirations.

Saigon and Phnom Penh collapsed before a communist onslaught at about the same time, but with very different results. While southern Vietnam succumbed to an orderly effort to remake it along Marxist lines, Cambodia, renamed "Kampuchea," slipped into three years of genocidal terrorism to purge Khmer society of elements that might block the Pol Pot regime's primitivist movement. The slaughter had nothing to do with Marxism or socialism, but it eliminated nearly all political opponents or likely opponents of the regime. Vietnamese invasion and the imposition of a Vietnamese-backed regime drove Pol Pot's Khmer Rouge into the hills as guerrilla forces. These forces joined a sometimes united front headed by Sihanouk, recognized by much of the world as the legitimate Khmer authority, while the Vietnam-backed puppets ran most of the country. Because of the historical significance of contemporary Vietnamese domination over Cambodia, the only government with the power to effect positive change is anathema to many Khmer.[18]

LAOS

Laos has been a backwater throughout its history. Prior to French rule, Laos had only brief episodes of political importance. Laotian history was marked by alternating domination by the Vietnamese or the Lao's southern cousins, the Thai. Traditional Lao political culture was shaped by both, but most Lao rulers adhered more closely to the less Sinic-influenced Thai models of government. Thus, the Laotians—like Cambodians—had a largely apolitical value system. Except for elites around the leaders, participation in governance was neither an expectation nor a hope.

Anti-French hostilities in Vietnam inevitably spilled over into Laos. Laos suffered a copy of Vietnam's troubles, except that the Pathet Lao, the local communists, never displayed an ideological drive comparable to their Vietnamese counterparts. Laotian political factionalism seemed a relabeling of traditional rivalries under foreign influences. When the Pathet Lao came into power in 1975 they were neither as thorough as their Vietnamese comrades nor as bloodthirsty as the Khmer.

Laos, at the end of 1985, remains a poverty-ridden communist backwater.[19] The Lao enjoy some advantages, especially reliance on their traditional ways and the latitude to pay lip service to Marxism's rigors while pursuing their more relaxed way of life. But Laos has no prospect of much democracy.

THAILAND

Thailand, with very different experiences with freedom, has a more complex legacy. Alone in Southeast Asia, Thailand avoided subjugation by foreign imperialists. A buffer zone between the British and French colonial empires, it maintained its independence by bending to the demands of both external powers while modernizing its government and society. This process was reminiscent of the ways in which the ancient Thai political culture grew from different Sinic and Indic influences. Though the Thai are an ethnic offshoot of China, and maintain substantial cultural ties with it, they also derived ideas from India-oriented regimes they conquered.

Though absolute rulers, modern Thai monarchs generally were perceived as fair. However, there was no significant effort made to introduce Western concepts of democratic rights, unlike in the Asian country Thai leaders emulated most, Japan. In the early 1930s a coup brought to power a group of militarists sympathetic to Japan's version of fascism. Thailand was on the losing side in World War II, but it did not pay a heavy price because the victors interpreted wartime Thai choices as necessary to preserve their independence in the face of Japanese threats. Right-wing officers remained in control until the late 1950s, when a succession of more moderate but still dictatorial officers began their musical chairs rotations.

In 1973 Thailand shifted toward shaky civilian rule, but this lasted only until 1976, when another coup partially restored the status quo ante and a succession of quasi-military governments. Nonetheless, these recent governments have been ostensibly "civilian," and signify some movement toward democracy as the military perceived the need to present at least the facade of a popularly supported government for both domestic and international appearance. It is unclear to what extent Thailand's edging toward greater democracy reflects Thai wishes for democracy or is a way to generate U.S. confidence that Thailand warrants defending.

The shaky "democracy" of 1985 was strong enough to withstand in mid-year yet another aborted coup attempt, but the monarchy felt compelled to lend its prestige to stabilize the regime.[20] The monarchy has long remained out of politics and has had a respected symbolic role, providing a sense of continuity and identity for the nation.

Thailand is a nation with weak democratic traditions making what for it is a significant effort to civilianize its government and open the way for political liberalization. If the present trend continues, Thailand will approach the democratic aspirations of such countries as South Korea and the Philippines.

BURMA

Burma is an odd mixture of layers of Indian, Sinic, Mon, Thai, and British colonial political cultures, upon which twentieth-century Burmese modernizers superimposed a distorted version of socialism. The Burmese were among the first Third World peoples to reject colonial rule by staging rebellions in the early 1930s that produced Burma's administrative separation from the British Raj in India, and internal autonomy by 1937. A reason for the progress was the sophistication of Burmese elites in political affairs. During World War II Burma became active politically, as it was as a theater of war, putting the nationalistic Burmese in a position after the war to press for independence, which was attained in 1948.

After independence Burma was troubled for years by rebellions of an assortment of communist groups and ethnic minorities. The problems led to the 1962 army coup that introduced General Ne Win's "Burmese Way to Socialism." This ill-defined and poorly implemented approach to Burma's difficulties produced a decade's experiment with isolationism. Though Burma partially emerged from its isolationist cocoon in the mid-1970s, it is unable to really move out in the world. Because of this hesitancy Burma has floundered, internally and diplomatically.

Since 1974, when over 90 percent of the Burmese electorate approved Ne Win's socialist constitution in a referendum, Burma has been a "Socialist Republic." This may reflect popular support for the Rangoon regime, an ideosyncratic government predicated on the whims of Ne Win and his cadres. The nearest parallel to Burma's confused single-mindedness may be North Korea's version of universal truth, though Burma's ways are far less ruthless, and nonaggressive. Each in its own way is trying to fashion an exemplar of a state. In Burma's case, preoccupation with the virtues of its unique insights into self-reliant progress produced a state that meanders, aware of its problems but held up by smugness about the ultimate correctness of its ways. The Burmese have little say in how their lives are run, but they do not seem perturbed by this. The ethnic minorities that persistently mount insurgencies on Burma's fringes use the rhetoric of self-determination, but few of them construe such rhetoric in democratic forms. Burma ranks low in the democratic scale, but it is not particularly heavyhanded, and it tries to project the image of a benevolent socialist state.

THE MALAY REALM

The Malay Realm is comprised of four states with common Malay roots (Malaysia, Indonesia, Brunei, and the Philippines) and one with mixed Malay, Chinese, and Indian roots (Singapore). Though these states share ethnic bonds that influence their domestic political cultures and all are members in the Association of Southeast Asian Nations, (ASEAN), there are notable differences in their polities and versions of democracy.

MALAYSIA

Malaysia consists of peninsular Malaya and East Malaysia. British colonial rule over these areas was indirect. Minor Malayan states, each ruled by a paternalistic monarch in a political system influenced by successive waves of South Asian Hindu, then Muslim, styles succumbed to British pressures and accepted a protectorate status. Historically, the Malay states had been subordinated to some extent to external powers, so the situation was not new. British rule allowed considerable local autonomy as long as British economic interests were secured. British control over East Malaysia (Sabah and Sarawak) was economically more direct, but politically even more diffuse. Private British companies ran these areas using the same indirect rule techniques with an additional layer of private intermediaries between the Malays and the British colonial administration.

During the colonial period, which lasted until 1957 for Malaya and 1963 for East Malaysia, internal politics among the Malays became more complicated because many Chinese and, to a lesser extent, Indians were brought to Malaya as laborers. These immigrants, especially the Chinese, worked their way into closer relationships with the British and the economically advanced in Malaya's society. Consequently, frictions emerged between the Malays and non-Malays. Organizing the aspirations of these subgroups helped to develop their political consciousness. As a result of these processes, plus the education the colonial elites received at British hands and the experience of putting down a communist insurrection, there emerged a significant appreciation for democratic values, which was transmitted to independent Malaysia and Singapore.

Malaysia is an unusual mixture of tradition and innovation. Sultans rule each state in the Federation, but with popularly elected officials who participate in the federal parliament. Malaysia's monarchs, too, are elected by their fellow sultans for a five-year term. This has produced some high quality leadership and has democratic aspects. Yet, because Malaysia has many monarchists who wish to strengthen the powers of state and federal monarchs, plus those who would like a theocratic Islamic state, the status of democracy is insecure. By the end of 1985 Islamic fundamentalist Parti Islami, based in Malaysia's northern states, was gaining strength at the expense of the long ruling party, UMNO. This is complicated by the continuing tensions between Malays and Chinese within Malaysia. Prime Minister Datuk Seri Mahathir's November 1985 visit to Beijing was, in part, an effort to reduce those tensions.[21] In addition, Malaysian politics is troubled by charges of corruption, factionalism, inefficiency, and repression of dissent. However, dynamic reform efforts make it probable that democracy in Malaysia will make continued progress.

SINGAPORE

Singapore has, despite an ethnic Chinese majority, made great efforts to cultivate a harmonious multi-racial state. It has been led by the Peoples Action Party, headed by Lee Kuan Yew, as a self-governing entity under the British in 1959, or an autonomous part of Malaysia 1963–65, and as an independent state since 1965. Singaporean democracy is flawed by the dominance of a single party that frowns on disruptive tendencies beyond its purview. Singapore is, in many ways, a mini-Japan. Singaporeans, like Japanese, have tended to become "economic animals" who intentionally try not to make political waves at home or abroad. But Singapore's leaders, most of whom are ethnic Chinese, have the traditional Chinese tendency toward an "either with us or against us" factionalism which damages the prospects for Singapore's democracy.

Singapore worries over Lee's intentions of setting up his son as a possible heir apparent and his unsubtle quelling of dissent that might disrupt his pursuit of progress and prosperity. In large part these are an aging leadership's efforts to perpetuate its successes. Lee clearly has become more authoritarian over the years. But because of the record and the political apparatus for electoral government, the outlook for Singapore's democracy is at least as bright as that of Malaysia's.

BRUNEI

Brunei is an enclave on northern Borneo, comparable to a Malaysian state. Unlike its neighbors, Brunei makes no pretense at democracy. Though its sultan resisted efforts to transform Brunei into a fundamentalist Muslim state, he pointedly modeled his newly independent state (1984) after Persian gulf shiekhdoms. A factor influencing the Malay elite's authoritarianism is the fact that one quarter of the population are ethnic Chinese. Though ethnic Chinese are not encouraged to remain in Brunei, they have stayed and prospered. Their frustrations, coupled with the possibility of resentment over the sultan's notoriously conspicuous consumption, encourage the elite to remain authoritarian.

If Brunei were in the Middle East, the extravagant ways of its leaders would not necessarily jeopardize their status, but because it is surrounded by Asian countries that pay lip service to the quest for fairness, it seems only a matter of time before that urge will spread to Brunei too. However, unless its oil-based economy falters, Brunei probably can keep a lid on social tensions by force, payoffs, or expulsions. Consequently, the prospects for enhanced democracy in Brunei are bleak.

INDONESIA

Indonesia is one of the most complex states in Asia. If not for the Dutch colonization the islands of Indonesia with their racial, cultural, and religious divisions would hardly have coalesced into their present configuration. Within Indonesia are voices favoring a Hindu polity with its castes, an egalitarian Muslim polity, tribal polities from the sophisticated to the Stone Age, and regional "nationalisms." Superimposed on this cacophony is a layer of secular technocrats and ideologues trying to adapt Western theories to Indonesia's realities. This mixture of ideas is held by people of several racial extractions speaking numerous languages.

This did not predispose Indonesia to receptivity toward democracy. Moreover, the Dutch operated an oppressive system designed to extract resources efficiently and cheaply. Dutch rule exacerbated problems by undercutting stable social values, and weakening the ability of the islands to be self-sufficient in food. It is no wonder that the Dutch created strong anticolonial feelings among the island's small intellectual elite. This attitude could have contributed to the appeal of democracy if there had been a nearby democratic model to emulate, but such a model did not exist.

Indonesians looked to more radical reform movements: fascist Japan's "Asia for Asians" sentiments and international communism's promise of revolution. The Japanese succeeded first during their wartime tenure. Though the Japanese interlude left no lasting ideological imprint, it gave Indonesians confidence that they could cope with the Dutch. Also, some Indonesians who gained military experience under the Japanese infused those values into their own military. The returning Dutch were rejected and defeated. Independent Indonesia, formed in mid-1950, was led by Sukarno—an idealist with rather naive ideas about nonalignment. He displayed great concern for his people's needs, which he tried to address by a vaguely socialist approach at home and sympathy for local Marxists and Chinese communism. Though Sukarno was not a communist, he leaned toward his own paternalistic version of democratic centralism ("guided democracy") supported by Marxist anti-imperialist rhetoric. Sukarno's regime was inordinately inefficient, and it wasted its energy on confrontation with Malaysia.

The Sukarno era ended abruptly after an aborted communist coup in late 1965 thoroughly discredited what he represented. Chinese support for that foiled effort led right-wing Indonesians to take bloody revenge on Indonesia's ethnic Chinese minority. Shortly after that chaotic period the Indonesian military seized power in mid-1966. Since then the government has held periodic elections to legitimize the regime, venting and measuring frustrations, but they can hardly be called democratic. The rule of the Indonesian military and exmilitary under Suharto has been institutionalized as *Dwi Fungsi* (i.e., dual function), which rationalizes the military playing a major role in civilian society. Though there are several active political parties in Indonesia, the only "party" that really counts is ABRI, the Indonesian Army.[22]

It is easy to criticize the military for corruption and inefficiency. With its large population, size, and resource base, Indonesia could become one of the powers of Asia, but its performance has never approached its potential. On the other hand, given the centrifugal forces that threaten to tear Indonesia apart, it is amazing that it has been so cohesive. By the end of 1985, divisive forces seemed to be growing because of the new strength of Islamic renewal movements.[23]

"Indonesia" is still an idea that is being fulfilled via the national ideology of Pancasila. For its leaders to achieve reasonably ambitious goals on behalf of a nation-state that is only half-formed is a major accomplishment. Though many authoritarians in Asia use the excuse that their people are not ready for democracy, in Indonesia's case the argument rings true. An attempt to implement democracy throughout Indonesia would probably be chaotic now and for the foreseeable future.

PHILIPPINES

The Philippines stand in stark contrast to Indonesia. Despite major regional centrifugal tugs, the Philippines has a better developed desire for democracy. The differences are due to the ways the Philippines were colonized and decolonized. Prior to being colonized by Spain, the region was on the outer fringe of Asia. Though the Spanish arbitrarily gathered disparate groups and called them the "Philippines," they did not have to overcome major legacies of past glories as they subjugated the islands. Spanish culture was a unifying force, helping to uplift and "civilize" the Malay and Negritos who lived there.

Spanish colonial rule gave the Philippines an identity it never had before, but it exacted a heavy price. As in Latin America, Spanish rule was exploitative, and a landlord and serf class system emerged. When the Philippines first achieved independence in 1898 expectations for a brighter future were high among Filipino reformers. But the United States assumed the colonial mantle from Spain, ostensibly to help the Filipinos learn how to be democratically independent. This made no sense to Filipino reformers who saw their freedom snatched away from them in the name of preparing them for freedom. The result was what Americans call the Philippine "insurrection" and Filipinos know as the "Philippine-American War." U.S. victory produced another 40-plus years of colonialism for the Philippines and a great deal of bitterness toward the United States as mentor. As bitter as Filipinos were about U.S. hypocrisy, they nonetheless learned a great deal about U.S.-style democratic processes, especially by being compelled to use those processes in order to regain their freedom. When the Republic of the Philippines was formed in 1946 it had developed a much better appreciation for democracy than any other Asian country. Nearly half a century of American proselytizing of U.S. democratic values infused in the Philippines an almost indigenous and deeply rooted familiarity with the basic value system that seems to be a precondition for an effective democracy.

What happened to bring the Philippines near disaster in 1985?[24] The first sign of major problems came in the postwar years in the form of a communist-backed rebellion led by the Hukbalahaps ("Huks"). The Huks were defeated, but the societal inequities that inspired their rebellion were not resolved. The Philippines are still plagued with an insurrection led by the communist New People's Army (NPA), which has grown markedly since 1979. The Philippine government talks a great deal about freedom, democracy, and economic reforms, and some progress has been made, but the social problems have festered and have been exacerbated by the callousness of the Marcos government.

Marcos initially appeared as deeply committed to freedom and democracy as any of the young state's leaders. After nearly 20 years of halfhearted political and economic improvements, he was elected in 1965 on pledges to get the Philippines out of the doldrums into which it had slipped under the leadership of aging cronies who had gone back to the corrupt and often violent patterns of the colonial era. In his first term Marcos had a fairly moderate record and he was reelected in 1969. At that point Philippines democracy was imperfect because of the persistent corruption and fraud, but it was a viable if at times chaotic democracy.

Marcos restricted civil liberties in 1971 and imposed martial law in 1972 on the pretext of combating a communist threat posed by the NPA. That threat, coupled with a Muslim insurgency, gave Marcos the rationale he needed to clamp down on the political opposition and build up his armed forces. However, these "threats" did not justify the scale of Marcos's crackdown on dissent. Widely viewed as a corrupt figure, managing the Philippines in a colonial fashion for the benefit of a small clique, Marcos was also seen by his harshest critics as in league with the United States in pursuit of allegedly "neoimperialist" economic and strategic goals. As a result, the Marcos regime and all it stood for (including the U.S. bases it hosts) was in jeopardy.

Nominally the Philippines remains a democracy that has political parties and conducts elections. However, those parties and elections have been widely discredited by the Marcos regime. Its involvement in the assassination of popular opposition figure Benigno Aquino, in August 1983, brought it to a new low. Anti-Marcos demonstrations, severe economic problems, and questions about Marcos's health made it only a matter of time before the situation in Manila unraveled. There was no acceptable heir apparent in Marcos's retinue, no viable opposition candidate of Aquino's stature, no certainty what the Philippine armed forces' leadership might do, and no reason for optimism about the Philippine economy, but there were ample signs that the NPA had grown to be a force capable of threatening the government. As 1985 ended the Philippines was preparing for a suddenly called election in early February 1986 to be contested by Marcos and Aquino's widow, Corazon. Virtually no one expected the election to be conducted fairly;[25] wealthy Filipinos reportedly sent money overseas. Public protests against the allegedly fraudulent election and the defection of military leaders forced Marcos to flee the Philippines on February 26, 1986.

After this trauma, Philippine democracy is very much alive, despite grave problems. It is precisely the vitality of Philippine aspirations for democracy, and an expectation that if Filipinos can manage their government democratically then many of the problems would be manageable, that gives reason to hope. Even at this crisis in Philippine history, it is fair to say that democracy remains more thoroughly internalized and assimilated among the Filipino elites than it is in any other Asian nation, excepting Japan.

SOUTHWEST PACIFIC/OCEANIA

Australia and New Zealand object to being lumped together, but they are unique in the Asia-Pacific region in that they alone share a full-fledged European cultural heritage and common ties to the British parliamentary tradition. They, along with Japan, are the only "stable democracies" in the region, and Australia and New Zealand are as solidly democratic as any country in the world.

AUSTRALIA

Australia's democratic health has been proven repeatedly in the postwar era. In 1973–74 the Gough Whitlam government introduced socialist programs at home and more innovative positions internationally. In 1975–76 the Liberal–National Country coalition led by Malcolm Fraser steered the country back toward the center-right. The pendulum swung once more to the center-left in 1983 and 1984 elections, which elected and reelected the current prime minister, Robert Hawke of the Labor party.

These recent swings, which have been more dramatic than Australia's past experiences with a fairly stolid electorate, illustrate two positive facets of Australian democracy. First, it is strong enough to encompass a wide divergence of opinion without undue strains. Freedom of speech, press, and belief are strong in Australia and encourage a high degree of political diversity. That diversity provides the momentum for the political changes that have tested Australian democratic processes. Second, in the face of such changes, the democratic processes have proven resilient, enabling peaceful and orderly transitions into and out of power, with opponents shifting into the loyal opposition.

NEW ZEALAND

New Zealand can be described in the same terms as Australia with the important difference that the democratic process has been even more thoroughly tested in recent years in Wellington. A small country populated mainly by people of European extraction with about 10 percent of Maori Polynesian minority, it has followed large-

ly pastoral pursuits for many years. Postwar politics were dominated by the conservative National party, with a couple of minor exceptions. In 1984, however, in a clear example of generational
change, David Lange of the Labor party ran a campaign appealing for
new policies in domestic and foreign affairs. Lange's domestic shift,
which focused on adapting New Zealand to market forces and lessen-
ing its protectionist positions, was generally well received at home
and abroad. But his foreign policy shift to the left of center on nuclear issues caused much controversy. By excluding U.S. nuclear ships,
Lange has put the Australia-New Zealand-U.S. (ANZUS) pact on
hold and severely strained U.S.-New Zealand relations. Some New
Zealanders have attacked him, but in general Lange seems to have
struck a responsive chord among New Zealanders. By the end of
1985 the government was on the verge of passing legislation banning
nuclear-armed or -powered ships from New Zealand ports, an act
likely to escalate U.S.-New Zealand and domestic tensions.[26]

As Lange frequently has pointed out to American and Australian critics of his position, he was elected to implement his policies in
a free, fair, and democratic election by an informed electorate. His
point is that it is foolhardy for New Zealand's allies to try to force
change in a freely arrived at widely supported decision. Allied coercion could injure New Zealand's democracy. As this delicate
problem is handled in the next year or two, all parties concerned
should be careful not to damage New Zealand's respect for the value
system that it shares with Australia and the United States.

OCEANIA

The states of Oceania are very diverse. Only two of them, Papua
New Guinea and Fiji, are of moderate international significance.
Both enjoy fledgling democracies. They both seem to be gaining
experience and have had no major upheavals, but it is too soon to
pass judgment on either because they have not faced significant tests
of their democracies' strength. Fiji is the more sophisticated of the
two, composed of people of Indian, Chinese, and European extraction as well as Melanesian Fijians. However, this diversity also has
planted seeds of factional and ethnic dissent, which could prove a
serious threat to stability. Papua New Guinea enjoys democracy
among its elites, but as a country which has moved in a very disjointed

fashion from the stone age to the edge of the twenty-first century in about 50 years, its democratic roots are shallow. Nonetheless, among its urbanized and modernized elites, a viable democracy exists— demonstrated in the reasonably orderly change of prime ministers late in 1985. The main problem for Papuan New Guinea's democracy will be how it copes with bringing the bulk of its people into the modern era while simultaneously conveying the values undergirding democracy.[27]

The rest of Oceania consists of several ministates that enjoy a degree of political pluralism, if not true democracy, and a few protectorates that supposedly are learning about self-rule. The major exception is the large French colony of New Caledonia, which was rocked in 1984–85 by violent efforts to overthrow the French and attain independence. Clearly New Caledonia lacks internal democracy, though the French citizens vote as part of France. There is no sign that this colonial anachronism's troubles will be resolved in the near future.

CONCLUSION

Democracy, or at least more open and moderate government, may be said to be progressing in most countries of the region. It should be emphasized, however, that they are not simply copying Western-style democracy but are looking to development within the framework of their own conditions and traditions. Japan is an important model, especially for states of the Confucian tradition, but each state goes somewhat its own way in the pursuit of freedom and fairness in government.

NOTES

1. In addition to the limited cross-section of sources cited in this analysis, readers desiring brief surveys of political conditions in each country should consult the latest editions of the U.S. Department of State's "Background Notes" series. For additional background reading, readers should consult the Asian materials in Amnesty International's Annual Reports, the U.S. Department of State's *Country Reports on Human Rights Practices,* Freedom House's *Freedom at Issue,* and the occasional reports issued by the American Friends Service Committee.

2. For an excellent assessment of Japanese political development, see J.A.A. Stockwin, *Japan: Divided Politics in a Growth Economy* (New York: W. W. Norton & Co., Inc. 1975).

3. *Washington Post Weekly (WPW)*, December 2, 1985, p. 18 presents a concise contemporary analysis of the LDP's inner workings.

4. *Christian Science Monitor (CSM)*, December 2, 1985, p. 13 succinctly summarizes such threats to Japan.

5. Richard Nations, "Spirit of Compromise," *Far Eastern Economic Review (FEER)*, May 12, 1985, p. 18 and *CSM*, April 2, 1985, p. 18 assess the LDP's succession intrigues.

6. For representative coverage of these events, see Robert Manning, "Who Killed Henry Liu?" and Carl Goldstein, "A Cause for Concern," *FEER*, November 22, 1984, pp. 34 and 36; Carl Goldstein, "Out in the Cold," January 31, 1985, pp. 14–15; March 21, 1985, Carl Goldstein, "Who Called the Shots?" pp. 34–35; and Carl Goldstein, "An Order to Kill?" April 4, 1985, p. 21.

7. Mary Lee and David Bonavia, "Socialist Balancing Act," *FEER*, October 10, 1985, pp. 36–41 offers an informative survey of this experiment.

8. *Asian Wall Street Journal Weekly (AWSJW)*, September 30, 1985, p. 2.

9. The nature of Deng's version of the Chinese Communist party is thoroughly analyzed in the *WPW*, October 28, 1985, p. 18.

10. Mary Lee, "Winter of Discontent," *FEER*, December 5, 1985, p. 16. An important statement of Chinese dissident democratic views was analyzed in the *WPW*, October 28, 1985, p. 18.

11. A useful and timely introduction to Korean politics is Young Whan Kihl's, *Politics & Policies in Divided Korea* (Boulder: Westview Press, 1984).

12. Excellent barometers of such political pressures are the publications of dissident groups. One widely available example is *Monthly Review of Korean Affairs* published by the Council for Korean Democracy in Arlington, Virginia.

13. Useful source materials for North Korean developments are the documents issued by the Democratic People's Republic of Korea's (DPRK) United Nations Mission in New York.

14. The year 1985 marked the tenth anniversary of Saigon's collapse. Two useful surveys of its consequences were *FEER*'s insightful cover story, Paul Quinn Judge, "Hanoi's Bitter Victory," May 2, 1985, pp. 30–40 and *Time*'s well illustrated cover story, "Vietnam," April 15, 1985, pp. 16–59.

15. *FEER*, September 29, 1985, p. 16 and Paul Quinn Judge, "Acceptable Face of Capitalism," November 7, 1985, pp. 32–33.

16. An important analysis of that presence is Denis Warner's "Vietnam, The Double-Edged Sword in South-East Asia," *Pacific Defence Reporter* (June 1985):15–18.

17. Useful year-end assessments of Hong Kong's nervousness are in *CSM*, 14/4, 1985, p. 22 and December 24, 1985, p. 9, and Emily Lou, "Advice Before Consent," *FEER*, January 2, 1986, pp. 10–11.

18. Examples of the problems plaguing the government and its opponents are analyzed in *FEER*, September 12, 1985, pp. 32, 34, and *CSM*, September 5, 1985, p. 13.

19. Excellent insights into 1985 Laos are provided by Sombath Somphone in *AWSJW,* December 16, 1985, p. 15 and François Nivolon, "Letter from Vientiane," *FEER,* January 2, 1986, p. 64.

20. The importance of that failed coup is assessed in *AWSJW,* September 16, 1985, pp. 1, 22 and *FEER,* September 26, 1985, p. 19.

21. Timely analyses of Malaysia's tensions are in *CSM,* December 2, 1985, pp. 13, 18 and Mary Lee, "The Chinese Question," *FEER,* December 5, 1985, pp. 29–30.

22. See *FEER*'s cover story on ABRI, October 24, 1985, pp. 23–30.

23. *CSM,* December 2, 1985, pp. 13–18.

24. *FEER* had two excellent cover stories on the Philippine's decline in 1985: Guy Sacerdoti, "On Your Mark, Get Set," April 4, 1985, pp. 30–37 and Guy Sacerdoti, "Marx, Mao, and Marcos," November 21, 1985, pp. 52–62, 111–13. See also "The Sick Man of SE Asia," *The Economist,* June 1, 1985, pp. 33–34, and Raul S. Manglapus, "The Philippines: Prospects for Democracy" in *Worldview* (March 1985):18–19.

25. A representative view is *CSM,* December 5, 1985, p. 15.

26. A cross section of such tensions can be traced in *FEER,* August 22, 1985, p. 40 and Colin James, "Alive But Fading Fast," October 10, 1985, pp. 40–41, and *CSM,* December 11, 1985, pp. 11, 15.

27. PNG's transition and political prospects elsewhere in the Pacific are treated in Ian Andrews, "Counting Out the Chief," *FEER,* December 5, 1985, p. 25, and Robert Marming, "Uncle Sam's Nephews," pp. 42–44.

8

Soviet Union and Eastern Europe

David E. Powell

The Communist countries of Europe—Albania, Bulgaria, Czech-oslovakia, the German Democratic Republic (GDR), Hungary, Poland, the Soviet Union, and Yugoslavia—have had little or no experience with democratic institutions or practices. Except for Czechoslovakia between World Wars I and II, government in this part of the world has been authoritarian, at times totalitarian. Today, the region is characterized by some diversity: Yugoslavia exhibits some features of a democratic state, and government controls are far from complete in Hungary and Poland. But no country in the region can be called "democratic," in the traditional sense of this term. All except Hungary, Poland, and Yugoslavia should be classified as "absolutist." In the following pages, we shall look for elements of democracy, or movement toward or away from it, in each of the region's states.

THE SOVIET UNION

According to official Soviet doctrine, "socialist democracy" prevails in the USSR: the two pillars on which it rests are state ownership of the means of production and a leadership that assumes it represents the will of the population. In addition, the Communist party allegedly ensures a wide range of freedoms, but only those ordinarily consecrated in the West but others such as guaranteed employment, free medical care, and free education. The Soviet Constitution also provides citizens with the right to submit proposals to state and public agencies, to criticize shortcomings in the work of these bodies, to bring suit against officials who abuse their power, and "to participate in the administration of state and public affairs." But all freedoms must be exercised in "the interests of society and the state," and it is the party—defined in Article 6 as "the leading and guiding force of Soviet society, the nucleus of its political system"—that decides what is, and what is not, permissible. "Democratic centralism" and a ban on factionalism guarantee that decisions taken by higher authorities are binding on party members and all other citizens throughout the country.

Dissidents and potential dissidents are deterred from challenging the regime by a network of laws, judicial practices, labor camps, psychiatric institutions, and party intervention into the legal process—as well as by the knowledge that they and their families will be exposed to harassment, imprisonment, or incarceration in a mental hospital. The principal statutes used to discourage dissent are Articles 70, 190(1), and 190(3) of the Russian Republic (RSFSR) Criminal Code, plus analogous sections of the other republics' criminal codes, which prohibit anything that is called "anti-Soviet." Precisely how many political prisoners there are in the USSR cannot be ascertained from the information available to Western scholars, although U.S. government sources put the figure at over 10,000.[1] Even the term "political offense" is unclear; recent years have seen more and more dissenters brought to court on nominally nonpolitical charges (e.g., "hooliganism," "assault," or "drug abuse"). A former political prisoner, Kronid Liubarsky, has tried to ascertain which kinds of political crimes are most prevalent. He recently estimated that some 33 percent of all Soviet prisoners of conscience are confined because of their religious beliefs; another 25 percent were members of national (i.e., ethnic minority) movements; 20 percent belonged to one or another of the various "democratic opposition groups" that demand official adherence to existing constitutional and legal requirements; another 15 percent had announced their intention to emigrate; and the remainder consisted of "small numbers from socialist opposition groups, workers' movements and a few men convicted for terrorist acts."[2]

The general thrust of reports emanating from the USSR indicates a continuation, and perhaps an intensification, of repression since the beginning of the 1980s. Virtually all of the unofficial organizations established since 1975, when the Final Act of the Helsinki Conference on Security and Cooperation in Europe was signed, have been decimated. Members of the various Helsinki monitoring groups that were set up in many Soviet cities were sent to labor camps or psychiatric hospitals; some are still incarcerated, while others were forced to emigrate, sometimes after having been sent into exile.[3] The country's best-known dissident, Andrei Sakharov, remains isolated in the city of Gorky, where he has been forced to live since January 1980. His wife, Elena Bonner, was permitted to travel to Italy and the United States for medical care; while abroad, however, she provided virtually no information about her husband's physical or emotional state, presumably out of fear that she would not be allowed to return to the USSR. The Soviet regime, it would appear, is determined to let the famous scientist die.

Anatolii Koriagin, a psychiatrist who is being punished for his revelations about the political abuse of psychiatry in the USSR, is reportedly near death. The dissident Ukrainian writer Anatolii Marchenko, who is said to be desperately ill in prison, continues to be denied access to proper medical care. At least four other Ukrainians—Uriy Lytvin, Valeriy Marchenko, Vasyl Stus, and Oleksiy Tykhy—who were incarcerated for their political activities, died in 1984–85 because of the harsh treatment they received. Aleksandr Shcharansky and Yuri Orlov, too, have been beaten, denied proper medical treatment, and kept in solitary confinement or at hard labor much of the time. They, along with many other prisoners of conscience, have been placed in cells with "ordinary" criminals who beat them, threaten them with homosexual rape, and subject them to other physical and psychological torments. Shcharansky was liberated in a prisoner exchange, February 12, 1986.

Almost all the members of an unofficial peace organization, "The Group to Promote Trust Between the USSR and the United States," have been placed under arrest, put into camps or psychiatric hospitals, or been forced to emigrate. The Gorbachev administration also continues to harass and punish members of unregistered religious organizations (e.g., Jehovah's Witnesses, Pentacostals, and Ukrainian Catholics [Uniates]), as well as members of ethnic groups who oppose Russification and discrimination against minority peoples. Finally, the regime continues to interfere with dissidents' mail and telephone service, and it jams most shortwave radio broadcasts from the West.[4]

Emigration of Jews, Germans, and Armenians is still permitted, but at extremely low levels. In the peak year of 1979, some 62,000 members of these ethnic groups were allowed to leave the USSR, but by 1984 the figure had fallen to less than 2,000. The number of Jews authorized to leave fell from a high of 51,320 in 1979 to just 896 in 1984. The number of exit visas issued during the first nine months of 1985 was slightly higher than the 1984 level—795, as compared with 721—but the overall totals remain quite low. Western specialists estimate that another 300,000 to 400,000 Soviet Jews would emigrate if given the chance, including some 10,000 "refuseniks," most of whom have been waiting for years to obtain an exit visa.[5]

The party apparatus still controls all organizations; it has made no ideological concessions to liberalism, relies on censorship and propaganda, and has intensified its efforts to militarize society. But if one looks to the economic sphere, the picture is slightly different. For example, there continues to be a flourishing private sector in agriculture; individual household private plots constitute only 3 percent of all land under cultivation, but they produce some 27 percent of all agricultural output. Decentralized schemes of agricultural management, such as the "link" and "brigade" approaches, provide more opportunity for private initiative. There is also a private, quasi-legal sector known as the "second economy," which is responsible for upwards of 15 percent of the country's Gross National Product (GNP). However, these institutions and practices are tolerated only because they compensate for some of the inefficiencies of centralized management, not because of any commitment to democracy.

To combat lack of initiative, indiscipline, and continuing stagnation in the planned economy, the authorities have permitted a good deal of debate over the need for economic reform. Among the most authoritative criticisms of the economic system were two articles by the prominent economist Tatiana Zaslavskaia. One of her essays, published in *Izvestiia* on June 1, 1985, called attention to the fact that central planning has remained virtually unchanged since the days of the first Five-Year Plans, even though the country's productive forces "have been transformed beyond recognition." A second article, which appeared in *Ekonomika i organizatsiia promy-*

shlennogo proizvodstva (EKO) at about the same time, went even further.[6] Zaslavskaia argued that socialism's promise to use resources rationally, promote rapid economic growth, and guarantee equitable distribution of goods and services is no longer being fulfilled. Individual and bureaucratic self-interest—e.g., "localism" (*mestnichestvo*) and "departmentalism" (*vedomstvennost'*)—have produced major distortions in the economic system, largely because the old forms of management are no longer suitable in the current economic environment. While all socialist systems require some degree of centralized administration, Zaslavskaia contended, the Soviet economy is characterized by "excessively detailed regulation." (Two years earlier, in a secret report apparently prepared for the USSR's political and economic leaders, Zaslavskaia used even sharper language.[7] The economy, she wrote in 1983, "has long since passed the point where it could be regulated effectively from a single center.")

Many other scholarly essays published in 1985 depicted the Soviet command economy as outmoded, incapable of allocating resources efficiently or stimulating more rapid economic growth. Perhaps the most remarkable of these writings is an article published in *EKO* in May 1985 by B. P. Kurashvili. He rejected the practice of trying to fulfill instructions "from above" as no longer appropriate, suggesting in its place an arrangement whereby enterprises could make their own choices of suppliers and customers. Their economic interaction would not be determined by central authorities; instead, economic activities would be "guided by the regulating power of the market." The appearance of Kurashvili's article, along with others criticizing the regime's basic assumptions, is remarkable. The authors do not simply advocate modifications that would streamline—and therefore strengthen—the system of central controls. Instead, they recommend basic, broad structural reform in the Soviet economic mechanism—that it be radically reformed and maybe even replaced with some kind of "market socialism."

There is little evidence, however, that the party leadership is receptive to these suggestions. For example, the major statement on economic policy issued during 1985—a decree on "new methods of management," promulgated in August by the party's Central Committee and the USSR Council of Ministers—called only for "improvements" in the centralized, directive system, not for any movement toward reliance on market mechanisms. It stated that production targets will continue to be set in physical terms and that they will be determined by existing branch ministries.[8] Mikhail Gorbachev himself has talked about reforms, but he has confined himself largely to calling for "intensification" of economic efforts and replacing older officials with younger, more energetic cadres. The General Secretary's conception of "reform" seems to be to improve central management, rather than replacing it. While he has talked about "significantly expanding independence and responsibility in management and associations," he speaks more often, and more forcefully, about traditional methods of central role.[9]

Even if it is too early to know whether the public discussion cited foreshadows basic political and/or economic change, it is important that these articles have appeared at all. The debate in 1985 was far more open and pointed than in earlier years. Market reform ideas have been given intellectual and/or political legitimacy. Although it may be some time before we know whether Gorbachev is able—or even whether he wishes—to introduce basic changes in the economic mechanism, the current discussion is far-ranging and vigorous by traditional Soviet standards. "Freedom of speech" is still understood in narrow terms, but the fact that official Soviet media publish attacks on central planning per se and permit reformist proposals (which in earlier times would have been censored, denounced as "revisionist," and perhaps even led to criminal charges) should command our attention.

The USSR boasts something of what is commonly called economic or social democracy. There is considerable equality of opportunity and more than a modicum of social security is guaranteed. Education and health care are free; housing and public utilities are extremely inexpensive; disparities in wealth and incomes are small in comparison with the situation in most Western countries; unemployment is nonexistent, at least according to official definitions; an elaborate "safety net" is in place, providing job security, maternity benefits, disability insurance and old-age pensions; and both women and members of the non-Russian nationalities have been brought into the mainstream of social and economic life.

However, the value of Soviet social accomplishments is less than clear-cut. For example, admission to institutions of higher learning often depends on the payment of bribes; youngsters whose parents are well-off or well-connected are far likelier than others to be admitted to a school of their choice. Similarly, while health care is formally free, money and "connections" are often needed to cope with shortages of medicines, indifferent care by doctors and other public health personnel, and the poor quality of most medical equipment. Many clinics, diagnostic devices, medicines and other facilities and services are available only to high-ranking officials of the party, the military, or the KGB. Another feature of the medical system that would outrage civil libertarians is the fact that alcoholics and drug addicts can be subjected to compulsory treatment.[10]

Upward mobility, which tended to be quite rapid in the Stalin era (partly because of the dictator's purges), is now far more difficult, as people in positions of influence maneuver to provide their children with so many advantages that it sometimes looks as if social status has become an inherited trait. Women, while no longer solely responsible for shopping, cooking, cleaning, and child rearing, still do most of the work in each of these areas. They are overrepresented in occupations characterized by low status and remuneration, while they are significantly underrepresented in prestigious occupations and at the managerial level of most fields. This is especially so in the political sphere, for they comprise only 25 percent of party membership, 2.5 percent of membership in the Central Committee, and have no one of their sex in the Politburo or Secretariat. Finally, the minority nationalities are under constant pressure to assimilate, through policies that promote ethnic intermarriage, limit the number of books and journals in native languages, and reinforce the thrust toward Russification by means of schooling, economic incentives, job mobility, and political control.

Cultural affairs, like economic issues, were debated in 1985. Conflicting views over the direction that public policy should take were presented in the media; some commentators called for the rehabilitation of writers and artists of the early twentieth century, while others demanded that "cultural workers" be more faithful to the canons of socialist realism. Thus, it was announced that the homes of the writer Mikhail Bulgakov and the poet Marina Tsvetaeva, whose works were reviled during the Stalin era, would be transformed into museums celebrating the achievements of their former occupants. In addition, *Pravda* and *Izvestiia* published articles urging that the paintings of several turn-of-the-century, avant-garde artists be displayed. The film *Rasputin,* which was produced a decade ago but withheld from theaters for ideological reasons, was released in June 1985. The movie offers an almost sympathetic picture of Tsar Nicholas II, and it appears to attribute more importance to Rasputin's malevolent influence than to broader socioeconomic forces in bringing about the Bolshevik Revolution.[11]

But these signs of flexibility in dealing with cultural affairs were more than counterbalanced by demands for firmer direction of the arts. One article in *Sovetskaia Rossiia,* perhaps responding to *Rasputin,* called for increased governmental control over imported films, as well as those produced in the USSR.[12] A leading scholar reminded historians and writers alike of the need to place greater emphasis in their works on "patriotism, internationalism, and implacability toward alien ideology." Probably the most authoritative statement made during the year was an editorial in the country's principal literary newspaper, which declared:

> The ideological struggle between socialism and capitalism and the threat to peace and security from imperialist reaction dictate to every Soviet writer fidelity to his public and patriotic duty, the need for a clear-cut ideological position, political vigilance and a dependable grounding in Marxism-Leninism.[13]

While it is still too early to know what Gorbachev's plans are for belles lettres, theater, and other forms of cultural expression, there is no reason to expect him to break with tradition and "let a hundred flowers bloom." In view of the authorities' intense concern with "military-patriotic education" and the inculcation of socialist values into each citizen, it will be difficult to make room for a liberal policy in the cultural sphere.

Some would challenge this conclusion, pointing in particular to a speech made in December by Evgeny Evtushenko. Speaking to a group of writers, the poet called for greater candor and openness in Soviet literature, mentioning topics that the press studiously avoids. But despite earlier hints that the media might provide more coverage of previously forbidden subjects, the official response to Evtushenko was far from enthusiastic. In fact, it provided fresh evidence of the censorship about which he had complained: the editors of *Literaturnaia gazeta* printed only the milder portions of the speech, simply ignoring the more awkward questions that had been raised.[14]

Two of Evtushenko's published statements were especially noteworthy. First alluding to the USSR's experiences with the "cult of personality," he expressed the hope that "self-flattery will be forever rejected [in our country]." Second, while discussing writings that criticize the arms race and human rights abuses in the West, he reminded his audience that "humanity begins with our native land." "Only not concealing and not hushing up things in our native land can give us the moral right to be universal," he declared. While these are important statements, they are a far cry from other sentiments expressed in the speech, but which the censors deleted from the published text. Among other things, Evtushenko suggested that writers be permitted to deal with various "forbidden subjects," e.g., the harm wrought by agricultural collectivization and Stalin's purges, the existence of food rationing in parts of the country, and the system of special stores to which only members of the elite are granted access. "Articles rhetorically calling for publicity are not the same as publicity itself," he concluded. He was right, of course; the fact that his remarks were so thoroughly bowdlerized is a reminder of the limits of intellectual freedom in the USSR.

EASTERN EUROPE

ALBANIA

In the period since Enver Hoxha's death in April 1985, his successor, Ramiz Alia, has begun to open up Albania to the rest of the world. Hoxha had kept his countrymen isolated from the capitalist West, condemned the communist governments of Yugoslavia, the USSR, and China as incorrigibly "revisionist," and ruled Albania as though it was his own personal fiefdom. In contrast, Alia has already put together a number of trade agreements, cultural exchanges, and joint economic ventures with Italy, France, and Greece, and he has expressed interest in expanding trade with West Germany.

This is not to argue that the new party leader is contemplating a demarche as radical as the one introduced in China by Deng Xiaoping. Nor is there any indication that he is some sort of "closet liberal" or a technocratic reformer. Indeed, all the evidence available suggests that he is an autocratic Marxist-Leninist ruler with a highly developed antipathy toward democratic institutions and policies. Like his predecessor, Alia dominates Albania's only political party, relies on the Sigurimi (the security forces) to maintain his own power and that of the party, and cloaks the inherently undemocratic nature of the system with repeated declarations about "the indivisible unity of the Party and the people." Citizens may not engage in independent political activity, cannot express their religious beliefs, and are severely restricted in most other areas of life.

Still, the Alia regime has taken a few steps that will reduce Albania's isolation and allow its citizens more exposure to the outside world. Some of the economic officials who had been running the country for decades have been dismissed, and others have been "encouraged" to retire. These individuals, largely uneducated but always politically reliable, have been replaced by younger cadres. Furthermore, the government has expanded and modernized its television broadcast system, and it permits its citizens to watch Italian, Greek, and Yugoslav broadcasts. Students at higher educational institutions are no longer being evaluated simply on the basis of ideological loyalty and family connections, but are now judged, to a far greater degree, according to conventional academic criteria.[15]

Other signs of change include the following: (1) a leading writer, Ismail Kadare, was given permission to travel abroad several times and was allowed to appear on French television; (2) two dozen French journalists were permitted to visit Albania in September; (3) Alia himself has urged writers and artists "to resist the prevailing attitude of complacency over average standards and sometimes also over mediocrity," adding that improvements in this sphere are "very urgent matters and a necessity"; (4) a second ferryboat line to Italy has been opened, plans to initiate air service to and from Italy have been announced, and a railroad line between Albania and Yugoslavia is being completed; when it opens in early 1986, it will connect Albania for the first time with the European railroad network; and (5) some athletes have been permitted to participate in international competition outside the country.[16]

Alia's policies are not without risk; indeed, any of them might produce results other than those desired by the regime. (This is no hypothetical problem: in June, two Albanian sportsmen defected to Yugoslavia while on their way home from the European weightlifting championships.)[17] It is not surprising, therefore, that some Albanian leaders have already expressed concern over the changes, arguing that they are undercutting the official control system. As the head of the Union of Working Youth of Albania (UWYA) put it in July, foreign and domestic enemies are always ready to take advantage of "the slightest lull" on the part of the authorities in Tirana.

They exert a continued ideological diversion by means of the air-waves, the post, commercials, tourists, and [other foreign] visitors. It is a fact that they manage to plant the poisonous seed among some immature young people. Barely do we lower our iron guard, and young people assume they can wear shoulder-length hair and tight pants. Or as soon as we begin to neglect the struggle against religion and against reactionary propaganda, the revival of various religious rites becomes evident.[18]

While shoulder-length hair and tight pants are not likely to threaten the party's monopoly of political power, they definitely indicate a relaxation of totalitarian controls. Similarly, the suggestion of a religious revival among Albania's youth indicates that Alia's policies have been less intrusive than those of his predecessor.

BULGARIA

There was little reason for optimism about the prospects for democracy in Bulgaria in 1985. The three major developments that unfolded during the year—involving the government's alleged role in the international narcotics trade, its participation (or nonparticipation) in the plot to kill Pope John Paul II, and the brutal effort to assimilate the Turkish minority—all point to the Bulgarian rulers' contempt for democratic processes.

According to the U.S. Drug Enforcement Agency (DEA), the government of Bulgaria has been actively involved in the trafficking of narcotics since 1970. Using the official import-export agency Kintex, the Bulgarians have been helping Turkish smugglers ship morphine base and heroin to the West, in exchange for the transport and delivery of weapons to left-wing terrorist groups in Turkey and elsewhere. There is also evidence linking Sofia to a broader conspiracy among Warsaw Pact states, designed to undermine and destabilize Western societies.[19]

Allegations of Bulgarian complicity in the plot to kill the pope are more difficult to prove. Sofia rejects any suggestion that its citizens had anything to do with the attempted assassination. Official spokesmen term the allegation part of "a smear campaign" directed against the socialist states and denounce the Italian judicial system for its "arbitrariness." But even though the testimony of Mehmet Ali Agcah himself has been contradictory and his behavior at times

bizarre, it is difficult to ignore all the evidence that has been presented linking Sofia to the shooting. Throughout 1985, a complex of
factors—court depositions, the cross-examination of witnesses, the
Bulgarian government's unwillingness to cooperate with Italian
officials, and the defensive-aggressive nature of Bulgarian denials
and countercharges leveled at Western "imperialist circles"—give
credence to the theory that Sofia was intimately involved in the
assassination attempt.[20]

The third dimension of the regime's assault on humane values
and democratic freedoms involves its harsh treatment of the country's
ethnic minorities.[21] Slightly less than 10 percent of the population is
of Turkish nationality; beginning in late 1984 and continuing with
greater and greater ferocity throughout 1985, the government has
tried to compel these individuals to abandon their self-identity and
"voluntarily" adopt Bulgarian names. Turkish villages have resisted
the authorities' demands, and the latter in turn have resorted to
force; ultimately, both the police and the army were needed to
suppress the resistance. Turkish officials, as well as Western diplomats and journalists, have estimated that some 1,000 ethnic Turks
have been killed; many more have been wounded or imprisoned.

According to the official Bulgarian line, there is no Turkish
minority in the country. So-called "ethnic Turks," it is argued, are
really Bulgarians who have been deceived by the "propaganda" of
Ankara or "its local nationalist agents." Bulgarian citizens who have
requested permission to emigrate to Turkey have been told that they
would be resettled instead in remote areas of Bulgaria, "where they
can live more calmly and will find their happiness." The ultimate
goal seems to be "to encourage assimilation by separating them from
the proximity of the mosque and an environment that is primarily
Turkish in language and custom."

Even while Bulgarian police and army units have been rounding
up ethnic Turks and forcing them to adopt Slavic-sounding names,
some of the latter have responded by resorting to terror. The regime's
excesses lead the victims (or other Bulgarian Turks acting on their
behalf) to engage in antistate violence—which in turn leads to still
harsher reprisals and to more terrorist activities. Bomb attacks in
1984 and 1985 killed about 30 people.[22]

Nonetheless, one can still find some Bulgarian voices speaking
out against dictatorship and calling for greater freedom. Economic
modernization and technological diffusion have already contributed

to the erosion of the official control system. For example, the appearance of videocassette recorders and tapes has made it possible for ordinary citizens to obtain and distribute materials that the authorities regard as ideologically harmful. Tapes are smuggled into the country, copies are made illegally, and they can be shown privately. Legislation designed to curb the illicit import and distribution of such materials was adopted in June, but it has not seriously restricted the activities of people who are determined to buy, sell, and/or watch tapes produced abroad.[23]

Other developments also call into question the regime's ability to exercise full control over the media. A particularly egregious example of lack of vigilance occurred during the summer, when one newspaper published an acrostic puzzle whose answer contained the message, "Dolu Todor Zhivkov" (Down with Todor Zhivkov).[24] More important was the appearance of an article by the well-known poet Hristo Radevski, criticizing the practice whereby editors make corrections in a text without the author's knowledge or consent.[25] He cited examples from his own experience, when his writings were "corrected" so heavyhandedly that he refused to allow them to be published or broadcast. He also mentioned a number of articles that had appeared under his name, but which were not really his work. Radevski was outspoken about "editorial staffers who are so afraid of making a mistake that in each original thought or in each fresh turn of a sentence they see an attempt aimed at undermining the foundation of socialism."

This attack on censorship was extraordinary, and only Radevski's stature made it possible for his remarks to appear in print. Still, the editors of the journal in which it was published clearly had reservations about their decision, for they appended a brief note to the end of the article, stating that "some of his generalizations are overdone," while others were "peremptory." The presence of these self-exculpating statements is no less puzzling than the decision to authorize the publication of Radevski's attack.

CZECHOSLOVAKIA

Since the invasion of Czechoslovakia on August 20–21, 1968, by half a million troops of the Warsaw Pact, the democratic promise of the "Prague Spring" has vanished, and Czechoslovakia once again is a dreary, illegitimate police state. The regime is propped up by 80,000 Soviet troops and a profound awareness among the citizenry that the reemergence of democratic institutions and policies would likely trigger another devastating encounter with the Brezhnev Doctrine. The government of Czechoslovakia today is highly authoritarian, contemptuous and fearful of democratic rights, and determined not to arouse the wrath of the Soviet leadership.

Two weeks before the seventeenth anniversary of the invasion, the country's principal unofficial human rights organization, Charter 77, issued a statement urging the government to cease harassing its critics. Since the invasion, it declared, the country has been "forcibly thrown back into the climate of the first half of the 1950s, when public discussion of any kind was impossible." The authors criticized the post-1968 leadership as people "whose main, or often only, quality [is] an unqualified adaptability and servitude to power."[26]

This is not the first time members of Charter 77 have spoken out, of course. For almost a decade now, the organization has criticized party and government officials, calling on them to cease tormenting Dubcek, his associates, and members of the creative intelligentsia who identify (or identified) with the Prague Spring. In a letter sent to President Gustav Husak and Prime Minister Lubomir Strougal on April 26, 1985, Charter 77 asserted that the country's progress since World War II was more than offset by the heavy cost in human lives, physical and psychological suffering, and the loss of personal dignity. Noting that achievements had been accompanied by "several waves of violence and persecution," the letter charged that "the results of today do not vindicate the cruelties of the past."[27]

A few months earlier, the same human rights advocates had expressed dismay at the USSR's decision to station short-range nuclear missiles in Czechoslovakia. These weapons, it declared, "have been appearing on our territory against the will of the majority of the population."[28]

However, those who speak out against the regime's policies, sign their names to unofficial documents, or circulate illicit literature put themselves and their families at risk. The authorities dismiss the dissidents' arguments and accuse them of acting on behalf of Western intelligence services. To deflect Western influence and to reinforce official messages, ideological specialists in Czechoslovakia have introduced programs of "counterpropaganda." These activities help to intimidate and isolate dissidents, as well as potential dissidents.

Some 1,100–1,200 men and women have signed Charter 77's "declaration of intent," originally issued in January, 1977. In addition to these persons who have publicly committed themselves by signing their names, others cooperate with the organization in various ways. But even its most enthusiastic supporters in the West acknowledge that the group's recognition abroad "is greater than its influence among the population at home."[29] In view of the immense resources available to the authorities and the limited assets on which Charter 77 can draw, there is no reason to expect this imbalance to change in the foreseeable future.

GERMAN DEMOCRATIC REPUBLIC (GDR)

In 1985 the only glimmer of democratic intent appeared in the area of foreign policy, where the Honecker regime seemed to be trying to reduce its subservience to Moscow. But it is unclear whether that was actually the regime's desire, and even if it was, the effort hardly matched the steps taken by Albania, Romania, or Yugoslavia.

The East German "challenge" involved an attempt to maintain good relations with the Federal Republic of Germany (the FRG, or West Germany) during a period of Soviet–West German conflict. The GDR relies on Bonn for most of its hard currency, but during much of 1985, the USSR was busy criticizing the FRG for its "revanchist policies" and for having permitted NATO deployment of intermediate-range nuclear missiles on its soil. This left Honecker with two alternatives: joining Moscow in denouncing the FRG, or trying to insulate the "special relationship" with Bonn from broader East-West relations.

Some have argued that Honecker's goal is to obtain "as much autonomy as possible with as much dependence as necessary." The East German leader, it is said, has pursued this objective by calling for a return to "political dialogue" with the FRG and by reaffirming the importance of "smaller nations" in international affairs.[30] Unfortunately, the Soviet position on this issue is difficult to discern; the press in the USSR has published some commentaries that challenge Honecker's view, along with others that have embraced it. The draft of the new party Program, released on October 26, asserts that "all states, big and small, regardless of their capabilities, geographic situation and social systems,"[31] can help to reduce tensions in the world and curb the arms race. If, as seems likely, this is now the official Soviet line, GDR policy in no way represents a challenge to the USSR.

Within East Germany, evidence of liberalization is slight. The only area in which institutions or individuals appear to have some freedom is the religious sphere. The Lutheran and Roman Catholic churches have managed to retain a considerable measure of autonomy, and high-ranking officials of both bodies have taken issue with various government policies. But this hardly matters, inasmuch as the regime ignores or rejects most of the churches' complaints.

At its annual meeting in September, the Synod of the Lutheran churches listed its major grievances against the secular authorities: (1) official discrimination against practicing Christians; (2) the increasing militarization of society (i.e., the growing emphasis on the acquisition of military skills in schools, and the linking of educational and job opportunities with participation in military activities); (3) the lack of a civilian alternative for conscientious objectors, who currently are compelled to work in military hospitals or are assigned to military construction projects; (4) neglect of construction and restoration work on churches; and (5) restrictions on freedom of movement, not only to the West, but also to other East European countries.[32] (During the meeting, one pastor linked these restrictions with the "emigration mentality" that he said pervades East German society. This atmosphere, he asserted, causes people "to wonder whether they really wanted to remain in the GDR.")

The Catholic church, which has a smaller following than its Lutheran counterpart, has only recently begun to play a role in East German politics. Partly motivated by the emergence of an unofficial peace movement supported by the Lutheran church, Catholic spokesmen have begun to speak out on questions relating to the arms race, arms control, and the militarization of the educational system. In January 1985, the church issued a pastoral letter urging young Catholics to "be different" from those around them; and on the fortieth anniversary of the end of World War II, Joachim Cardinal Meisner denounced "the division of Europe, the world, and above all, our homeland."[33]

But the authorities have succeeded in restricting the activities of clergymen to such a degree that their political influence is marginal at best. Religious newspapers—which, unlike other media, are not under the direct control of the state—have been delayed, withdrawn from circulation or, under government pressure, subjected to self-censorship when they tried to publish letters dealing with "political" questions.[34]

There is abundant evidence that the government of the GDR systematically violates its citizens' rights and has failed to fulfill the promises made in 1975 when the Helsinki Final Act was signed. The special U.S. government commission set up to monitor compliance with the agreement has reported numerous instances of East German restrictions on religious freedom, foreign travel, the right to emigrate (including efforts to achieve family reunification), and other rights presumably guaranteed by the Final Act. Much more than harassment and bureaucratic delays are involved here. The International Society for Human Rights (ISHR) estimates that there are 7,000 political prisoners in the GDR, while the "13th of August" working group (a human rights organization located in West Berlin) puts the figure at 10,000.[35] The authorities show no signs of altering their policy toward human rights, including those specifically "protected" by the Helsinki accords.

HUNGARY

Three decades have passed since the Red Army crushed the Hungarian Revolution of 1956, Imre Nagy was executed, and Janos Kadar came to power. During this interval, Kadar and his colleagues have cast off the Stalinist mold and transformed Hungary into a far more open country. While no informed observer would ever confuse Kadar's regime with a genuinely democratic political system, the character and degree of change introduced in Hungary since 1956 are far from inconsequential. Western businessmen and tourists can be seen in large numbers, Western films and plays frequently appear in Hungarian theaters, Hungarian citizens are freer than most of their East European counterparts to travel abroad, and people are permitted to engage in certain political activities that would be inconceivable elsewhere in the Soviet bloc. On March 15, the day set aside to commemorate the democratic revolution of 1848, a group of young men and women actually was allowed to organize an unofficial procession. (They were, however, accompanied by policemen, who were instructed to make sure that these "inexperienced young people" did not view this concession as evidence of "the withering away of the state.")[36]

By Western standards, of course, Hungarians are far from free: opposition political parties are banned; the Hungarian Socialist Workers' party is organized according to the principles of "democratic centralism"; an elaborate censorship apparatus is in place; and citizens who have committed no crime (but who are viewed as politically unreliable) may be placed under "police surveillance," an arrangement which severely restricts their activities. As is true elsewhere in Eastern Europe, Western newspapers and magazines are available only in selected research institutes or in hotels catering to visitors from the capitalist world, access to certain literary and scholarly works is limited, and children and adults alike are given a distorted picture of historical and current events.

Restrictions such as these inevitably give rise to frustration and anger, especially among intellectuals. While some manage to find loopholes in the censorship apparatus—Hungarians are experts at "getting around the system, rather than confronting it," a British journalist has remarked[37] —most scholars and writers can express their true feelings only in underground publications. A particularly eloquent example of such writings appeared in Budapest in early 1985:

> We protest against censorship, because it is a sign of the infringement on our national sovereignty; it is contrary to the principle of popular sovereignty and to the basic principles of every democracy; it falsifies our past in the interest of power. . . .[38]

However appealing this argument might seem to a Westerner, Hungarian party and government leaders reject it categorically. A report prepared in October 1984 for the party's Central Committee touched off a campaign to restrict cultural imports from the West; since then, various officials have insisted on closer supervision over culture and the arts. Thus, the deputy minister of culture called for stern measures to combat "undesirable ideological and political phenomena in artistic life," while the minister of the interior spoke out against what he saw as a growing danger from "internal 'oppositionalist' and hostile elements." Those who seek "to weaken and erode the system have recently . . . become more active," the latter official charged. Asserting that certain unnamed dissidents were "teetering on the verge" of criminal behavior, he warned that the state would not hesitate to take repressive measures against those who overstep "the limits of tolerance [and] damage the vital interests of the people."[39]

Even while this harsher political atmosphere was being fash—ioned—or, perhaps, because of it—the country's leaders implemented at least one "democratic" reform. They held elections in which voters were given a choice of candidates. The new electoral system, adopted in 1983, requires that there be at least two candidates for each parliamentary and local government seat, and the elections of June 1985 were the first to be held under the new law.[40] Official spokesmen described the arrangement as "a significant step forward in the development of socialist democracy," a change that had "far-reaching significance" for Hungarian political life.

But it is extremely unlikely that the new system has altered, or will alter, the distribution of power within the country. Several factors justify a skepticism. First, each candidate had to sign a written statement pledging his or her support for the Patriotic People's Front (PPF), the party's principal front organization. This approach, of course, has much in common with Soviet-style elections; indeed, before the various candidates had been chosen, one Politburo member was able to predict with some assurance that there would be no "fundamental differences" among those running for office. Second, the authorities specifically excluded from the nominating process any persons who might "abuse democracy" by focusing on the nation's social and economic difficulties in order to gain "popularity and cheap success." Third, 35 of the 387 seats in parliament were placed in a special category, with candidates permitted to run unopposed. As might be expected, the country's most important political leaders were included in this group in order to guarantee that they would be "elected." Finally, no matter who won or lost the elections, the outcome could not have tipped the balance very far in the direction of popular sovereignty. Government bodies, from local councils up to Parliament itself, continue to have very little political power; the party remains "the leading force" in Hungarian society.

Nevertheless, both the nominations and the elections provided the population at large with an opportunity to express their feelings toward some of Hungary's most prominent citizens. The nominating meetings were open to the public, and in most electoral districts there was vigorous debate with respect to various candidates' credentials. A few well-known incumbents were denied a place on the ballot because they lacked support in their home districts, while a number of others required special intervention by the party, the PPF, or the police to ensure their nomination.

The elections, too, produced what can only be termed "upsets." During the campaign period, the secretary general of the PPF declared proudly that "for years there has been voting in Hungary; now there will be an election." Large numbers of people evidently understood the difference. Thus, of the 71 candidates who had been chosen from the floor at nominating meetings—individuals who ran in addition to, or instead of, men and women put forth by the PPF—a remarkable 35 percent were elected. Several major political figures, including both party and government functionaries, lost their seats, presumably because of popular hostility toward them. In fact, the majority of parliamentary candidates taking part in contested elections (that is, all but the 35 who ran unopposed) received less than 60 percent of the vote.

What does the new electoral mechanism imply about movement toward greater democratization? Very little, it would appear. Steven Koppany has aptly described the current political system as "a liberally autocratic regime wanting desperately to be liked by the people under its control." Hungary continues to be a one-party state, and it is difficult to be impressed by competitive elections when the country's legislative bodies are virtually impotent, and all the candidates pledge to carry out the same program. Still, ordinary citizens were given an opportunity to signal their dislike of certain public figures, and a number of important officials and former officials experienced humiliating losses. As the West German newspaper *Die Welt* concluded, the electoral reform provided "a little touch of democracy," but not much more.[41]

POLAND

The Polish government is rigidly authoritarian: it is led by an army general; it is the object of constant Soviet intimidation; and it relies almost exclusively on military, paramilitary, police, and secret police units (as well as the threat of intervention by the USSR) to enforce its rule. At the same time, the Polish political system may well be the freest in the entire region; the Catholic church commands the loyalty of virtually the whole population, former activists of the banned trade union Solidarity are permitted to engage in certain forms of political activity, and a vast array of underground books, journals, and newspapers is available to interested persons of all social strata and political position. The scope of this "independent" publishing industry is astonishing: one "company" regularly prints books in editions of 4–5,000 copies, and more than 600 titles are available from underground publishers, including works of fiction and poetry, memoirs, and studies in the fields of history, economics, philosophy, and political science.[42] These materials have attracted so many readers that the authorities often respond to their messages by printing rebuttals in the official media. Even if this is not the sort of open "dialogue" that Solidarity of the Committee for the Defense of Workers (KOR) had hoped for, it is nonetheless a remarkable phenomenon in a communist country.

The church continues to represent the major source of political opposition. During the year 1985, the most important episode involving church-state relations was the trial and conviction of four officers of the Security Service who had abducted and murdered Jerzy Popieluszko, a popular Warsaw priest who was an outspoken critic of the regime. The court made no effort to link the actions of the four with higher authorities in the security apparatus, other government agencies, or the Polish United Workers party (PUWP), however, despite abundant evidence linking the four to more powerful officials.

During the trial and afterward, the government spoke out repeatedly against the church, accusing various priests of "extrareligious" activity; e.g., attempting to introduce religious emblems in state-run schools and other public institutions, sponsoring a youth movement outside the auspices of the official youth organizations, and "infiltrating" the latter, and taking political positions in the guise of conducting pastoral work among the faithful. At the same time, priests and lay persons who took part in protest activities were harassed, arrested, fined, and/or imprisoned more frequently, and there were several attacks by "unknown" assailants against the most militant members of the clergy.

The murder of Popieluszko only complicated the authorities' efforts to bring the church under control. A kind of cult sprang up around the memory of the priest; his grave (at the church where he used to preach) is said to have become "a national shrine visited by millions of ordinary people, curious tourists, and even representatives of foreign governments." For some, he has become a symbol of religious piety, for others, of patriotism, and for still others, "of the determination to defend the ideas of human dignity and civil rights." The inscription on his tombstone is itself a challenge to the illegitimate regime, describing him as "a Martyr for the Faith and the Fatherland."

Nor has the murder deterred other clergymen from speaking out on issues affecting the church or parishioners; if anything, it has reinforced their convictions and their willingness to follow in Popieluszko's footsteps. In a sermon delivered at the murdered priest's church, the Reverend Teofil Bogucki declared that the country was "defending itself against the invasion of atheism and communism from the East, as well as indifference and laicism from the West." Similarly, Josef Cardinal Glemp told an audience of 70,000 Catholics that "human rights" and "basic justice" were being threatened in Poland, and as recently as November 9, the nation's Catholic bishops called upon the government to free all political prisoners and permit ordinary citizens to play a more meaningful role in politics.

A second sphere in which the regime of General Wojciech Jaruzelski has been unable to exercise total control involves the electoral process.[43] On July 16, Solidarity's underground leaders appealed to all Poles to boycott the parliamentary elections scheduled for October 13. To take part in the voting "after four years of repression, lawlessness, and arrogance," they said, would be tantamount to "renouncing social and national aspirations and assuming co-responsibility for the crimes of martial law." During the "campaign," national and local spokesmen for Solidarity repeatedly urged citizens not to vote; one open letter, signed by some of the most prominent members of the union, asserted that a boycott "would show common disapproval of the lying and violence and of the imprisonment of political opponents" by the regime.

The proposed boycott was only partially successful. According to official reports, 79 percent of all registered voters cast their ballots on election day. (Nonvoters were dismissed as consisting largely of "blackmarketeers, criminals of various kinds, alcoholics, and drug addicts.") Underground sources put the turnout at only 66 percent, but no matter which of the two figures one uses, the fact remains that a significant number of people stayed home. Thus, the elections resulted in a stalemate. The government proved to be able to withstand all pressure to modify its conduct, while the opposition managed to prevent the authorities from increasing their control over the public in general.

The regime has responded to other actions carried out by Solidarity—publishing underground newspapers, circulating petitions, distributing leaflets, and "symbolic displays of resistance during various public events"—more harshly than it handled the boycott issue. On March 28, General Jaruzelski warned that he would resort to "surgical methods" if Solidarity activists continued to "harm the socialist state." In May, three of the union's most prominent figures—Wladyslaw Frasyniuk, Bodgan Lis, and Adam Michnik—were sentenced to prison terms ranging from two-and-a-half to three years. They were convicted for "participating in the activities of an illegal union . . . and undertaking actions designed to incite public unrest." Other men and women associated with Solidarity have been detained by the police, subjected to illegal searches and seizures, and suffered other kinds of harassment or beatings.

The Jaruzelski regime appears to be regarded by most Poles with a mixture of contempt, anger, and resignation. On April 6, the newspaper *Polityka* acknowledged that political alienation in contemporary Poland was widespread and showed no signs of abating.

> Certain major social groups . . . consider the social order to be unjust and at the same time inefficient. . . . They do not feel any solidarity with the state in its present form, they approach it from detached positions, and sympathize with those who actively oppose it.

Official and unofficial surveys alike indicate that the credibility of the press and its spokesmen is low. In one study, barely one-fourth (26.1 percent) of a nationwide sample agreed with the statement that the journalistic profession "serves society and helps people understand the world," and only 16.6 percent believed that journalists were expressing their true opinions in their stories. Other investigators have acknowledged that "a growing number of people have withdrawn into private life—often those who were most involved on the side of Solidarity—and have chosen 'internal emigration.' . . . They feel they have been cheated." Not surprisingly, many of these individuals "are full of doubts and reservations. They . . . are sensitive and suspicious; they have reservations about the intentions of the authorities and the activities of state institutions."[44]

Finally, the year 1985 witnessed a number of developments that further curtailed academic freedom in Poland.[45] In July, the

Sejm adopted several laws limiting the autonomy of higher academic institutions, increasing the role of older, "more reliable" faculty members, placing severe restrictions on students' self-government committees, and giving the minister of science and higher education the authority to dismiss rectors, deans, and other administrative personnel. In late November, the government began a purge, removing on political grounds more than three dozen officials from their positions in various universities around the country.

Some members of the Sejm spoke out against these changes. One deputy said he viewed the new legislation with "sorrow and horror" and predicted that the new arrangement would bring "irreversible damage" to the nation. While statements such as these were brushed away by Parliament, it is important to note that there was, in fact, a debate—a mere vestige of democracy, but something that could never happen in the USSR or in Czechoslovakia.

ROMANIA

Although they pursue an independent line in foreign policy, Romania's leaders maintain extremely tight control over the country's population. Indeed, Romania generally is regarded as the most "Stalinist" of the states of Eastern Europe—except, perhaps, for Albania. In recent years, stricter limits have been placed on the acquisition and use of private property, as well as the right to change one's residence, have contact with foreigners, gain access to Western literature, and study or travel abroad. The law currently requires those who wish to emigrate to pay a special tax—in hard currency, even though it is illegal for them to possess it in the first place. Since 1983, private ownership of duplicating machines has been prohibited, and citizens must now register their typewriters with the police (providing, in the process, a sample of typed material so that the authorities can trace down "socially harmful" documents or letters).

Other controls are equally or more invasive. Because of energy shortages and President Nicolae Ceausescu's determination to repay the country's hard-currency debt, citizens were forbidden to drive their own automobiles during the first months of 1985. Apartment dwellers were permitted to use only one small bulb, and temperatures were officially set at 61 degrees, although they apparently went no higher than 55 degrees in reality. Conditions at work places, including hospitals, were just as spartan: unofficial reports attribute numerous deaths, primarily among young children and the elderly, to lack of heat in medical centers. People over the age of 70 are actually denied admission to hospitals, and birth certificates for newborn children are not issued until the infant has lived for three weeks. (The latter device is designed to exclude from official infant mortality data those children who are most vulnerable to the cold.) Laws that were passed in the 1960s, prohibiting abortions and sharply restricting divorces, were supplemented and reinforced by the passage of still harsher measures. Today, "Draconian penalties await physicians who do not abide by the anti-abortion law, childless couples are charged higher taxes, and Romanian women are forced to undergo monthly gynecological tests to make sure that no pregnancy goes undetected."[46]

The extremely severe curbs that had been placed on the practice of religion years ago are now being more strictly enforced. Clergymen are, as a rule, under constant surveillance, and the children of religious believers are often denied admission into official youth groups, which severely restricts their educational and career opportunities. Unauthorized religious gatherings are regularly broken up by the police unless they are conducted in the strictest secrecy.[47]

Some of the antireligious methods employed by the regime are astonishingly crude. For example, word reached the West in 1985 that some 20,000 Bibles donated a decade ago to the Transylvanian Magyar Reformed church—with the permission of the Romanian government—had been seized and then recycled into toilet paper. Even more destructive is the program, begun in 1982 and continuing to this day, of demolishing some of the country's greatest cultural monuments—churches, monasteries, cathedrals, and synagogues. Since 1984, perhaps a dozen churches and synagogues, including some dating back to the seventeenth century, have been razed in the historical center of Bucharest. The ostensible purpose of this state-directed vandalism is to make way for an elaborate complex of buildings that will house the offices of the Communist party and the Romanian government, and to create a grand "Boulevard of the Victory of Socialism." Similar work is being carried on in many provincial cities and towns. There is considerable evidence, including some references in published literature, of opposition to the destruction, especially among architects and art historians.

The world of belles lettres presents a somewhat more complicated picture. Most writers and playwrights have become docile
apologists for the regime and contribute to an elaborate "cult of
personality" in honor of Ceausescu. A smaller number have refused
to bend, however; using Aesopian language, they sometimes manage
to slip controversial materials past the censors. One such story, by
Augustin Buzura, dealt with a blind woman whose sight was restored
by a doctor. Instead of expressing joy, the woman begged the physi-
cian not to tell her relatives. As the author himself put it:

> The woman's reaction is not so strange. In the end, how many
> people do not prefer the darkness, [the] complete darkness, which
> [offers] an excuse for their cowardice, weakness, illness [or] igno-
> rance? For how many people is the light [in fact] a blessing?
> Because it is not so comfortable to live with your eyes wide open, in
> stark daylight, without alibis, excuses or justifications.

Reacting to this and other writings, the authorities rebuked Buzura
and all but barred him from further appearances in print.[48] By
Romanian standards, this was an unusually mild punishment.

The fate of another outspoken writer, the poet Dorin Tudoran,
was more disquieting. Perhaps the country's leading dissident, he
resigned from the Writers' Union (WU) and the Communist party
some years ago because of excessive political interference in literary
matters. After he sent abroad a series of articles that could not be
published in Romania, he was deprived of any opportunity to earn a
living. In 1984, he applied for permission to emigrate, but his re-
quests were denied repeatedly. When he began a hunger strike on
April 15, 1985, the police responded by cutting off all mail and
telephone contact between Tudoran and his supporters in Romania
and the West. Romanian officials refused to disclose his whereabouts
or his fate; in fact, on several occasions, spokesmen for the regime
have even denied that the writer ever existed.[49]

Finally, the country's ethnic minorities, especially the 1.8–2.5
million Hungarians (the lower figure is the official estimate) are also
the object of discrimination. One Western journalist has written of
Romania's "cultural genocide of minorities—the dispersal or exile of
their intelligentsia; official curtailment of their educational, language
and religious opportunities; and a campaign of intimidation against
their cultural and religious leaders."[50] Ceaucescu's treatment of his

Hungarian subjects has been so harsh that it has elicited numerous protests from abroad; the press in Kadar's Hungary has been especially outspoken. Still, the fact that the situation of ethnic minorities is worse than that of other Romanian citizens should not obscure that Ceausescu seeks to deprive all of his countrymen of what Westerners would regard as elementary democratic rights.

YUGOSLAVIA

With its mixed capitalist-socialist economy, its foreign policy of nonalignment, and its remarkably open press, Yugoslavia seems to have much in common with genuinely pluralist systems. Reality, however, is a good deal more complicated. Only one political party exists—the Communist party or League of Communists—and its decisions are binding on all governmental bodies, organizations, and individual citizens. The electoral system offers voters no choice and there is no Yugoslav equivalent to the U.S. Bill of Rights. Political discourse, while robust by East European standards, has never been permitted to go beyond boundaries established (and frequently reinterpreted) by the regime. In fact, the year 1985 witnessed a hardening of official policy toward freedom of speech, freedom of religion, and freedom of association.

There continues to be a flourishing debate among scholars, journalists, government bureaucrats, and party officials over the most basic of questions—what role should the party play in Yugoslav society? More often than not, public discussion of this issue spills over into a related topic—the need for economic reforms. There is widespread agreement that the country is going through a crisis of immense proportions: it currently has a hard-currency debt in excess of $24 billion, is experiencing a rate of inflation somewhere between 80 percent and 100 percent, and upwards of 1.3 million of its men and women are unemployed.

One can also find heated discussion over the merits of private enterprise in socialist Yugoslavia. Critics emphasize the ideological argument, condemning "the exploitation of man by man." They contend that the private sector should have no place at all in a socialist state; permitting it to expand, they say, would amount to the restoration of capitalism. Those who advocate a greater role for private enterprise are far less interested in ideological purity; they are more concerned with finding jobs for the unemployed and improving the quality of life of all citizens. Lashing out at his opponents as "Maoists" and "ultraleftist dogmatists," one party official has charged such people with believing that "socialism could be achieved through misery."[51] Neither side in the controversy has made much progress in changing its adversary's point of view.

Public opinion appears to be on the side of the ideological purists; indeed, several studies of workers' attitudes indicate that a majority supports the goal of greater social and economic equality. In one survey carried out in Slovenia, 75 percent of the workers polled said they favored reducing differences in personal incomes; a similar study conducted in Serbia put the figure at 57 percent. It is easy to understand why ordinary people feel as they do: far from being a classless society, Yugoslavia is characterized by significant social stratification. According to one estimate, the total amount of money earned by the wealthiest 10 percent of the population is equal to the amount earned by the lowest 45 percent.[52]

The fact of such wide differences in income is said to have become "the source of widespread dissatisfaction among a large part of society." If the gap were to widen, one scholar has suggested, it "would inevitably increase social tension" and might even threaten the country's political stability. The real problem is the difficulty involved in reconciling Marxist theory with economic reality. Officials, scholars, and citizens alike understand that the profit motive could be harnessed to pull Yugoslavia out of its crisis; but greater reliance on market forces is likely to increase social and economic differentiation, and egalitarianism remains one of the most attractive features of socialism. How to find "the correct balance between these two . . . contradictory philosophies" is, in a sense, what the country's political debate is all about.[53]

Exchanges of this kind are evidence of a lively and free press. At the same time, however, there definitely are limits to official tolerance. This was made clear in 1984–85, when 28 intellectuals were arrested on charges of engaging in subversive activities.[54] Participants in Belgrade's "Free University" (the Yugoslav equivalent of Poland's unofficial "flying universities"), had met from time to time in each other's apartments to discuss the country's social and economic problems. The state prosecutor argued that their meetings were secret and illegal—"conspiratorial" and aimed at "overthrowing the existing political system" Most of the accused were released almost immediately, but six persons were indicted in February 1985. Three men—a writer, a sociologist, and a journalist—were tried and convicted of "spreading propaganda hostile to the state." They were sentenced to prison terms ranging from one to three years.

Their attorney, too, wound up in jail, presumably because he revealed that the state had fabricated evidence to strengthen its case. (He had been accused in 1981 of disseminating "hostile propaganda"; after he put up a spirited defense on behalf of his three clients, the old charge was resuscitated.) He was sentenced to a seven-month term and disbarred for ten years. While it probably is too early to conclude that the trial put an end to the fiction that Yugoslavia is a country of progressive socialism, it is nonetheless true that the regime's reputation for tolerance has been badly tarnished.

There were also a number of trials involving ethnic and/or religious dissent, and a few that dealt with purely political issues. "Nationalists" in Serbia, "terrorists" in Croatia, "Islamic fundamentalists" in Bosnia-Herzegovina, and ethnic Albanians in the Kosovo region were the major targets in 1985, just as they had been in the past. Members of various minorities accused the regime of discriminating against them, while law enforcement officials and political leaders saw demands for greater autonomy as a threat to the delicate balance that obtains in Yugoslavia. Of course, conflict is virtually inevitable: programs that one religious or ethnic community perceives as vital to its needs are often viewed by others as an assault on their identity or integrity. Similarly, policies that the federal authorities regard as a needed curb on fissiparous tendencies in the republics may look like an unwarranted intrusion into purely local affairs.

Each of the six republics has its own government, its own political and economic priorities, and its own approach to matters ranging from cultural policy and the handling of nonconformist intellectuals to the development of public transportation and the construction of steel mills. Clearly, decentralization of decision making is both a prerequisite to, and a guarantor of, Yugoslavia's pluralist system. This applies to human rights as well as economic policy. For example, writings or behavior may be perfectly acceptable (or even encouraged) in one republic while they serve elsewhere as a reason for arrests or for applying pressure on the editors of newspapers and scholarly journals.

In any event, police and prosecutors throughout Yugoslavia were especially vigilant in 1985, and there was a disparity between "crime" and punishment. One 18-year-old high school student was sentenced to six-and-a-half years in prison for writing poetry that was deemed "hostile" to the existing order. A number of ordinary citizens who had worked in Western Europe or the United States were jailed simply because they maintained contact with "hostile" emigres. A Catholic priest was imprisoned for having "insulted Tito's memory" while hearing confession from his parishioners. Another priest in the city of Split was put in jail for having visited sick and dying people "without authority." (According to the law, clergymen are permitted to make hospital visits only if they are specifically requested to do so by patients.)[55]

These cases, like the others we have discussed, point to pervasive insecurity in high party and government circles. More important, they threaten to dissolve the regime's uncertain commitment to basic human rights.

NOTES

1. See *Country Reports on Human Rights Practices for 1984,* report prepared by the Department of State for the House Foreign Affairs and Senate Foreign Relations Committees (February 1985), p. 1,124.

2. Liubarsky's estimates are cited in *Soviet Analyst,* Vol. 14, No. 8 (April 17, 1985), p. 7. Ukrainians seem to have been singled out for especially harsh treatment. According to the U.S. government, Ukrainian men and women account for some 40 percent of all political prisoners in the USSR, although members of this ethnic group comprise only 16 percent of the country's population. See the *Eighteenth Semiannual Report by the President to the Commission on Security and Cooperation in Europe on the Implementation of the Helsinki Final Act, Special Report No. 130* (October 1, 1984–April 1, 1985), p. 6. Hereafter, this source will be cited as *Special Report.*

3. *Special Report,* p. 7. For a comprehensive list of these individuals and their fates, see *Radio Liberty Research* (hereafter cited as *RL*), *RL* 245/85 (July 30, 1985).

4. *USSR News Brief, No. 20* (October 31, 1985); *Smoloskyp,* Vol. 7, No. 27 (Spring–Fall 1985); North Atlantic Assembly, *The Bulletin, No. 35/36* (January 1–May 31, 1985), pp. 11–13, 19–22; Ibid., No. 37 (June 1–August 31, 1985), pp. 4–5, 10–11, and 15–16; Peter Reddaway, "The Case of Dr. Koryagin," *The New York Review of Books* (hereafter cited as *NY Review*), Vol. XXXII, No. 15 (October 10, 1985), p. 10.

5. Data supplied by the Soviet Jewry Research Bureau, National Conference on Soviet Jewry (October, 1985). See also *Special Report,* p. 25.

6. *EKO,* No. 7 (1985), pp. 3–23.

7. The report is available in English in *Survey,* No. 1 (1984), pp. 83–109.

8. *Pravda,* August 4, 1985.

9. *Pravda* and *Izvestiia,* June 12, 1985.

10. For details on these issues, see David K. Shipler, *Russia* (New York: Penguin Books, 1983), pp. 163–79, 192–223; David K. Willis, *Klass* (New York: St. Martin's Press, 1985). For a discussion of bribery and corruption in higher education, see *RL* 153/85 (May 13, 1985).

11. See *Pravda,* September 9, 1985; *Izvestiia,* October 21, 1985; *New York Times* (hereafter cited as *NYT*), November 15, 1985; *RL* 314/85 (September 19, 1985).

12. *Sovetskaia Rossiia,* October 25, 1985. See also ibid., July 18, 1985.

13. *Literaturnaia gazeta,* March 14, 1985.

14. The full text of Evtushenko's speech is available in *NYT,* December 19, 1985; the abbreviated text appears in *Literaturnaia gazeta,* No. 51 (1985). For suggestions that the Soviet press be more "open," see *Izvestiia,* March 23, 1985 and *Pravda,* March 27, 1985.

15. See *Radio Free Europe Background Report* (hereafter cited as *RAD BR) 115* (October 4, 1985) and *RAD BR/56* (June 26, 1985).

16. *RAD BR/115,* op. cit.; *RAD BR/120* (October 15, 1985).

17. *RAD BR/54* (June 25, 1985).

18. Cited in *RAD BR/88* (August 26, 1985).

19. U.S. Department of Justice, Drug Enforcement Administration, Office of Intelligence, *Special Report: The Involvement of the People's Republic of Bulgaria in International Narcotics Trafficking* (May, 1984); *NYT,* July 13, 1985.

20. For a discussion of these developments, see *Bulgarian Situation Report* (hereafter cited as *SR*) *9* (August 1, 1985). For the Soviet response see *Literaturnaia gazeta, No 10* (1985) and *Sovetskoe gosudarstvo i pravo, No. 9* (1985), pp. 88–93.

21. The following paragraphs draw heavily on *NYT,* May 19, 1985; May 24, 1985 p. 34; August 7, 1985; and October 31, 1985; New York *Times Magazine,* December 8, 1985; *Bulgarian SR/7* (May 24, 1985), *Bulgarian SR/8* (June 29, 1985); and *RAD BR/26* (March 29, 1985); *Special Report,* p. 15; *The Bulletin,* No. 35/36, pp. 23–24, No. 37, pp. 18–19.

22. See the remarks of Rada Nikolaev in *Bulgarian SR/7.*

23. *Bulgarian SR/8.*

24. *Bulgarian SR/9* (August 1, 1985).

25. *Bulgarian SR/8.*

26. *Czechoslovak SR/15* (September 24, 1985).

27. *Czechoslovak SR/9* (June 3, 1985).

28. Ibid.; *Czechoslovak SR/15.* See also the interview with Anna Marvanova, an active member of Charter 77, in the *Wall Street Journal,* December 18, 1985. The dissident organization has also spoken out against U.S. policy toward Nicaragua. See *Czechoslovak Newsletter,* Vol. X, No. 12 (December 1985), p. 1.

29. *Czechoslovak SR/10* (June 27, 1985); *Czechoslovak SR/14.*

30. Guenther Gaus, cited in *RAD BR/66* (July 16, 1985).

31. *Pravda* and *Izvestiia,* October 26, 1985.

32. For a discussion of the Synod, see *RAD BR/114* (October 4, 1985). See also *RAD BR/86* (August 23, 1985) and *The Bulletin,* No. 35/36, pp. 15–16.

33. *RAD BR/35* (April 22, 1985).

34. See *Special Report,* p. 13.

35. Ibid., pp. 13, 14.

36. See *Hungarian SR/7* (June 8, 1985).

37. Timothy Garton Ash, "The Hungarian Lesson," *NYR,* Vol. XXXII, No. 19 (December 5, 1985), p. 5.

38. Cited in *Hungarian SR/7.*

39. *RAD BR/51* (June 5, 1985); *RAD BR/117* (October 11, 1985); *Hungarian SR/3* (March 8, 1985).

40. This discussion of the election relies heavily on *RAD BR/41*; *Hungarian SR/8* (June 21, 1985) and *SR/9* (August 7, 1985).

41. Cited in *Hungarian SR/8.* See also Judy Dempsey, "Hungary's Elections: A Half-Step Towards Pluralism?", *The World Today* 41 (August/September 1985):139–40.

42. See *Polish SR/5* (March 22, 1985).

43. This and the following paragraph are derived from *Polish SR/13* (August 16, 1985), *SR/14* (September 13, 1985), *SR/18* (November 8, 1985), and *RAD BR/123* (October 25, 1985).

44. Cited in *Polish SR/15* (September 27, 1985) and *SR/17* (October 25, 1985).

45. This and the following paragraph are drawn from *NYT,* November 30, 1985 and December 1, 1985, as well as *Polish SR/13* (August 16, 1985) and *SR/17.*

46. *Romanian SR/6* (March 25, 1985) and *SR/10* (June 26, 1985).

47. For details, see *Romanian SR/12* (August 13, 1985). Protestant fundamentalists are subjected to especially severe persecution. See *NYT,* December 15, 1985.

48. See *Romanian SR/6.* For additional evidence of Buzura's boldness, see *Romanian SR/9* (May 30, 1985).

49. For details, see *Romanian SR/10.*

50. *Wall Street Journal,* June 14, 1985; *NYT,* June 12, 1985.

51. Cited in *Yugoslav SR/5* (April 22, 1985).

52. *Yugoslav SR/9* (August 12, 1985).

53. *Yugoslav SR/5.*

54. For details on this affair, see *Yugoslav SR/1* (January 24, 1985) and *SR/2* (February 12, 1985).

55. See, inter alia, *Yugoslav SR/6* (May 28, 1985); *The Bulletin,* No. 35/36, pp. 13, 22, and *No. 37* (June 1–August 31, 1985), pp. 11, 16–17.

9   Conclusion

    Unless the writers of the preceding chapters have allowed themselves to be misled by optimism, the general tendency in most countries of the world, perhaps even including the Near East, has been in the direction of democracy, or at least in the direction of somewhat more pluralistic, less regimented, more open political systems. In most cases, change has been slight; it cannot be expected to be rapid except occasionally, as democratic ways have to grow slowly under authoritarian forms to make possible a breaking out, like a crab shedding its shell when it has grown too much for the confines of the old one. Outside of Latin America, there were in 1985 no dramatic shifts from one regime type to another, but there have been concessions here and there, especially some relaxation of controls of expression and of the economy. Perhaps the most significant fact is negative, the resistance of democratic governments to economic constriction approaching disaster. There has been remarkably little tendency to turn to extremist parties promising to overturn the evil system, much less to call upon the generals to straighten out the mess.

    If any reduction of the power or scope of the undemocratic state is regarded as an edging, however slight, toward democracy, or toward making it less inconceivable, very many countries have moved during the past year. Perhaps most of all, there seems to have been a perceptible decline of the legitimacy of dictatorial or military rule and a greater need for arbitrary rulers to make at least pretended concessions to principles of popular rights. There have been setbacks, and the trend is not strong, but if years to come are as favorable to democracy as 1985, within a decade we will see a much reformed political world.

In Western Europe and North America, democracy continues in good health. Problems have been no more than usual, and more economic than political. Democratic institutions seemed to have solidified in two of the nations where they were most questionable, Spain and Portugal. Malta was a dark spot but a small one. The striking fact of West European politics has been the weakening of forces threatening to democracy. The ebb of communist parties has been much greater than would have been predicted a few years ago. Only in Italy, where the party is farthest from Marxism-Leninism and Soviet direction, has communism remained a major political force; and even there, the predictions made in the 1970s about the inevitability of communist power seem far outdated. In the United States, democracy has failed the test of fiscal responsibility, but there has been a continued recovery from Vietnam and Watergate and a remarkable restoration of badly shaken confidence in government. Latin America was the region in which democracy scored most victories. In Uruguay, Brazil, and Guatemala, elected civilians replaced military presidents. There were no serious threats of military usurpation of any democratic government. The prospects may become less bright as the novelty wears off, but their moderation despite economic pressures is encouraging.

Sub-Saharan Africa showed some changes in the democratic direction. The military government of Nigeria was replaced by a less dictatorial one, and Guinea moved away from the absolutist rule of Sekou Toure. In South Africa apartheid was at least under increasing attack, and a few concessions were intended to ease its stringency. Cameroon and Tanzania saw some relaxation of authoritarianism, but other countries, such as Liberia, saw negative developments. No one expected a florescence of liberal institutions, at least not unless or until economic decline is turned around.

Of all the world's regions, the North Africa–Near East showed the least apparent movement, probably because of continued conflict in the area, including aftermaths of war in Lebanon and the continuation of the six-year-old war between Iran and Iraq. The atmosphere of violence was doubtless conducive to the continued growth of Islamic fundamentalism, a drive for rejection of Western influences (including democracy), and substitutions of traditional Islamic institutions and law.

In South Asia, the Tamil insurrection in Sri Lanka contributed to further erosion of democracy in that country, which in happier times was one of the better functioning democracies of the Third World. Elsewhere the trend seemed to be somewhat as in Latin America. Indian democracy, which had seemed shaky because of communal antagonisms in the last months of Indira Gandhi's rule, was reaffirmed and strengthened by her son and successor, Rajiv Gandhi. The other two populous countries of the region, Pakistan and Bangladesh, while remaining definitely authoritarian, gave testimony to the strength of the democratic ideal by adopting some institutions of consultation and representation.

The democracy of East Asia, Japan, has continued on track with little change; so far as its stability has been in doubt because of its newness, it has matured and solidified in another year of life. More striking has been the turn of events in China, where the economic reforms of Deng Xiaoping have been extended and broadened. The freedom of the peasants to raise what they will and to sell most of their produce on the market, plus the availability of licenses for many small private businesses and loosening of planning controls over state enterprises inevitably has a political accompaniment, including more latitude for the press, less political advertisement and indoctrination, and more freedom of religion. While slackening controls, the ruling party did nothing, however, to restrict its power, which was evident in the one-child campaign—a remarkable demonstration of the ability of the state to impose its decision in an intimate aspect of life strongly contrary to the wishes of many persons. It may be speculated that a continuation of economic liberalization must eventually raise a class able to assert some political influence, but this is not certain.

Elsewhere, there have been signs of change in Vietnam, Burma, Taiwan, and other countries, while the Marcos dictatorship in the Philippines came under attack as never before.

Least of all in the Soviet sphere have there been official concessions to democracy—except in Hungary, where elections to the virtually powerless "parliament" were contested, although all candidates had to be party-approved. But in the Soviet Union itself change seemed to be in the air, less from what the government did—such as slight moves to economic reform—than from the fact that it permitted more critical and controversial writing than for many years past, since the days of Khrushchev. If this meant the Gorbachev government was prepared to consider the deep reforms suggested by writers in the official press, far-reaching changes might be in the offing. In Eastern Europe there were also hints of greater independence, which meant in some cases a slight relaxation of controls, especially over the economy, as in the Hungarian deviation. It is not to be assumed that governments of Eastern Europe desire to be independent of the Soviet Union or to deviate from its economic and political model; and Soviet forces on the ground are present not so much to coerce the governments as to support them, because their existence in present form is probably contingent on the Soviet connection.

So far as there is any retreat from central direction in the Soviet Union and Eastern Europe it seems to be due mostly to economic problems and a recognition that central planning is not a complete answer in the face of accumulating problems and general slowdown. This seems broadly true; economic needs have been the most obvious and probably most important cause for retrenchment of the state. For China, Maoism was a disaster in material terms. A revolutionary regime, demanding complete obedience and sacrifice, must justify itself either in terms of national need—as in a struggle for independence—or the promise of a materially better tomorrow for the masses of its citizens. But Maoist political action led to impoverishment and even hunger for many. After his death, ideology was due to give way to practicality, although the rapidity and depth of change must be ascribed to the personality of the leader, Deng Xiaoping. The justification of Deng's reforms is that production has risen with almost incredible rapidity when peasants and small entrepreneurs were freed to produce for their own benefit; and this is the chief reason for supposing that the reforms may continue although many party cadres see themselves as losers. In somewhat the same way, the Vietnamese government, having demonstrated great ability to manage a war, showed equal inability to manage a peacetime economy. Reluctantly, nearly a decade later, it may be undertaking something of a retreat from total control.

Much the same thing has occurred in many countries of the Third World. Governments and bureaucracies prefer nationalized industry for the power it places in their hands and the jobs it makes available, but nationalized enterprises have generally worked badly, worse in less developed than in more developed economies. They have usually produced losses, and sometimes, as in Tanzania, have been tragic failures. The small Asian countries that have achieved high growth rates by encouraging private enterprise—Taiwan, Republic of Korea, Singapore, and Hong Kong—have provided a persuasive contrary example. The mentality of the Third World consequently has shifted considerably from statism and the virtue of controls to the desirability of permitting more freedom of trade and production. And so far as economic controls imply political power, a degree of economic freedom implies something of political freedom and pressure for democracy.

The difficulty of arbitrary governments in guiding the economy is not only a question of inefficiency of bureaucracy and planning mechanisms and problems of management of production. It is also related to the need for motivating and securing the cooperation of producers and potential producers, determining value without market mechanisms, of promoting the free flow of information, and fostering of investment, both of capital and entrepreneurship, in ways beneficial to the economy. This has been most evident in Latin America, where military governments of such countries as Argentina, Uruguay, Brazil, Peru, and Panama, finding themselves in economic difficulties, have felt the need for broader participation in decision making. To obtain it—and to relieve themselves of responsibility—they saw no way but to call elections and put the government in the hands of elected, that is, legitimate leaders.

If disillusionment with state direction of the economy—which is also seen in the mode for privatization of public enterprises in Western Europe and the United States—is surely the largest factor in the widespread tendency toward reduction of the role of the state and the admission of more pluralism and democratic elements, it is not the only one. With the ceaseless growth of the global information society, it becomes harder for governments and elites to isolate themselves from world opinion. On the international scene, democracy has no philosophic competitor.

International acceptance is also increasingly desired to qualify for aid in various forms. In Latin America, especially Central America, the pressure of U.S. policy for the holding of proper elections has played a part. Behind the convictions of the Reagan administration has been the preference of Congress for decent civilian governments; it is much easier to secure economic and military aid for governments that seem worth supporting. To improve eligibility for U.S. assistance has been crucial in the acceptance by the military of civilian governments in such states as El Salvador and Guatemala, and it has facilitated military return to the barracks in South America.

For the United States to favor democratic institutions abroad, and especially in what may be regarded as its sphere of influence, is not new, but it has become more accepted in recent years. Twenty years ago, it was widely considered to be irresponsible interventionism for this country to try to tell other countries what sort of political system they should have. However, international concern for human rights came to the fore in the 1970s, and it has been formally legitimated by numerous international organizations. There has also been a growing sense of the rightness, or righteousness, of democracy, as the only decent form of government, something we can be proud of promoting in the world. This sense of the legitimacy of democracy, or the illegitimacy of government based simply on force, as military dictatorship, and mystic claims to rulership by an organization, such as a political party, are hard to sustain in the modern age unless that rulership can show exemplary results.

If democratic ideology has become more convincing and aggressive, so to speak, and its rivals have become less so, there are many reasons. Possibly the most important is the lack of success of centrally planned economies, as already mentioned, and of state enterprise in general. Any political system that can point to strong economic growth is pardoned many a sin; an oppressive government with a stagnant economy is merely oppressive. Another factor is the wearing out of ideologies necessary or at least very useful, to sanction repression and arbitrary government. Fascism, of course, has been hopelessly discredited and can appeal only to something like a lunatic fringe. Communism, too, has exhausted its revolutionary capital and also the exaltation of victory in World War II. Radicalism looks desperately for new inspiration. The ideological hunger is rather pitiful; splinter groups cling to Maoism long after it has been essentially repudiated by its Chinese beneficiaries; West Indians even make a cult of the deceased and rather discredited Emperor Haile Selassi of Ethiopia.

This broad trend is understandable, perhaps inevitable, in historical terms. Democracy is basically nonviolent, rationalistic, and voluntary; nontraditional absolutist ideologies are more violent, emotional, and revolutionary in purpose. Despite many a conflict, the world has been relatively pacific by comparison with past centuries since World War II, especially since the Vietnam war unwound in 1972–73. The world economy has been reasonably stable, and the international atmosphere has tended toward the pragmatic. The climate has warmed, albeit slightly and slowly, for democracy.

During the century from the end of the wars of the French Revolution in 1815 until the First World War in 1914, Europe enjoyed a long peace interrupted by only minor wars and a fairly steady advance of production and living standards thanks to the progress of science and technology. It was also a time of the growth and spread of liberal ideas and representative and constitutional government. In the optimism of the age, the conviction grew that as the world became more civilized traditional powers would give way to popularly elected regimes, more or less in the pattern of British parliamentary government, and movements for constitutionalism diffused even to Russia, Turkey, and China. There was no real ideological competition for the philosophy of legal, responsible government based on the will of the people. Traditional monarchy was outworn and socialism represented an extremist fringe.

But four years of carnage in the name of patriotism demoralized and disillusioned European civilization. The war made it possible for the Leninists to thrust Russia back to an absolutism more like that of the seventeenth than of the late-nineteenth century; and antirationalist fascism overturned traditional and representative institutions in Italy, and subsequently in Germany and other countries where democracy lacked solid foundations. By the mid-1930s the great contest seemed to be between fascism (or Nazism) and communism; democracy looked like the wave of the past.

Defeat in the Second World War and the shame of the death camps destroyed the credibility of fascism, but the other totalitarianism of the Soviet Union emerged with great strength and prestige. The Western democratic side also came out of the struggle with vitality and confidence. There consequently developed a new contest between authoritarianism in the form of Marxist-Leninist communism and the liberal or democratic states, led by the United States. Appropriately called the "Cold War" because it was a conflict for survival carried on without much active fighting, it has lasted, with varying intensity, to this day and will probably continue, in changing forms, for a long time.

It has sometimes seemed as though the historical current favored the absolutists or totalitarians, with their ability to direct resources for the expansion of power and to organize the discontents of a world in ferment. The intensity of the contest made politics more violent and democratic institutions more difficult; on the one side was the revolutionary drive for power and collective, that is, state control; on the other was the fear of total loss of freedom if the totalitarians should prevail.

If the authoritarian revolutionaries had the advantage of initiative and purposefulness, they suffered the disadvantage that a revolutionary force of renovation upon achieving its state power becomes a bureaucratic apparatus of status and exploitation. The ideology of renewal and change can make the system of control efficient only as long as there is faith in the new dawning. As the Leninist ideals become ever less relevant, the authoritarian state becomes less effective, and it finds itself facing a choice between maintaining controls at the cost of economic progress, or permitting the relaxation essential for economic progress at the price of ideological and political loosening.

In this age, the authoritarian state has to base itself on either the promise of efficiency—that by capable management it improves the quality of life—or some kind of emergency or national need for unity and sacrifice. Failing economically, authoritarianism thrives in violence, which generates fear and hatred, evokes extremist politics, and destroys orderly democracy. Thus revolutionary warfare in Central America has led to an absolutist regime in Nicaragua and probably would have brought about radical governments of Left or Right in neighboring countries but for the insistence of the United States on more or less democratic or at least non-Marxist institutions. The bitter Arab-Israeli clash has all but excluded democracy in the Near East; even in Israel, democracy is for the Jewish population. The Iranian revolution and the subsequent war between Iraq and Iran have also heated tempers and generated the most dynamic of contemporary ideological movements, past-oriented Islamic fundamentalism. Civil conflict in South Africa may likewise lead to some form of absolutism—indeed, the regime of apartheid in defending itself becomes antidemocratic, admitting censorship and police violence.

But these hot spots are not a large part of the contemporary political universe; the overall picture is one of relative calm. It is consequently understandable that the tendency toward more pluralistic and open societies prevails in more of the world. The main antagonist, the Soviet state, has become unsure of its outlook and purposes; and it has become clear that, in a nonemergency, a more or less free or mixed economy functions more efficiently than one that the political leaders try to manage. Much of the global competition is a technological race, in which the opener societies have an inherent advantage. In complex modern societies, it is increasingly necessary to permit circulation of information and to consult different views and interests, that is, to have a responsible, more or less democratic government.

It may be, then, that the world moves toward a condition like that at the beginning of this century, when it was generally assumed that parliamentary constitutionalism was the political goal of mankind. It seems clear that personal, military, or party dictatorships will have to grant more rights and soften or relinquish political controls in order to keep their societies viable and competitive in the modern world. It may be reasonably assumed that this trend will continue, however gradually in view of human conservatism and sporadically in view of the unpredictability of politics. The trend toward democracy, that is, will probably continue unless or until there is a major breakdown of the world economic order or a big new explosion of violence to charge an authoritarian passion or new antidemocratic ideology.

Bibliography

Alexeyeva, Ludmilla. *Soviet Dissent.* Middletown, CT: Wesleyan University Press, 1985.

Benjamin, Roger, and Stephen L. Elkin. *The Democratic State.* Lawrence, KA: University of Kansas Press, 1985.

Cohen, Carl. *Democracy.* Athens, GA: University of Georgia Press, 1971.

Dahl, Robert A. *Polyarchy: Participation and Opposition.* New Haven: Yale University Press, 1971.

Gastil, Raymond D. *Freedom in the World: Political Rights and Civil Liberties 1985-1985, 1985-1986.* Westport, CT: Greenwood Press, 1986.

Harrison, Selig S. *The Widening Gulf, Asian Nationalism and American Policy.* New York: The Free Press, 1978.

Huntington, Samuel P. "Will More Countries Become Democratic?" *Political Science Quarterly* 99, Summer 1984.

Jackson, Robert H., and Carl G. Rosberg. "Democracy and Tropical Africa." *Journal of International Affairs* 38, Winter 1985, pp. 295-306.

Jackson, Robert H., and Carl G. Rosberg. *Personal Rule in Black Africa: Prince, Autocrat, Prophet, Tyrant.* Berkeley: University of California Press, 1982.

Journal of International Affairs 38, Winter 1985, Special Member, "Dilemma of Democracy."

Layne, Linda (ed.). *Elections in the Middle East: Implications of Recent Trends.* Bolder, CO: Westview Press, 1986.

Lijphart, Arendt. *Democracies: Patterns of Majoritarian and Consensus Government.* New Haven: Yale University Press, 1984.

Peeler, John A. *Latin American Democracies: Colombia, Costa Rica, Venezuela.* Chapel Hill: University of North Carolina Press, 1985.

Pickles, Dorothy. *Democracy.* Baltimore: Penguin Books, 1970.

Roskin, Michael. *Other Governments of Europe: Sweden, Spain, Italy, Yugoslavia, and East Germany.* Englewood Cliffs: Prentice-Hall, 1977.

Rustow, Dankwart A. "Elections and Legitimacy in the Middle East," *Annals of the American Academy of Political and Social Science.* November, 1985.

Scalapino, Robert A., Sezaburo Sato, & Jusuf Wanandi (eds.). *Asian Political Institutionalization.* Berkeley: Institute of East Asian Studies, University of California, 1986.

Sklar, Richard C. *Democracy in Africa.* Los Angeles: African Studies Center, 1983.

Ungar, Sanford J. *Africa: The People and Politics of an Emerging Continent.* New York: Simon & Schuster, 1985.

Wesson, Robert. *Democracy in Latin America: Prospects and Problems.* New York: Praeger, 1982.

Wiarda, Howard J., and Harvey F. Kline (eds.). *Latin American Politics and Development.* Boulder, CO: Westview Press, 1985.

Index

About the Contributors

Larry Diamond is Senior Research Fellow at the Hoover Institution. His articles on Nigerian politics have been published in *Foreign Affairs* and other journals. His study of the failure of the First Nigerian Republic, *Class, Ethnicity and Democracy in Nigeria*, is forthcoming. He is currently editing a four-volume study of experiences with democracy in the Third World, with Seymour Martin Lipset and Juan Linz.

Dennis A. Kavanagh is professor of politics at the University of Nottingham in England. His most recent books include *British Politics: Continuities and Change* (1985), *The British General Election of 1983* (1984), with David Butler, *Political Science and Political Behaviour* (1983) and the *Politics of the Labour Party* (1982).

Douglas C. Makeig, a Senior South Asian Specialist with the Federal Research Division, Library of Congress, is responsible for monitoring political and security issues affecting all seven countries of the region. He is currently conducting research on Indo-Pakistan relations. The views expressed in this article are those of the author and do not necessarily reflect those of the Library of Congress or the U.S. Government.

John D. Martz is professor of political science at Pennsylvania State University. He has published fourteen books on Latin America, especially Venezuela and Colombia, and has written many articles for journals and contributed chapters to multi-authored books.

Edward A. Olsen is professor of National Security Affairs and coordinator of Asian Studies at the Naval Postgraduate School, Monterey, California. He is the author of numerous books and articles on Asian affairs, including *US-Japan Strategic Reciprocity* and *The Role of the Armed Forces in Asia.*

Glenn E. Perry is professor of political science at Indiana State University. He is the author of *The Middle East: Fourteen Islamic Countries* (1983) and the editor of *Palestine: Continuing Dispossession* (1986). His articles on Middle Eastern affairs have appeared in several journals, and he has contributed to various multi-authored books.

David E. Powell is a Research Associate at the Russian Research Center, Harvard University. He is the author of *Antireligious Propaganda in the Soviet Union* as well as numerous articles dealing with Soviet and East European affairs. He has books underway on alcohol abuse and militarism and pacifism in the Soviet Union and Eastern Europe.

Martin P. Wattenberg is an associate professor of political science at the University of California, Irvine. He is the author of *The Decline of American Political Parties, 1952–1984* and has published numerous scholarly articles on elections and voting behavior.

Robert Wesson is Senior Research Fellow of the Hoover Institution, Stanford University, and professor emeritus of political science of the University of California, Santa Barbara. He is the author of a number of books on Soviet politics, Latin America, international relations, and comparative government, including *Modern Government: Democracy and Authoritarianism.*